TANKS
OF WORLD WAR II

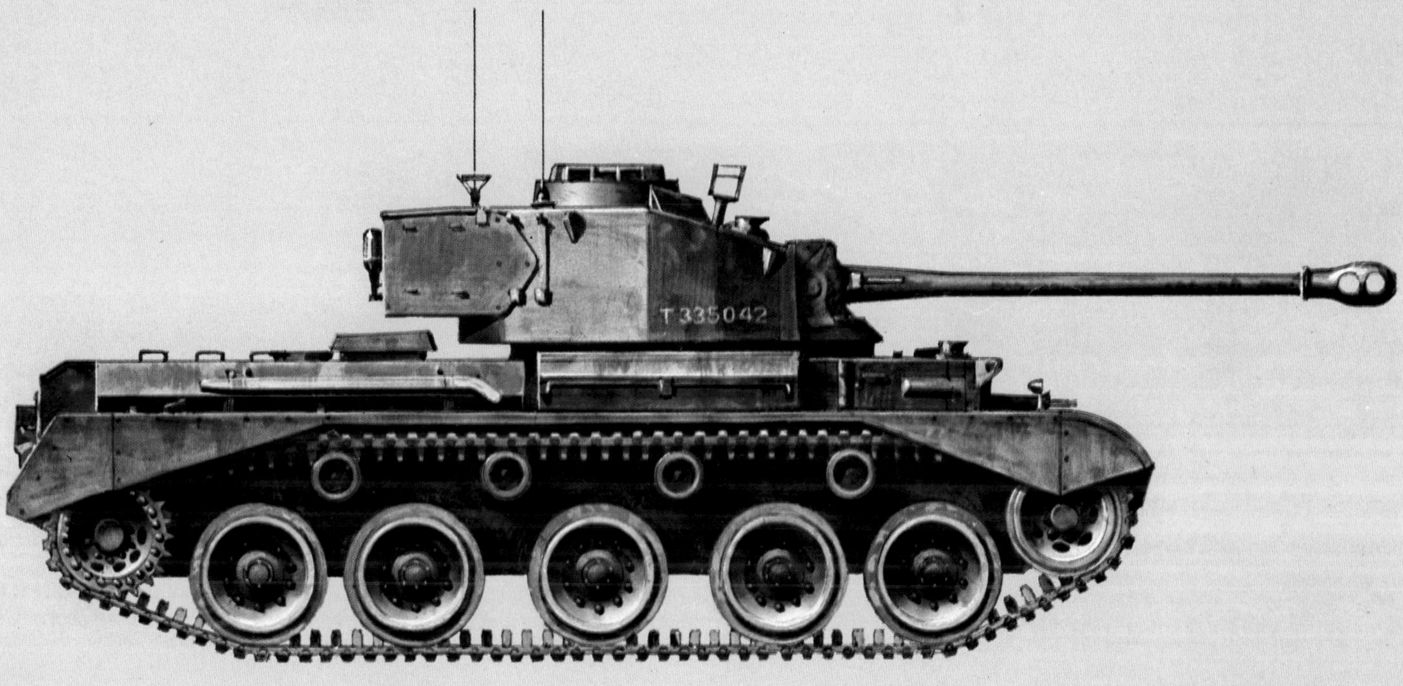
T 335042

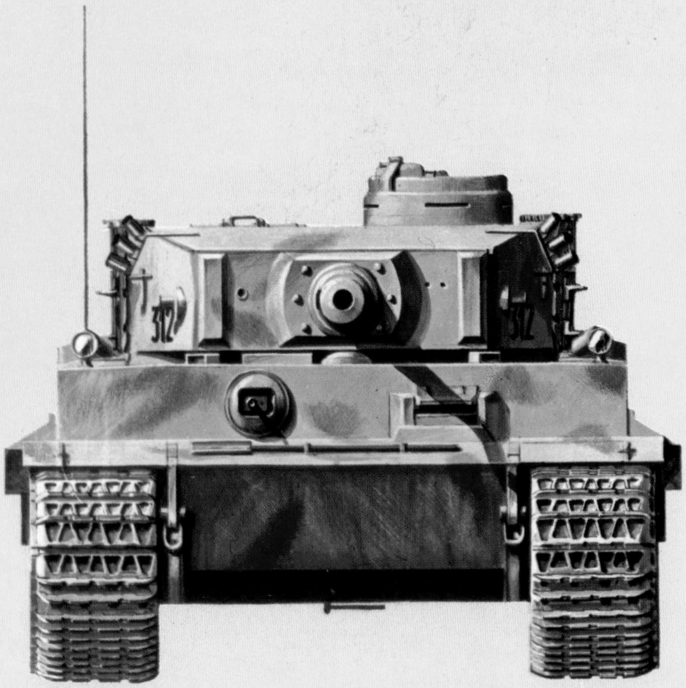

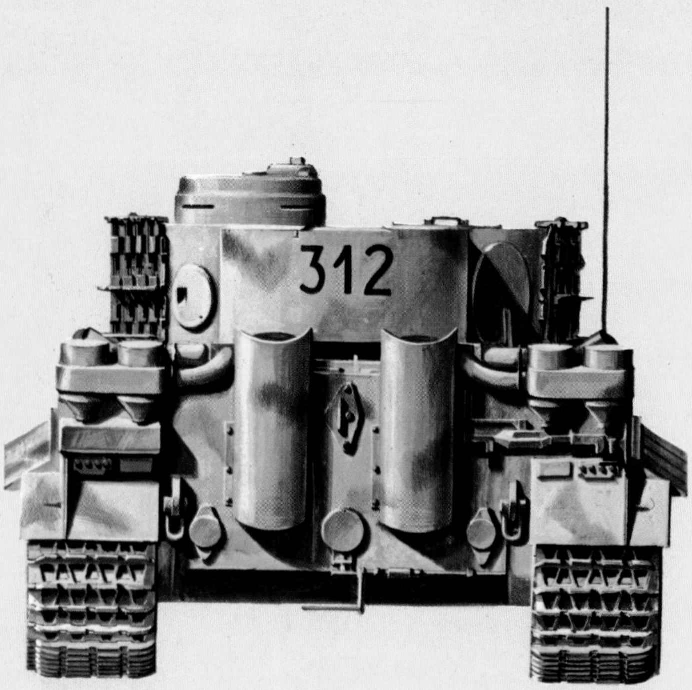
312

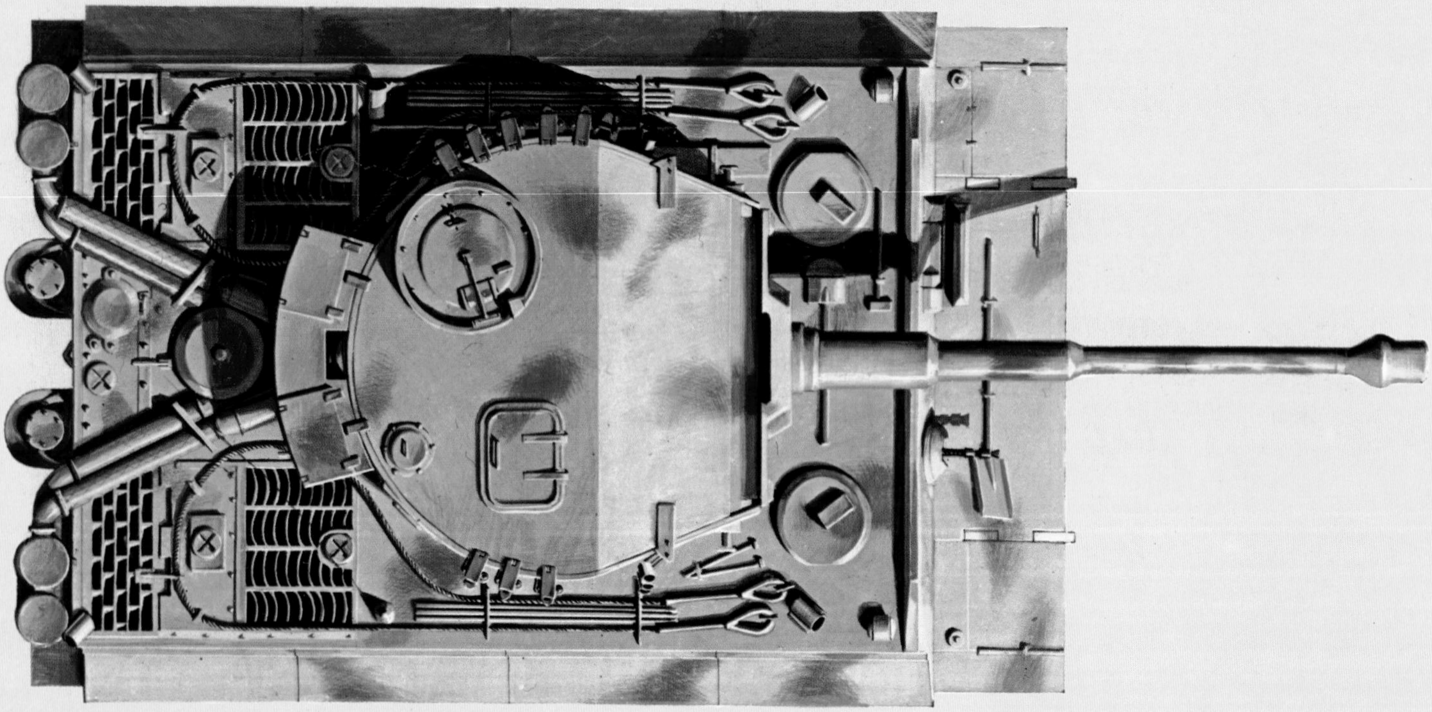

TANKS
OF WORLD WAR II

CHRIS ELLIS

CHANCELLOR
PRESS

First published in 1981 by Octopus

This edition published in 1997
by Chancellor Press, an imprint of
Reed International Books Limited
Michelin House, 81 Fulham Road,
London, SW3 6RB

ISBN 1 85152 725 7

Printed in Malaysia

Page 1: Comet A34 of the British 11th
Armoured Division, 1945. It equipped
the 23rd Hussars.

Page 2–3: Early production PzKpfw VI
Tiger Ausf H of the Wehrmacht.

Page 4: T-34/76B of the Red Army's
Guards Tank Regiment.

Page 5: Sd Kfz 234/2 Puma of the elite
German Panzer Lehr division, Falaise
Gap, Normandy, 1944.

Page 208: IS-2 of the Red Army's 11th
Armoured Corps, as used in the final
attack on and occupation of Berlin in
April 1945.

Chris Ellis would like to thank Liz
Romanovitch who typed the
manuscript and Elizabeth Elliot who
compiled the technical data.

Contents

Introduction

The technology of the late 1930s was harnessed in World War 2 to make weapons more formidable and effective than ever before. Big bombers, submarines, and monoplane fighters were among the notable weapons of war which made their mark on history. But on land it was undoubtedly the armoured fighting vehicle that captured popular imagination, and it was the tank which dominated military tactics in virtually all theatres of war except the jungles of south-east Asia. It has often been said that war gives the greatest momentum to change; certainly the fierce competition to outfight the other side in the six bitter years of conflict between 1939 and 1945 caused the most rapid and sometimes unbelievable developments in design. In the case of tanks, design made far more progress in this short period than it had done in the 30 years during which armoured fighting vehicles had been in existence. Indeed, it might be said that, though there have been big strides in tank design since 1945, they have not been so rapid or fundamental as were the developments in World War 2.

The first tank, in the modern meaning of the word, was developed in Great Britain in 1915, though there had been other armoured vehicles before that. 'Little Willie', followed by 'Big Willie' or 'Mother', was produced to overcome a major tactical problem encountered on the Western Front. By 1915 the Allies and the Germans had settled down to a muddy conflict in France and Belgium in two facing rows of trenches, with each side blasting the other with huge gun barrages and trying vainly to attack and take the opposing lines. Infantry were stopped in this objective by a 'new technology' weapon of the period, the machine gun. A well-sited machine gun could cut down hordes of advancing infantry, and so the fighting on the Western Front soon reached stalemate. The answer in the eyes of the more imaginative, Britain's Winston Churchill among them, was to develop a machine immune to machine gun fire and stable enough to cross the enfiladed area of 'no man's land', either silencing the enemy machine guns with its own weapons or even carrying infantry inside it to deposit unscathed in the enemy trenches.

The result of this thinking was a crawler track vehicle able to cope with the mud and shell holes, with guns in sponsons in the side which could answer the fire from the enemy trenches. The French soon came along with an early design of theirs, the Renault FT, which put the gun in a traversing turret, and this rapidly became the norm in all future tank designs of consequence. Many were sceptical about the value of the tank. Lord Kitchener, British War Minister at the time, dismissed it as a 'pretty mechanical toy', for there was still an entrenched school of thought that horsed cavalry would always win the day. In many armies this thinking prevailed right up to 1940 when the early tank battles of World War 2 finally showed that warfare was going to be all 'mechanical'.

In truth the early tanks did have limitations, and these were often limitations of technology. Construction was still at the plate and girder stage, armour plate was relatively unsophisticated, engines were feeble in the main, sprung suspension was still a thing of the future, and guns were 'pop guns' by the standards of a few decades later. The idea of carrying men in armoured vehicles to fight as infantry was one that hardly got off the ground, mainly because the rough ride and poor ventilation in the vehicle left the occupants in no state to get out and fight when they arrived at the enemy lines. However, the ideas were there and the Battle of Cambrai in November 1917, and the Battle of the Aisne in 1918, showed how effective massed tank actions could be.

In the peacetime euphoria of the early 1920s, there was mass demobilization and tanks were not high on any defence priorities. By the time a new generation of designs had been evolved in the late 1920s there was a world slump and many promising types were abandoned or delayed. But the men who had operated the tanks or had seen them in action, went on thinking and writing. In Britain they were men like B.H. Liddell-Hart and J.F.C. Fuller, and in Germany, Von Seeckt and Heinz Guderian, who could see that future wars would be entirely mechanized. The British champions of the tank, against much establishment opposition, managed to get an Experimental Mechanized Force organized in the late 1920s and this was really the prototype of all the armoured divisions of World War 2. The German military leaders, forbidden to have tanks by the terms of the 1919 Versailles Peace Treaty, nonetheless made do with cardboard outlines mounted on motor cars to get their troops used to the idea of tank warfare. By the time Hitler and the Nazi Party took full power in 1933, the ideas of the German armoured warfare pioneers were fully endorsed by the new leadership, and real full-size armoured divisions (known as panzer divisions) were established, with a rational series of tank designs, the PzKpfw I-IV, each complementing the other.

The British, meanwhile, were trailing behind – not short of ideas, but short of decisions at high level. The British General Staff were not sure what sort of war they would be fighting in the future, but finally settled on an 'infantry tank' class which was really a slightly updated version of the original British tank type, able to cross 'no man's land' at walking pace in support of infantry. The other class was to be a 'cruiser tank', able to roam the battlefield and take on enemy tanks, rather like cruisers at sea. However, the delays entailed in working out these concepts and coming up with designs meant that when the war started Britain was woefully short of any vehicles in these new categories – in fact, the first were just coming into service and Britain was over-dependent on inadequately armed and armoured light tanks which had been built between the wars, mainly for colonial patrol work.

The Germans did not play by the rules of Britain or France (France had similar 'infantry' and 'cruiser' tank ideas under other names), and the German panzer generals, among them Guderian and a new star, Erwin Rommel, showed that armoured warfare in France in 1940 would be fast-moving, with no fixed lines, mechanized armoured infantry in half-tracks following the tanks to hold the ground, with dive bombers 'softening up' objectives ahead of the tanks. Effective gun support was given at all levels, while a new class of armoured vehicle, the assault gun, supported the infantry. Tank-against-tank actions were often avoided and high velocity anti-aircraft guns were used in the anti-tank role, with enemy tanks sometimes being lured on to concealed guns.

All this, then, changed the pattern of warfare for the Allies, who began to use similar methods of attack, complete with half-track armoured infantry carriers, tactical aircraft like the Typhoon, Thunderbolt and Stormovik, and, above all, bigger guns and heavier armour than had ever been contemplated before the war. In fact, tank development for the rest of the war became one big race to mount bigger and better guns in ever more heavily armoured tanks. Thus the British, who had standardized on the 2pdr gun in 1939, went rapidly to the 6pdr, 75mm, and 17pdr in a desperate effort to outshoot German tanks which were being similarly upgunned at a prodigious rate. Typical of late war German tanks

was the mighty King Tiger (Tiger II) with its 88mm gun and enormously thick armoured superstructure. But as tanks got bigger and heavier they also became slow and unwieldy, and by 1944–5 the tables had been turned on the Germans who were fighting a defensive war on their own doorstep against superbly armed Allied armoured divisions with huge resources and a new 'generation' of tanks designed as a result of combat experience.

The key to success for the Allies was the huge output of excellent American tanks. The USA had almost no tanks before the war, but being neutral until 1941 they were able to spot trends quickly and see that bigger tanks and guns were going to be essential. This led to the very successful M3 and M4 medium tanks, and excellent supporting self-propelled (SP) guns. Similarly, the Russians, with a big but motley collection of outdated tanks and only a hazy doctrine of armoured warfare, were able to build on the best of the lessons they had learned in the 1930s to come up with their KV (and later IS) heavy tanks, and the magnificent T-34, which was the most significant design of the whole war.

This book includes 40 of the greatest and most important tanks of the war and describes their development against this general background. The colour illustrations show the great variety of models and colour schemes and should make this a most handy ready reference book for all armour enthusiasts and model tank makers.

Light Tank M24 Chaffee supplied to the Japanese Self-Defence Force post-war. From 1945 onwards Chaffees were used by many of the Allied nations. Britain and France had them first, but post-war they went to numerous nations including Italy and Japan. Many were still in use at the start of the 1980s. The French Army had a version in 1950 with a new French 75mm gun. In the late 1970s the Norwegian Army took updated Chaffees into service as a 'new' type since they were still considered to be effective and cheap as a light tank type. Also shown is the M19 Gun Motor Carriage. This vehicle was originally designated T65E1 and had a twin 40mm M2 AA mount set at the hull rear and the engines moved forward to the hull centre. Design commenced in mid-1943 and 904 vehicles were ordered in August 1944, when it was standardized as the M19, although only 285 were completed. M19s were standard US Army equipment for many years post-war, and the example shown was supplied to the Japanese.

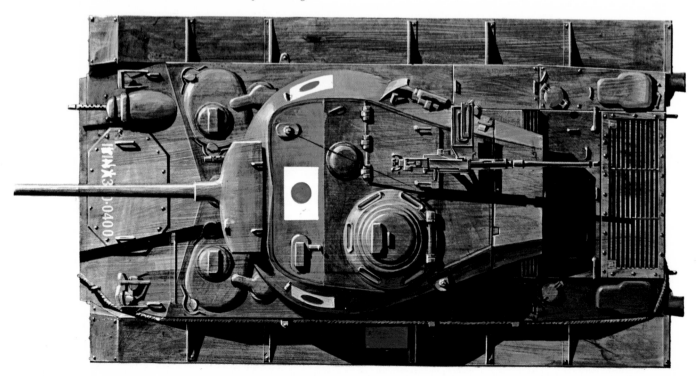

0   1   2 m

Gistudio – Tatangelo

Light Tank M24 Chaffee

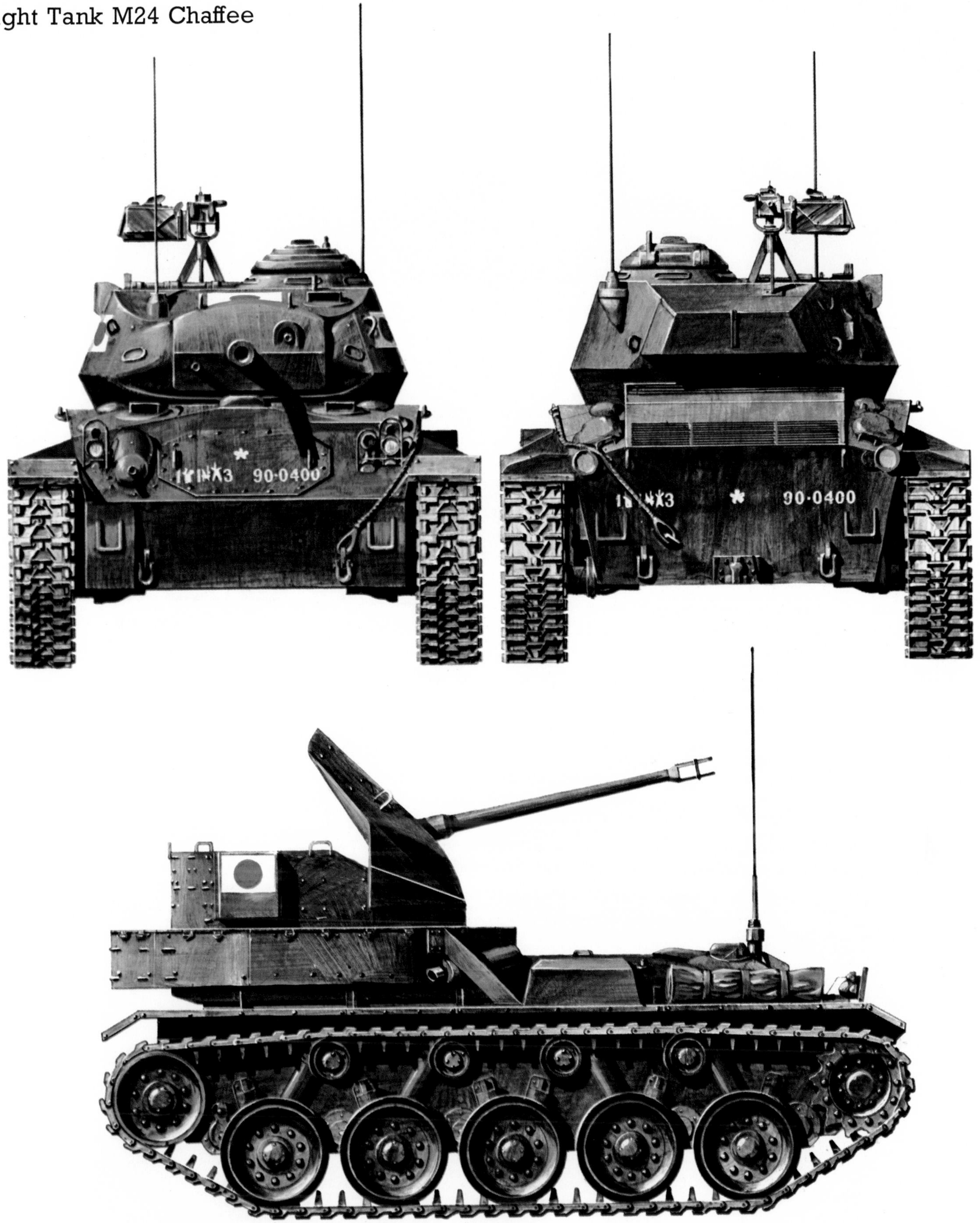
90-0400
90-0400

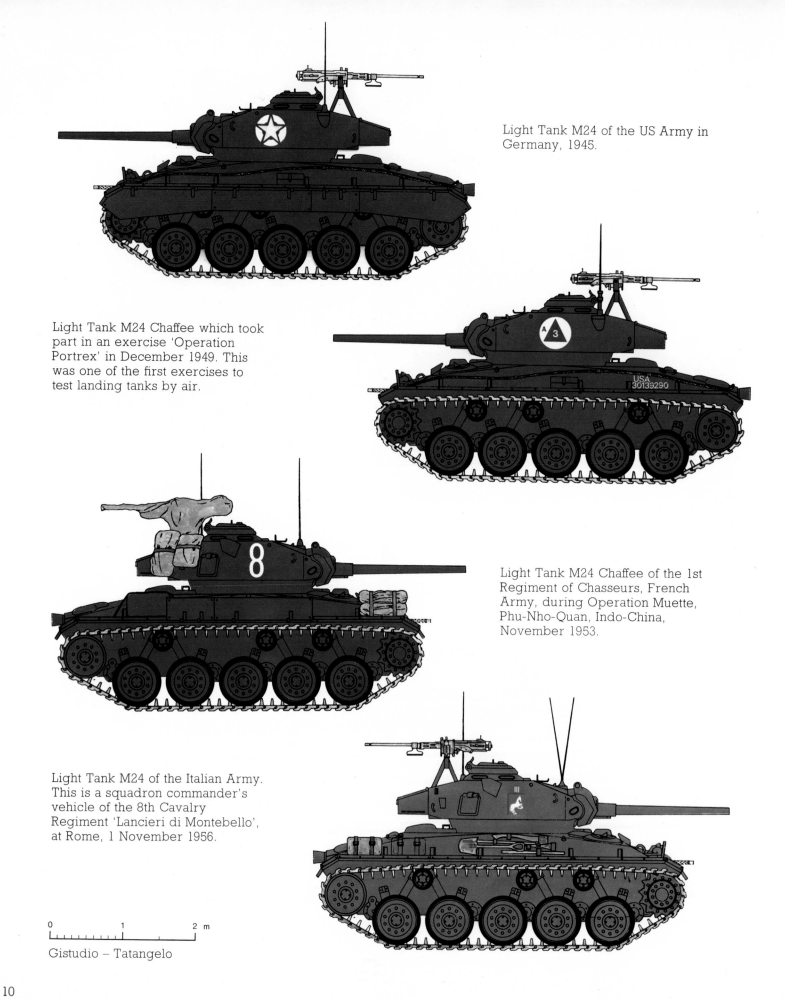

Light Tank M24 of the US Army in Germany, 1945.

Light Tank M24 Chaffee which took part in an exercise 'Operation Portrex' in December 1949. This was one of the first exercises to test landing tanks by air.

Light Tank M24 Chaffee of the 1st Regiment of Chasseurs, French Army, during Operation Muette, Phu-Nho-Quan, Indo-China, November 1953.

Light Tank M24 of the Italian Army. This is a squadron commander's vehicle of the 8th Cavalry Regiment 'Lancieri di Montebello', at Rome, 1 November 1956.

0   1   2 m

Gistudio – Tatangelo

M24 Chaffee

Light Tank M24 Chaffee of the
Austrian Army in the 1960s.

Light Tank M24 Chaffee of the
Greek Army, as paraded for the
anniversary of the 1821 revolution,
Athens, 1962.

Light Tank M24 Chaffee of the
Pakistan Army, marked for
operations during the Bangla Desh
war of liberation, near Dacca, 1971.

Light Tank M24 Chaffee of 3rd
Reconnaissance Squadron, South
Vietnam Army, Tan-Son-Nhut
airport, 1972.

M24 Chaffee

In April 1943, the US Ordnance Department, in conjunction with Cadillac (makers of the M5 series), began work on an entirely new light tank design. This was to incorporate the best features from earlier designs with all the lessons learned from previous experience. The twin Cadillac engines and Hydramatic transmission which had been so successful and trouble-free in the M5 series were retained, but the engine was to be more accessible. A weight of 18 short tons was envisaged with an armour basis of only 25mm to save weight, although all hull faces were to be angled for optimum protection. Maximum turret armour was 37mm and the old vertical volute suspension was replaced by road wheels on torsion arms to give a smoother ride. The first of two pilot models, designated T24, was delivered in October 1943 and proved so successful that the Ordnance Department immediately placed a production order for 1,000 vehicles which was later raised to 5,000. Cadillac and Massey-Harris carried out production, commencing in March 1944 and these two plants between them had produced 4,415 vehicles (including SP variants) by the end of the war in 1945.

The 75mm M6 gun was adapted from the heavy aircraft cannon used in the Mitchell bomber, and had a concentric recoil system which saved valuable turret space. The T24 was standardized as the Light Tank M24 in May 1944. The first deliveries of M24s were made to American tank battalions in late 1944, replacing M5s, and the M24 came into increasing use in the closing months of the war, being used in the crossing of the Rhine. It remained the standard American light tank for many years afterwards and took part in the Korean war.

Parallel to the need for a new light tank was the desire to produce a standard chassis as the basis of what was known as the 'Light Combat Team' – a complete series of tanks, SP guns, and special purpose tanks. Basing all these on a single chassis greatly simplified maintenance and production and many variants were produced to meet this concept. Each had engine, power train and suspension identical with that of the M24, and the different models are outlined here.

M19 Gun Motor Carriage: Produced for the AA Command, this vehicle had a twin 40mm M2 AA mount set at the hull rear and the engines moved forward to the hull centre. Design commenced in mid-1943 and 904 vehicles were ordered in August 1944, but only 285 were completed. M19s were standard US Army equipment for many years after the war.

M41 Howitzer Motor Carriage: This featured the M24 chassis with the engine mounted centrally to allow a 155mm howitzer to be set in an open mount at the back. It was known unofficially to the troops as the 'Gorilla'. Some 250 were ordered but only 60 were complete when the war ended and the contract was cancelled. It had a crew of 12, 4 riding in the vehicle and 8 in an accompanying ammunition carrier.

M37 Howitzer Motor Carriage: This vehicle was intended at first to supplement, then to replace the M7 HMC. Of the 448 which were ordered, 316 were delivered when contracts were cancelled at the war's end. It carried 90 rounds of ammunition and had a seven-man crew.

T38 Mortar Motor Carriage: Essentially this was the M37 with the howitzer removed, the embrasure plated in, and a 4·2in mortar mounted within the superstructure. A pilot model was made but the project was cancelled when the war ended.

T77E1 Multiple Gun Motor Carriage: Potentially this was a most effective AA tank with remote-controlled quad ·50 cal. machine guns in a domed-shaped turret, based on USAAF aircraft armament control equipment. A prototype, the T77, was tested in July 1945, after which a computing system was added to the sights, this form being designated T77E1. It was intended to produce this vehicle to replace half-track AA types but when the war ended the project was cancelled and no production of this variant took place.

MODEL M24 Chaffee

COUNTRY OF ORIGIN USA.

WEIGHT 18·36 tonnes (18 tons).

LENGTH 5·48m (18ft).

WIDTH 2·75m (9ft 2in).

HEIGHT 2·45m (8ft 1in).

GROUND CLEARANCE 0·43m (1ft 5in).

ARMOUR 25–63mm.

ENGINES Twin Cadillac, 110hp each, gasoline.

MAXIMUM SPEED 56km/h (34mph).

RANGE 160km (100 miles).

CREW 5.

ARMAMENT 1 × 75mm gun, 1 × ·50 cal. MG, 2 × ·30 cal. MG.

AMMUNITION 75mm, APC, HE and WP (smoke): 48 rds, ·50 cal.: 420 rds, ·30 cal.: 4,125 rds.

TRENCH CROSSING 2·43m (8ft).

TRACK WIDTH 0·40m (1ft 4in).

MAXIMUM ELEVATION 60°.

FORDING DEPTH 1·01m (3ft 4in).

Char B1-B1 bis

General J.E. Estienne, the original pioneer of the French tank arm in 1915, initiated the requirement which resulted in the Char B. In 1921 Estienne, as head of tank development, asked five firms to submit designs for a 15-ton vehicle with a 75mm or 47mm gun in the nose – essentially an updated version of the Schneider and St Chamond tanks of World War 1. Schneider-Renault, FAMH and FCM all built mock-ups, and in 1926 it was decided by the *Section Technique* to authorize a prototype combining the best features of the various mock-ups. Suspension was taken from the FCM tank while the mechanical features were those of the Schneider-Renault design. The ARL (*Atelier de Construction de Rueil* – the French tank arsenal) were to supervise overall design, and the first prototype Char B was completed in early 1929, with two more being built in the next two years. This first model weighed 25 tons, had 25mm armour maximum, a 75mm gun in the nose beside the driver, two machine guns in the hull front and two more in the turret. There was a Renault 180hp 6-cylinder engine giving a 28km/h (17mph) top speed.

Prototype trials continued at a leisurely pace over the next few years and the vehicle, by now called the Char B1, was modified slightly to have 40mm armour and a resulting increased weight of 28 tons. In April 1935, 40 Char B1s – essentially the prototype design with a 47mm gun in the turret – were ordered as a stop-gap. In the interim a more heavily armoured model was to be produced with a 60mm armour maximum, an enlarged turret with an improved 47mm gun and an uprated 300hp engine. The overall weight increased from 28 to 32 tons and the new vehicle was designated Char B1 bis. It followed the Char B1 on the production line, and 365 were built by June 1940 when France capitulated.

Meanwhile a further improved model was designed, the Char B1 ter with longer hull and 75mm armour, and the prototype was built in 1937. However, it was decided to concentrate on building the Char B1 bis instead and only five of the B1 ter vehicles were produced.

The Char B1 bis was a fairly complex and advanced vehicle for its time; indeed its maintenance requirements were a potential disadvantage in times of war. Essentially the tank was built like a box; it had slab sides and suspension assemblies bolted to a frame of girders and cross-members, with heavy castings for main structural components. The driver sat in the nose and he also fired the short 75mm gun, which was placed in the hull to his right and had air-blast gear fitted to blow out the recoil fumes. The steering system was of the Naeder hydrostatic type giving very fine directional control by the tracks, the idea being that the vehicle was itself lined up by the driver to lay the nose gun. The gun sight was thus mounted below the driver's episcope and not beside the gun. The commander sat in the turret and fired the 47mm gun, the other crew members being a radio operator and a loader who was supposed to serve both guns. This arrangement of duties was a weakness of the concept, for the two men who controlled the vehicle, driver and commander, had to concentrate all their activities in action on firing the guns.

Many Char B1 bis vehicles fell into German hands in 1940 in common with other French equipment. By German standards the one-man turret made the vehicle unsuitable for first-line use, but a number of vehicles were used for internal security duties in France under the German designation PzKpfw B1 (f). Others had the guns removed and were used for driver training under the designation PzKpfw B1 (f) Fahrschulewagen. The other main tank adaptation was for a flamethrowing vehicle, where the 75mm gun was removed from the hull front and replaced by a flame projector. The flame fuel was carried in an armoured tank fitted to the hull rear. Designation for this variant was PzKpfw B1 bis (f) Flamm. Lastly there was a limited conversion in 1942 to make an SP gun.

MODEL Char B1 bis.

COUNTRY OF ORIGIN France.

WEIGHT 32·5 tonnes (32 tons).

LENGTH 6·3m (20ft 8in).

WIDTH 2·5m (8ft 2in).

HEIGHT 2·8m (9ft 2in).

GROUND CLEARANCE 0·48m (1ft 6½in).

ARMOUR 60mm.

ENGINE 6-cylinder Renault, 307hp, gasoline.

MAXIMUM SPEED 28km/h (17mph).

RANGE 150km (93 miles).

CREW 4.

ARMAMENT 1×75mm gun, 1×47mm gun, 2×7.5mm MG.

AMMUNITION 75mm: 74 rds, 47mm: 50 rds, MG: 5,100 rds.

TRENCH CROSSING 2.75m (9ft).

TRACK WIDTH 50cm (1ft 7in).

MAXIMUM ELEVATION 25°.

FORDING DEPTH 1·47m (4ft 10in).

The Char B1 bis was a heavily armoured and technically impressive type which was developed in the 1930s and was in wide service with the French Army when the war started in September 1939. The vehicle illustrated was from the 4th Armoured Division, commanded by General de Gaulle, and was destroyed in action at Abbeville on 31 May 1940.

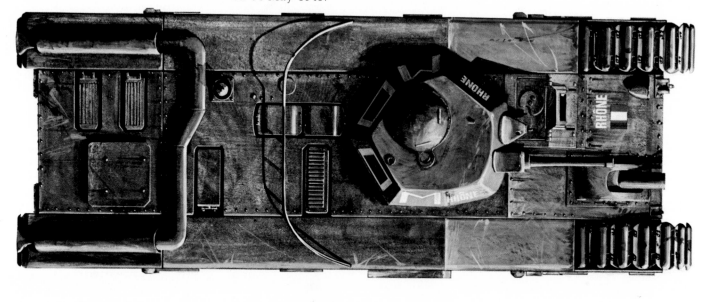

Claudio Tatangelo

Char de Bataille B1 bis

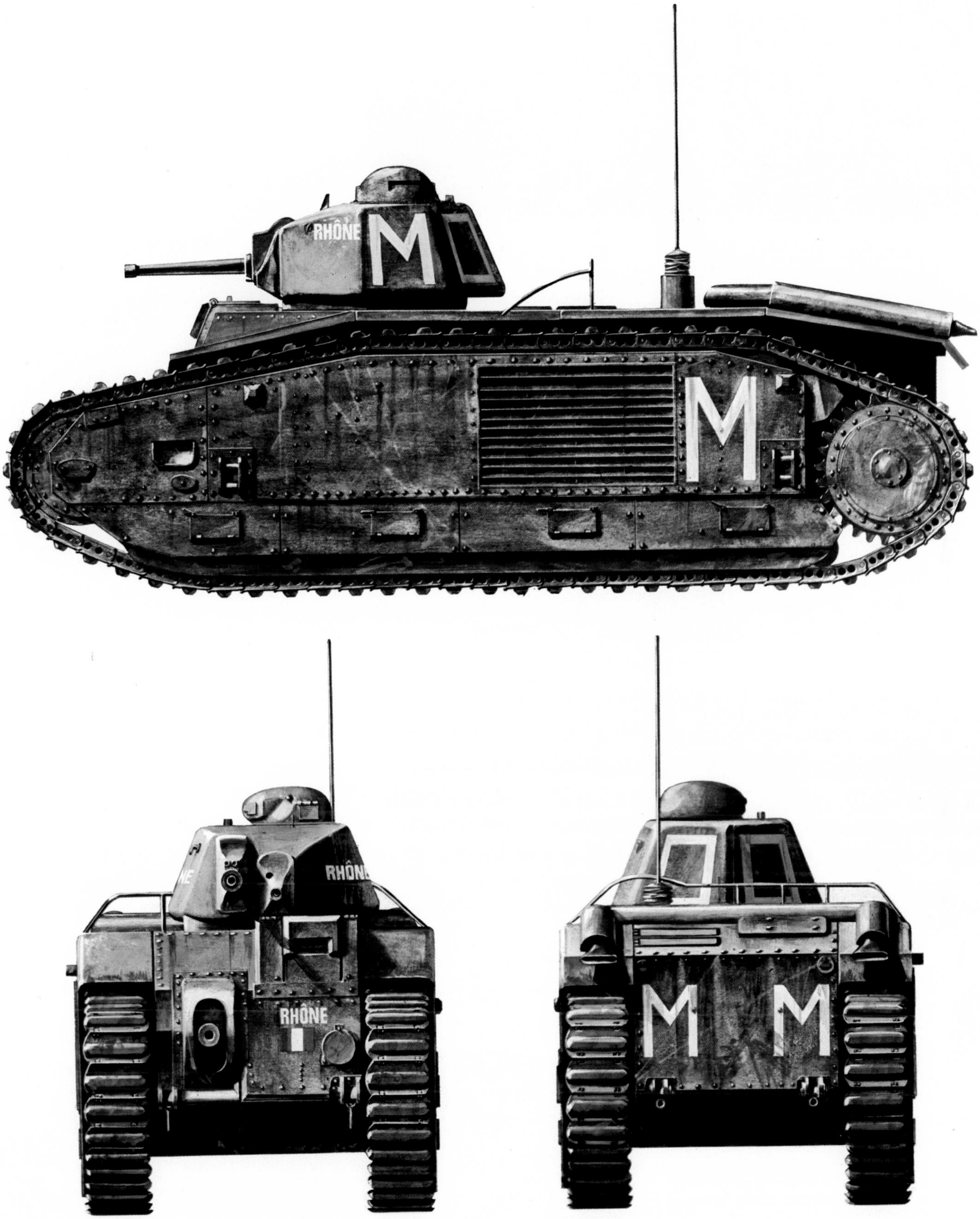
RHÔNE
M
M
RHÔNE
RHÔNE
M M

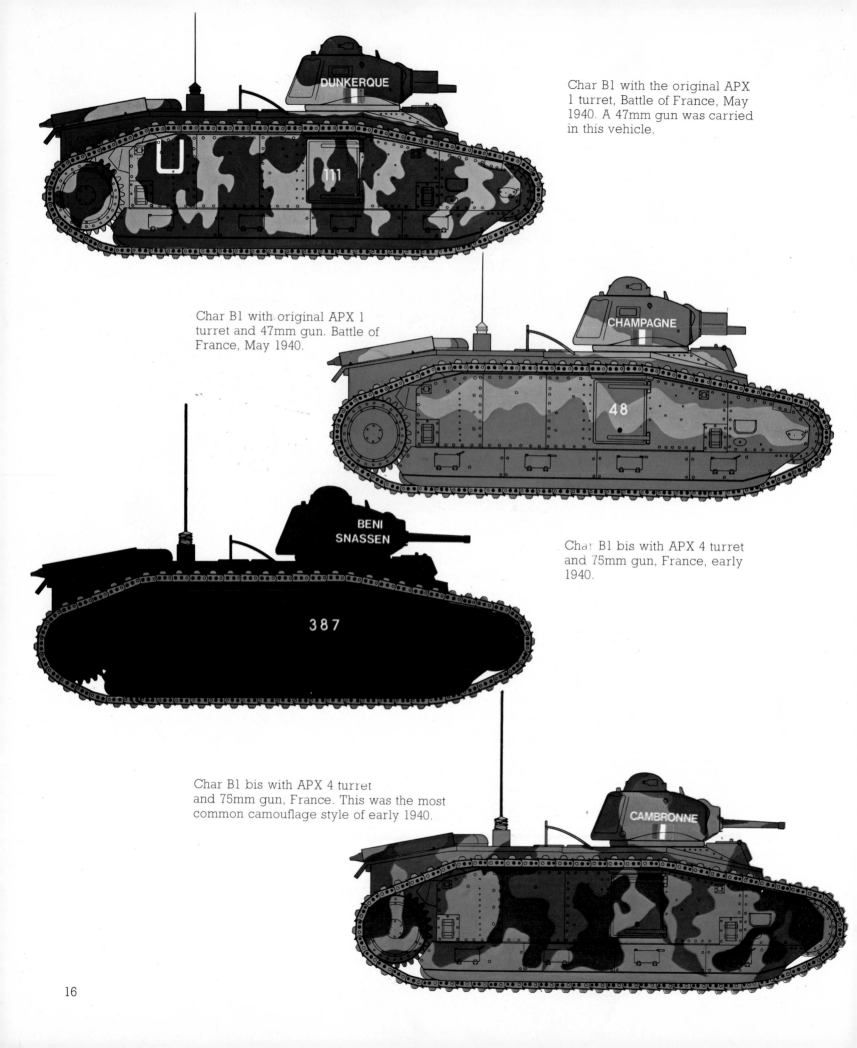

Char B1 with the original APX 1 turret, Battle of France, May 1940. A 47mm gun was carried in this vehicle.

Char B1 with original APX 1 turret and 47mm gun. Battle of France, May 1940.

Char B1 bis with APX 4 turret and 75mm gun, France, early 1940.

Char B1 bis with APX 4 turret and 75mm gun, France. This was the most common camouflage style of early 1940.

Char B1-B1 bis

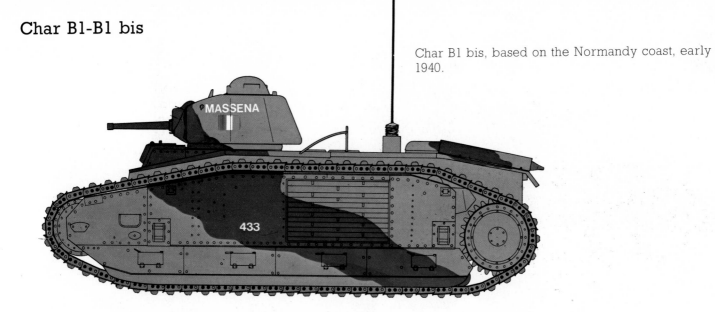

Char B1 bis, based on the Normandy coast, early 1940.

Char B1 bis used by the German occupation forces in France, captured by the British in 1944, and now displayed in the RAC Tank Museum, Bovington, England, restored to French colours.

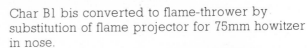

Char B1 bis converted to flame-thrower by substitution of flame projector for 75mm howitzer in nose.

Char B1 bis with turret removed and used as a driver training school vehicle by the Germans in 1941.

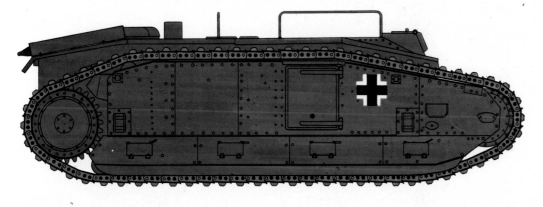

Claudio Tatangelo

Japan's standard medium tank for most of the war years was the Type 97 Chi-Ha, which had advanced features such as monocoque construction, diesel engine and well-sloped armour. However, it was flimsy, too small and too poorly used to be any match for the US M3 and M4 tanks which it most often encountered. Of special note is the radio aerial which it carried horizontally round the turret. The simple bell-crank and coil spring suspension was most effective for a vehicle of this size. The main drawing shows a vehicle of the 6th Company of the 9th Armoured Regiment, as recorded in action on 17 June 1944 at Saipan. The inset view shows the Type 97 7·7mm machine gun carried in the vehicle and pivot-mounted on the turret for AA defence.

0   1   2 m

Danilo Renzulli

Type 97 Chi-Ha

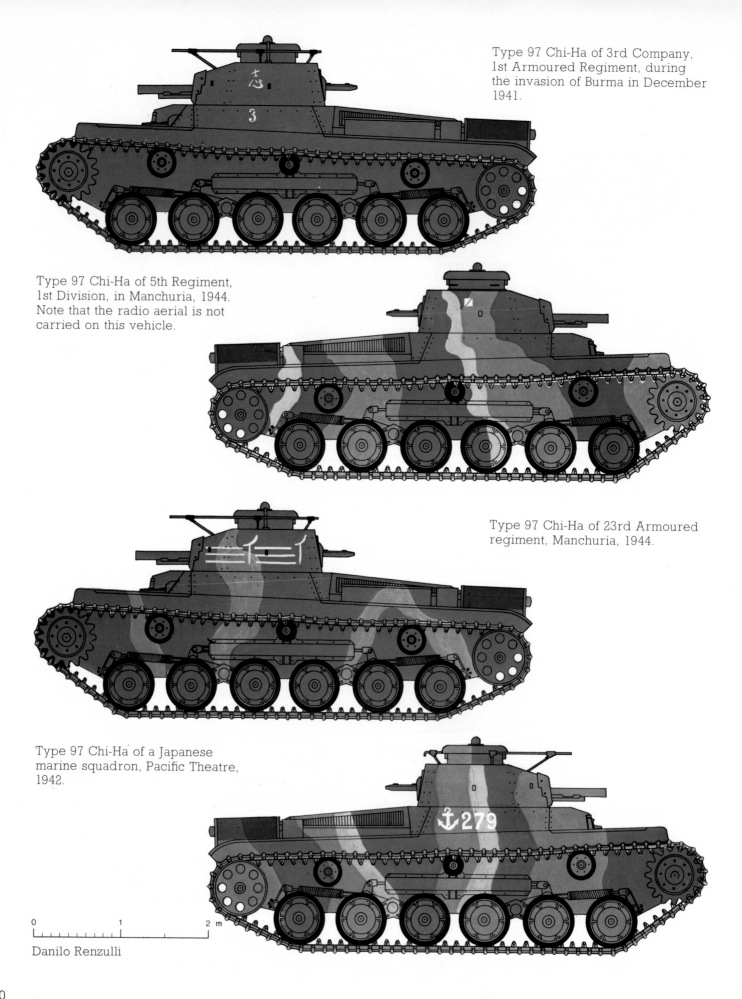

Type 97 Chi-Ha of 3rd Company, 1st Armoured Regiment, during the invasion of Burma in December 1941.

Type 97 Chi-Ha of 5th Regiment, 1st Division, in Manchuria, 1944. Note that the radio aerial is not carried on this vehicle.

Type 97 Chi-Ha of 23rd Armoured regiment, Manchuria, 1944.

Type 97 Chi-Ha of a Japanese marine squadron, Pacific Theatre, 1942.

0   1   2 m

Danilo Renzulli

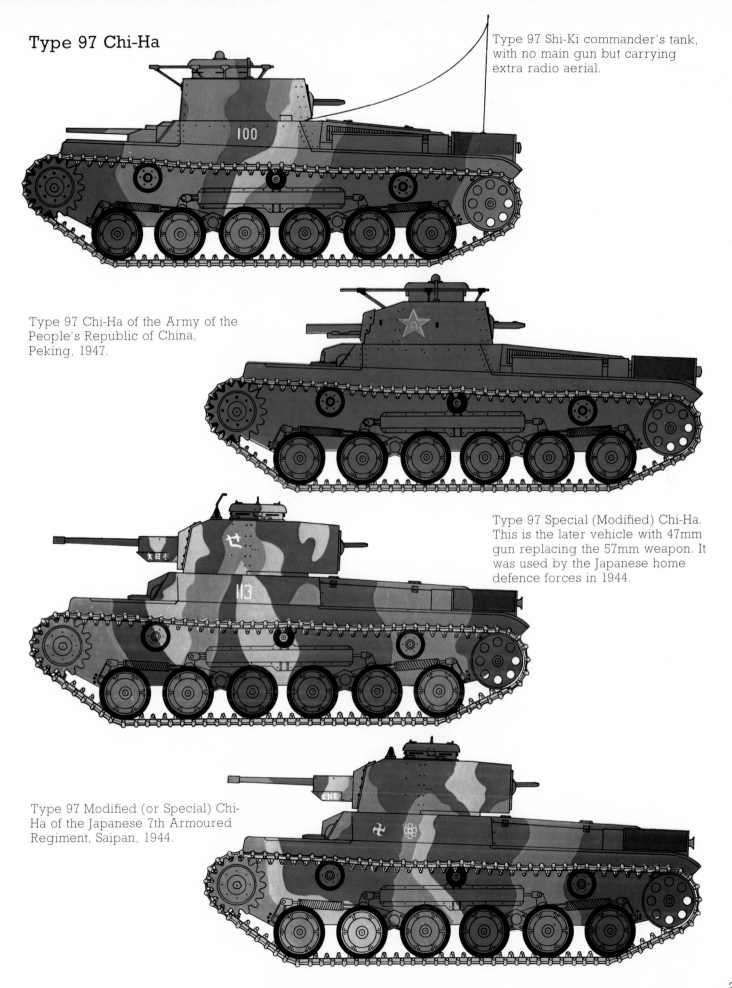

Type 97 Chi-Ha

Type 97 Shi-Ki commander's tank, with no main gun but carrying extra radio aerial.

Type 97 Chi-Ha of the Army of the People's Republic of China, Peking, 1947.

Type 97 Special (Modified) Chi-Ha. This is the later vehicle with 47mm gun replacing the 57mm weapon. It was used by the Japanese home defence forces in 1944.

Type 97 Modified (or Special) Chi-Ha of the Japanese 7th Armoured Regiment, Saipan, 1944.

Type 97 Chi-Ha

From 1929 onwards, the standard medium Japanese tank was the Type 89, which was inspired by the Vickers Model C tank sold to the Japanese government in 1927. Built by Mitsubishi Heavy Industries, the Type 89 was a good machine for its time, seeing extensive service in the Sino–Japanese wars of the 1930s. A development of the period was the adoption of diesel power for the Type 89, in which form it was known as the Type 89B: it was the first production tank with a diesel motor.

With a top speed of 25km/h (15mph), the Type 89B was slow and was used mostly in the classic infantry support role. Developments overseas – notably in Great Britain with its Experimental Mechanized Force – had shown that tanks could be deployed in an independent role. One result of this had been the appearance of the A6 tank in Britain with a 47mm gun and good top speed. Though the A6 never saw production it greatly influenced other powers when they came to design 'new generation' tanks. The Japanese formed a Mechanized Combined Brigade for operations in Manchuria, and found the Type 89B too slow to work with other vehicles. One result of this was to accelerate the development of a new light tank, the Type 95, while consideration was given to the urgent development of a faster up-to-date replacement for the ageing Type 89B. The field requirement was for a top speed of 35km/h (22mph), a 47mm gun, and a top weight of 15 tons, though the General Staff was anxious to limit expenditure and asked for a lighter vehicle.

Mitsubishi Heavy Industries were asked to make one prototype in competition with Osaka Army Arsenal. The Mitsubishi version was to full requirements of weight and speed, while the Osaka model was to the 'economy' specification with both reduced weight of 10 tons and speed of 27km/h (17mph). In both versions the suspension was seen as a means of saving weight, using coil springs and bell-crank type linkage for suspending the bogies. The hull structure was made in monocoque style, with some welding, and the conventional girder frame of the time was therefore eliminated. The superstructure was well sloped and low, and to a great extent both designs pioneered future design trends. Superficially both prototypes were similar in shape though the Osaka vehicle (Chi-Ni) resembled an enlarged Type 95 light tank, and the Mitsubishi vehicle (Chi-Ha) had a more generously dimensioned superstructure. The prototypes were ready for trials in 1937, and both proved faster than their specifications required. Though a 47mm gun was being developed, these prototypes had the same short 57mm gun as the Type 89B. The Chi-Ha had a two-man turret while the Chi-Ni had a one-man type like the Type 95 light tank.

When war was resumed between Japan and China in July 1937, budgetary limitations were subsequently discarded and the more expensive Chi-Ha prototype was selected for production. It was now designated Type 97 (Jinmu year 2597 – Western year 1937), taking its code from the last two digits of the Japanese year of adoption. Final changes as a result of trials included rubber tyres on the return rollers, periscope and episcope vision devices, and wireless installation. Early vehicles had the 57mm gun, considered satisfactory at the time, though the Nomonhan incident in 1939, when Russian tanks clashed with Japanese tanks on the Manchuria–Mongolia border, showed how superior the Russian guns were. This clinched the final adoption of the 47mm gun for the Chi-Ha, and a new turret was designed to take the longer weapon (Type 1 47mm gun of 1941). It increased the overall weight of the tank by 500kg (1,100lb).

'Type 97 Chi-Ha Modified' was the designation of the re-armed vehicle, and it became the most widely used of Japanese medium tanks in World War 2. In the event, despite the Chi-Ha's advanced design, Japanese tank forces had a most undistinguished war, partly because of the jungle terrain and partly because of the tactics employed.

MODEL Type 97 Shinhoto Chi-Ha.

COUNTRY OF ORIGIN Japan.

WEIGHT 16 tonnes (15·8 tons).

LENGTH 5·5m (18ft).

WIDTH 2·3m (7ft 6in).

HEIGHT 2·3m (7ft 6in).

GROUND CLEARANCE 0·40m (1ft 3½in).

ARMOUR 8–25mm.

ENGINE Type 97 V12, 170hp, diesel.

MAXIMUM SPEED 38km/h (24mph).

RANGE 210km (130 miles).

CREW 4.

ARMAMENT 1 × 47mm gun, 2 × 7·7mm MG.

AMMUNITION 47mm: 114 rds, MG: 4,035 rds.

TRENCH CROSSING 2·5m (8ft 2in).

TRACK WIDTH 0·9m (2ft 11in).

MAXIMUM ELEVATION 40°.

FORDING DEPTH 1m (3ft 3in).

Churchill

The story of the Churchill begins in September 1939 when there was a strong feeling at the War Office that conditions on the Western Front would not be very different from 1914–18. Accordingly, there seemed to be a need for a very heavy infantry tank invulnerable to known anti-tank guns and able to cross very wide trenches and negotiate ground churned up by shell fire. Designated A20, a specification was drawn up by Woolwich Arsenal, and Harland and Wolff were asked to build a pilot model. Armour thickness of 80mm, a top speed of 24km/h (15mph), ability to climb a 1·5m (5ft) parapet, and a crew of seven were among the requirements. Various combinations of armament were considered, but finally a 2pdr was selected for the turret, with another in the nose and machine guns recessed in the hull side at the front. Four pilot models were ordered in February 1940. However, the first pilot model on trials in June 1940 had gearbox trouble.

This coincided with the Dunkirk evacuation, when Britain was left with less than 100 tanks for home defence. Vauxhall was therefore asked to develop the A20 design further, scale it down slightly, and get it into production as rapidly as possible. A pilot model of the new design, A22, Infantry Tank Mk IV, was ready by November 1940. Due to the rushed development programme for this vehicle, there were numerous defects in the design which led to frequent breakdowns with the early marks. This necessitated considerable re-work programmes in 1942–3, the sending of Vauxhall engineers to units equipped with the tank, and numerous detail improvements to the mechanical components.

Named Churchill, the A22 was built in quantity by a production group under the direction of Vauxhall. The Churchill was of composite construction consisting of an inner skin of 125mm mild steel with an outer covering of armour plate bolted or riveted in position. Initially a cast turret was fitted, but later models had larger turrets of either cast,

welded, or composite construction. The engine and drive were at the rear, and the overall tracks with small sprung bogie assemblies allowed space between the lower and upper runs of track for stowage of ammunition and stores, making the Churchill an unusually roomy vehicle. Escape doors for the crew were fitted in each side. Transmission featured the new Merritt-Brown four-speed gearbox which provided controlled differential steering, the first on any British tank. The engine was a very reliable Bedford Twin-Six, adapted from two Bedford truck engines.

Armament of the Mk I was a 2pdr with a 3in howitzer in the hull front. Changing tactical requirements, however, led to an alteration of armament through the Churchill's production life. In common with the British cruiser tanks a 6pdr gun was fitted in 1942, necessitating a larger turret (Mk III). Experience in the desert fighting of 1941–2 led the British War Office to believe that speed and reliability were more important than heavy armour, and it was decided to stop Churchill production in 1943 when the A27 series of cruiser tanks became available. However, the Churchill's first combat actions, with the 1st Army in the Tunisian campaign, proved most successful and this earned the vehicle a reprieve. In 1943, the Churchill was again up-gunned (Mk VII) with the new British version of the 75mm gun. At the same time major design changes were made. Since it was built to meet British rail loading gauge restrictions, the Churchill suffered from the same disadvantage as other contemporary British designs in that it was too narrow to take the larger turret required for the 17pdr gun. Thus by 1944–5 it was under-gunned by German standards, but this drawback was offset to a certain extent by the vehicle's heavy armour protection.

An enlarged version was designed, named A43 Black Prince, with a 17pdr gun. But the war had ended when the prototype appeared and it never saw service.

MODELS Churchill Mk I–VIII.

COUNTRY OF ORIGIN Great Britain.

WEIGHT 39 tonnes (38·5 tons) up to Mk VI; 40·6 tonnes (40 tons) remainder.

LENGTH 7·43m (24ft 5in).

WIDTH All except Mk VII: 3·2m (10ft 8in): **Mk VII**: 3·4m (11ft 4in).

HEIGHT All except Mk VII: 2·5m (8ft 2in); **Mk VII**: 2·7m (9ft).

GROUND CLEARANCE 0·57m (2ft).

ARMOUR **Mk I–VI**: 16–102mm; **Mk VII and VIII**: 25–152mm.

ENGINE Bedford 350hp, gasoline.

MAXIMUM SPEED **Mk VII**: 20km/h (12·5mph); others: 25km/h (15·5mph).

RANGE 193km (120 miles).

CREW 5.

ARMAMENT All: 1–2 MG plus: **Mk I**: 1 × 2pdr, 1 × 3in; **Mk II**: 1 × 2pdr; **Mk III and IV**: 1 × 6pdr; **Mk V**: 1 × 95mm; **Mk VI and VII**: 1 × 75mm; **Mk VIII**: 1 × 95mm.

AMMUNITION Besa MG: 42 boxes of 225 rds, 2pdr (**Mk I, II**): 150 rds, 3in (**Mk I, IICS**): 58 rds, 6pdr (**Mk III, IV**): 84 rds, 95mm (**Mk V, VIII**): 47 rds, 75mm (**Mk VI, VII**): 84 rds.

TRENCH CROSSING 3·04m (10ft).

TRACK WIDTH 0·35m (1ft 2in).

MAXIMUM ELEVATION 20°.

FORDING DEPTH 1·01m (3ft 4in).

Infantry Tank Mk IV (A22) Churchill was originally developed from the concept of a 'shelled area' tank put forward in 1939 when conditions like those of World War 1 were expected on the Western Front. It was eventually developed somewhat differently after the events in 1940. However, it remained a slow and heavily armoured vehicle. In its Mk I form shown here it had a 2pdr gun in a cast turret and a 3in howitzer

in the nose, reflecting the influence of the French Char B which was produced to similar requirements in the 1930s. The example illustrated served with 14th Canadian Armoured Regiment and was used in the unsuccessful Dieppe raid of May 1942. The trunking and exhaust extensions were used to waterproof the vehicle for wading ashore from landing craft. They were discarded on reaching shore.

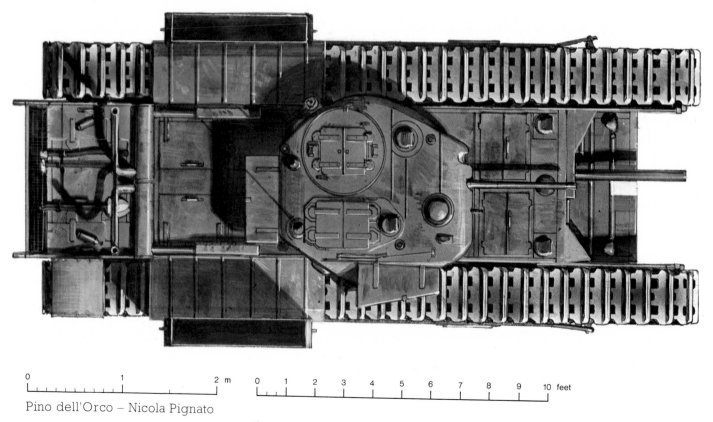

Pino dell'Orco – Nicola Pignato

24

Infantry Tank Mk IV (A22) Churchill I

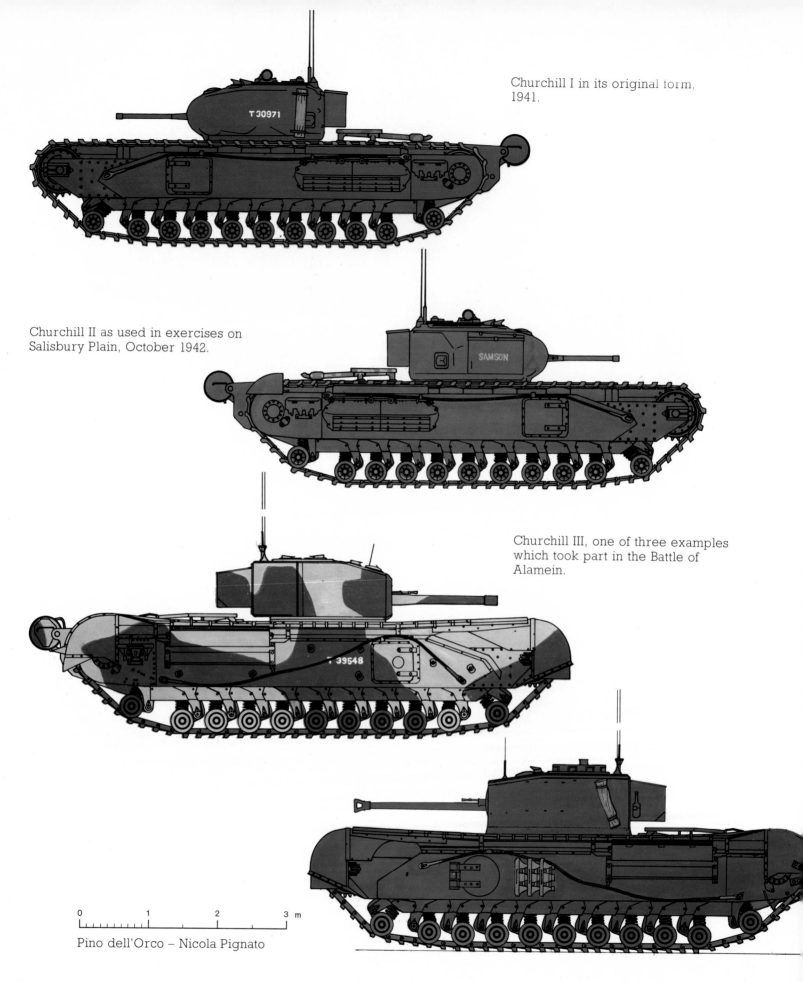

Churchill I in its original form, 1941.

Churchill II as used in exercises on Salisbury Plain, October 1942.

Churchill III, one of three examples which took part in the Battle of Alamein.

Pino dell'Orco – Nicola Pignato

Churchill

Churchill III (named 'Suffolk') of 142nd Royal Tank Regiment, Battle of Medjez el-Bab, Tunis, 6 March 1943.

Churchill IV, operating in England in 1942. This vehicle has the 6pdr Mk V gun which required a counterweight on the barrel. The 6pdr Mk III did not require this fitting.

Churchill IV supplied to the Soviet Army under Lease-Lend, 1943.

Churchill VII Crocodile. This was the specialist flame-thrower variant with armoured flame fuel trailer, and flame projector carried in nose. The Churchill VII was armed with a 75mm gun and had a heavy cast turret.

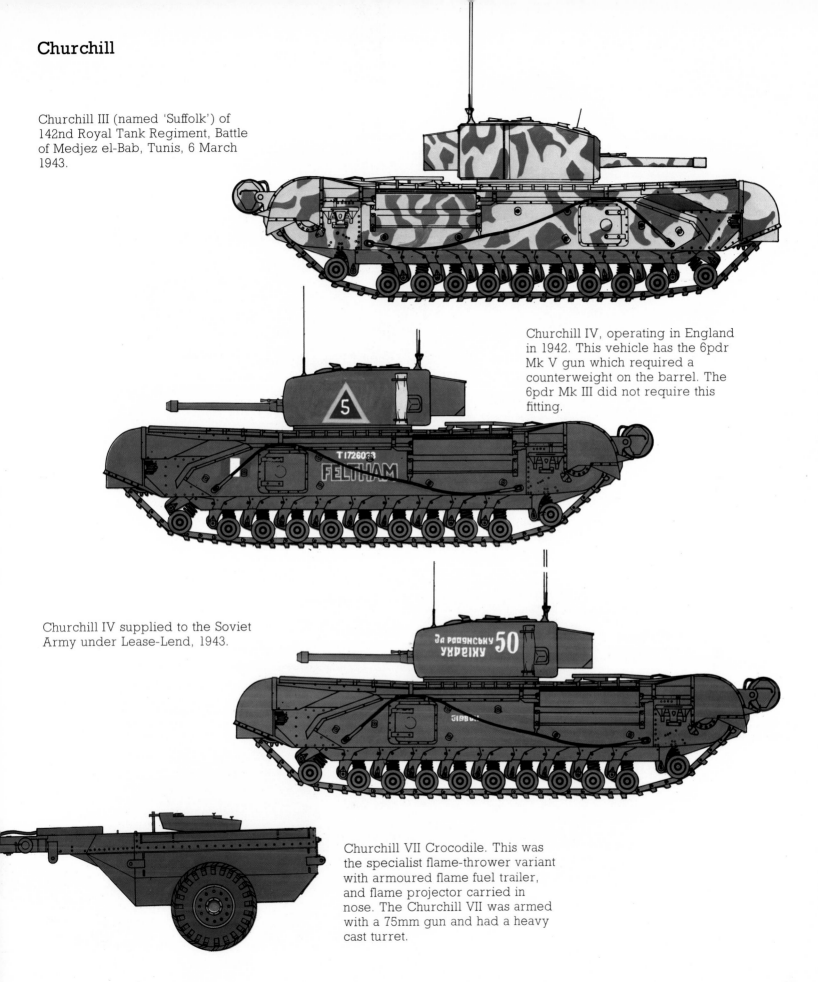

The Comet (A34) was the last British tank type to enter service before the war ended, though its planned successor, the Centurion, was just starting troop trials as the war finished. A feature of this design was the 'compact' version of the famous 17pdr gun, the 77mm, designed to fit the Comet's small turret ring which was not large enough to take a standard 17pdr. In essence the Comet was a redesign of the famous Cromwell tank, and Comets served the British Army well into the 1960s. The vehicle illustrated was in service with 11th Armoured Division in 1945, equipping the 23rd Hussars, the first unit issued with this tank.

Pino dell'Orco – Nicola Pignato

Cruiser Tank A34 Comet

52

THERESE
52
COBRA
T335042

T335042

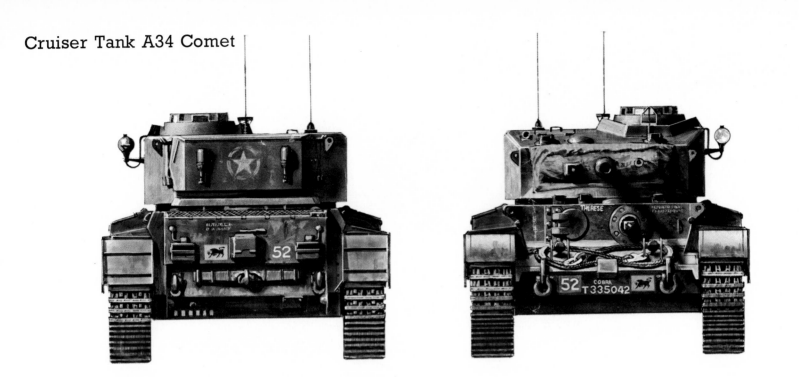

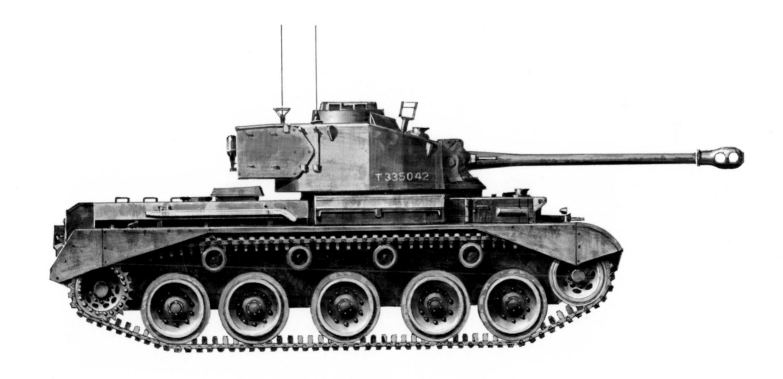

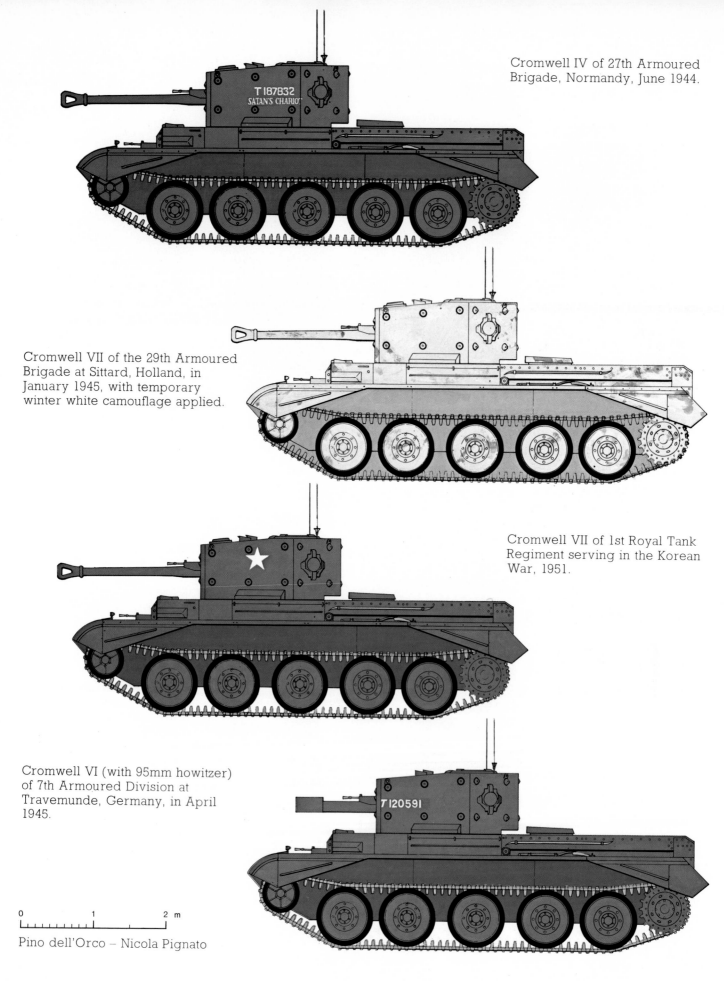

Cromwell IV of 27th Armoured Brigade, Normandy, June 1944.

Cromwell VII of the 29th Armoured Brigade at Sittard, Holland, in January 1945, with temporary winter white camouflage applied.

Cromwell VII of 1st Royal Tank Regiment serving in the Korean War, 1951.

Cromwell VI (with 95mm howitzer) of 7th Armoured Division at Travemunde, Germany, in April 1945.

0   1   2 m

Pino dell'Orco – Nicola Pignato

Cromwell and Comet

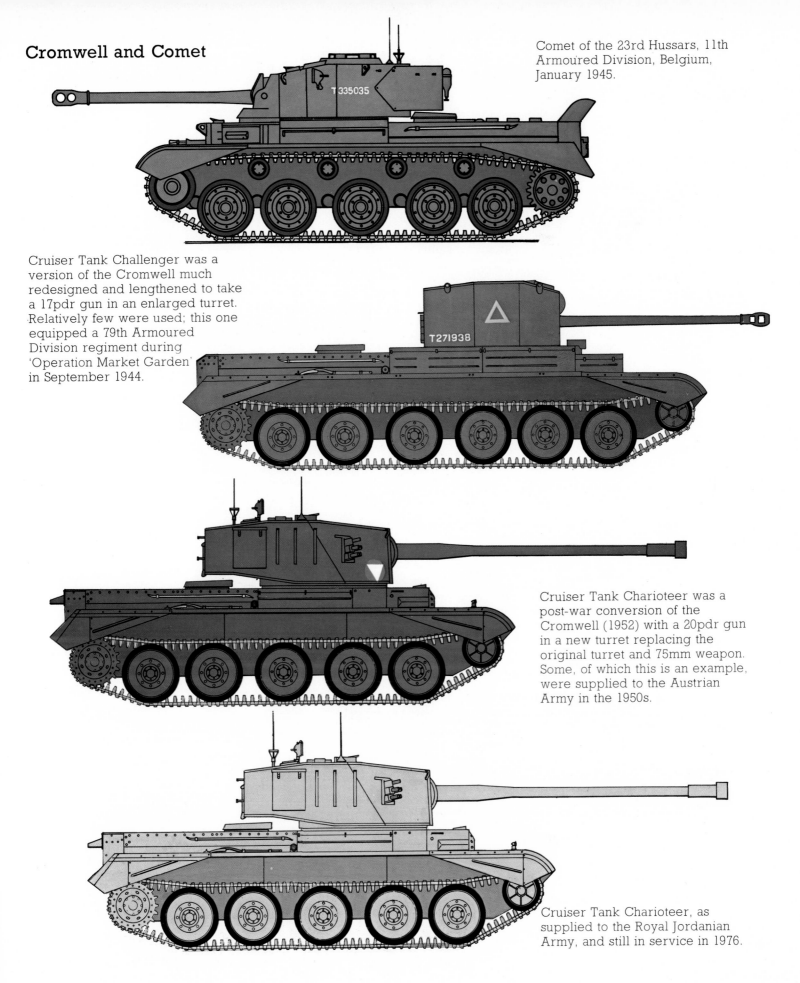

Comet of the 23rd Hussars, 11th Armoured Division, Belgium, January 1945.

Cruiser Tank Challenger was a version of the Cromwell much redesigned and lengthened to take a 17pdr gun in an enlarged turret. Relatively few were used; this one equipped a 79th Armoured Division regiment during 'Operation Market Garden' in September 1944.

Cruiser Tank Charioteer was a post-war conversion of the Cromwell (1952) with a 20pdr gun in a new turret replacing the original turret and 75mm weapon. Some, of which this is an example, were supplied to the Austrian Army in the 1950s.

Cruiser Tank Charioteer, as supplied to the Royal Jordanian Army, and still in service in 1976.

Cromwell and Comet

To replace the Crusader an enlarged cruiser tank was designed, having a larger turret able to accommodate the new 6pdr gun. Designated A27 it was intended to have a new powerful engine, the Meteor, adapted from the Rolls-Royce Merlin aero engine. Due to shortages of Merlin engines, however, early vehicles had the old Liberty engine and were called the Centaur.

The Meteor-engined version of the A27 design was designated A27M (M=Meteor engine). The Meteor engine as adapted from the Merlin for tank use had about 80 per cent of its component parts identical to the aircraft engine. Cromwell production began in January 1943 and the choice of such a powerful engine was fully justified by results; furthermore, plenty of power was available for any future developments of the A27 type.

Meanwhile, fighting in the Western Desert, coupled with the decisive appearance of the American-built M3 and M4 medium tanks in that theatre led to a requirement for a gun with 'dual-purpose' capability – able to fire HE or AP shot – as fitted in the very successful M3 and M4 mediums. Work on a British-designed version of the 75mm gun – virtually a bored-out development of the British 6pdr gun – able to fire American ammunition, was put in hand in December 1942 and Cromwells from Mk IV onward were produced with this weapon in place of the 6pdr. The first vehicles to be equipped were delivered in November 1943.

The Cromwell was the most important British-built cruiser tank of World War 2, forming the main equipment of British armoured divisions in 1944–5 together with the American-built M4 Sherman. However, even with a 75mm gun it was still, by 1944 standards, inferior to the best German tanks. With its Meteor engine it was then the fastest and most powerful of British tank designs, but the narrow hull prevented its being up-gunned further and considerable redesign was necessary to turn it into a vehicle capable of carrying the very desirable 17pdr gun armament.

All the A24/A27 series were structurally similar, with a hull and turret of simple box shape and composite construction – an inner skin with an outer layer of armour bolted on. Driver and co-driver/hull machine gunner sat in the forward compartment, and the turret crew consisted of the commander, gunner and loader who was also the radio operator. Tracks were manganese with centre guides, and engine and transmission were at the rear. An important innovation was the introduction on later models of all-welded construction in place of riveting, thus further simplifying mass-production.

The Leyland company took over production supervision of the Cromwell early in 1943 and they immediately began work on designing an improved version to overcome the limitations of the A27 design. Mechanically and dimensionally the improved vehicle, designated A34, was similar to the A27. To avoid the need for widening the hull to take the 17pdr gun, Vickers-Armstrong designed a new compact version of the 17pdr with a shorter barrel, shorter breech and lighter weight. It had a performance and penetrating power only slightly inferior to the 17pdr gun and fired the same ammunition. It was intended that the 77mm gun should go in the original A27 type turret with only small modifications, but after tests an enlarged turret was found necessary. The A34 pilot model was ready for tests in February 1944, and among modifications incorporated as a result of trials was a stronger suspension with the addition of track return rollers. Production deliveries commenced in September 1944; with the exception of a few trials vehicles issued earlier, the first A34s, then named Comet, were issued to battalions of the 11th Armoured Division after the Rhine crossing in March 1945.

The Comet proved fast and reliable, the first British tank to come near matching the German Panther in performance and gun power. However, it appeared too late to play a significant part in tank combat in the war.

MODELS Cromwell and Comet.

COUNTRY OF ORIGIN Great Britain.

WEIGHT **Cromwell:** 27·4–28·4 tonnes (27–28 tons); **Comet:** 33 tonnes (32·5 tons).

LENGTH **Cromwell:** 6·3m (20ft 10in); **Comet:** 7·6m (25ft).

WIDTH **Cromwell:** 2·9m (9ft 6in); **Comet:** 3·04m (10ft).

HEIGHT **Cromwell:** 2·5m (8ft 2in); **Comet:** 2·6m (8ft 9in).

GROUND CLEARANCE **Cromwell:** 0·41m (1ft 4in); **Comet:** 0·45m (1ft 5½in).

ARMOUR **Cromwell:** 8–76mm; **Comet:** 14–101mm.

ENGINE Meteor, 600hp, gasoline.

MAXIMUM SPEED **Cromwell:** 50–64km/h (32–40mph); **Comet:** 46km/h (29mph).

RANGE **Cromwell:** 278km (173 miles); **Comet:** 197km (123 miles).

CREW 5.

ARMAMENT **Cromwell:** 1 × 75mm gun, 2 × 7·92mm MG; **Comet:** 1 × 77mm gun, 2 × 7·92mm MG.

AMMUNITION **Cromwell:** 75mm: 64 rds, Besa MG: 4,950 rds, Vickers MG: 2,000 rds; **Comet:** 77mm: 61 rds, Besa MG: 5,175 rds.

TRENCH CROSSING **Cromwell:** 2·28m (7ft 6in); **Comet:** 2·43m (8ft).

TRACK WIDTH **Cromwell:** 0·33m (1ft 2in); **Comet:** 0·45m (1ft 6in).

MAXIMUM ELEVATION **Cromwell:** 20°; **Comet:** 20°.

FORDING DEPTH **Cromwell:** 0·91m (3ft); **Comet:** 0·91m (3ft).

Cruiser Tank A9/A15

The Vickers Medium Mk II and Vickers light tank types formed the main British armoured strength in the 1930s and a proposed Medium Mk III was dropped on the grounds of expense. In 1934, Vickers-Armstrong designed a new medium tank, designated A9, to meet General Staff requirements. It incorporated the best features of the discontinued Medium Mk III, but was much lighter so that it could be powered by a standard commercially made engine.

Two types of tank, 'cruiser' (essentially the old 'medium' class) and 'infantry', had been decided upon by the British War Office in 1936 when considering future requirements. The A9 thus became the Cruiser Tank Mk I. Trials of the pilot model started in July 1936 and production of 125 vehicles commenced a year later.

The A10 was mechanically and structurally similar to the A9, but it lacked the auxiliary front turrets which had been a distinctive feature of the A9. The requirements called for a lower speed but an armour basis of 24mm, later increased to 30mm with the addition of a machine gun alongside the driver.

The A10 had the same turret and the same boat-shaped hull as the A9, and the additional armour was achieved by bolting extra plates to the outside of the hull and turret structures. Another important step in the development of British tanks was the A13, since it started the long run of cruiser tanks with Christie suspension produced by the British.

Two Christie vehicles were purchased in 1936 and two prototypes were designed based on these, but larger. Tests revealed many mechanical problems, mostly stemming from the vehicle's high speed of more than 56km/h (35mph). Modifications included governing the speed down to 48km/h (30mph), altering the clutch and transmission, and using shorter-pitched tracks. By January 1938 most of the problems had been overcome and a production order was confirmed for 65 vehicles. Further detail modifications were made to fittings before production was started by Nuffield Mechanis-

ations and Aero Ltd, a company formed specially for munitions work by Morris. Deliveries started early in 1939, and the order was completed by summer 1939, the tank being named Cruiser Mk III.

Cruiser Mk IV was essentially an up-armoured version which followed the Cruiser Mk III in production and arose from a decision taken in early 1939 to increase the armour basis to 30mm for cruiser tanks. The extra armour plating was mainly on the nose, glacis and turret. The LMS Co. was next asked to work on an improved version of the A13, the Mk III. This was to be built with a 30mm armour basis, and to have a lower overall height.

To keep the profile to the required low height, a Meadows flat-12 engine was fitted, and a Wilson compound epicycle gearbox was incorporated. The driver's position was relocated to the right and the radiators for the engine were sited in the front of the vehicle on his left. The first production models, named the Covenanter, were delivered in early 1940, but this tank had problems with the cooling system.

The A15 Crusader stemmed from the same line of development that gave rise to the Covenanter. It was to be built to a 30–40mm armour basis, which was much superior to that of other designs, and had the well-proven Liberty engine. Approval to go ahead was given in July 1939 with an initial order for 200 tanks plus the pilot model. This latter was ready by March 1940. In mid-1940 the order for A15s was increased to 400, then to 1,062. Total output until 1943 was 5,300 vehicles.

Early troubles with the pilot model included poor ventilation, inadequate engine cooling and mechanical problems with the gear change. Though most of these problems were overcome, the Crusader, as it was named, always suffered from unreliability, and the speed with which it was put into production did not allow long development trials, particularly for desert operations. It was in this theatre that the Crusader became the most important tank from spring 1941 until early 1943.

MODELS Cruiser Tank Mk I A9 and Cruiser Tank Mk VI A15 Crusader.

COUNTRY OF ORIGIN Great Britain.

WEIGHT **A9**: 12·2 tonnes (12 tons); **A15**: 19·3 tonnes (19 tons).

LENGTH **A9**: 5·8m (19ft 3in); **A15**: 5·97m (19ft 8in).

WIDTH **A9**: 2·5m (8ft 4in); **A15**: 2·76m (9ft 1in).

HEIGHT **A9**: 2·5m (8ft 4in); **A15**: 2·23m (7ft 4in).

GROUND CLEARANCE 0·41m (1ft 4in).

ARMOUR **A9**: 14mm; **A15**: 7–40mm.

ENGINES **A9**: AEC 150hp, gasoline; **A15**: Liberty 340hp, gasoline.

MAXIMUM SPEED **A9**: 40km/h (25mph); **A15**: 44km/h (27·5mph).

RANGE **A9**: 285km (177 miles); **A15**: 380km (236 miles).

CREW **A9**: 6; **A15**: 5.

ARMAMENT **A9**: 1 × 2pdr, 3 × Vickers ·303in MG; **A15**: 1 × 2pdr, 2 × Besa MG.

AMMUNITION **A9**: 2pdr: 100 rds, Vickers MG: 3,000 rds; **A15**: 2pdr: 110 rds, MG: 4,500 rds.

TRENCH CROSSING **A9**: 2·4m (8ft); **A15**: 2·28m (7ft 6in).

TRACK WIDTH **A9**: 0·35m (1ft 2in); **A15**: 0·26m (10·7in).

MAXIMUM ELEVATION **A9**: 20°; **A15**: 20°.

FORDING DEPTH **A9**: 0·97m (3ft); **A15**: 1m (3ft 3in).

The Crusader was the fastest and best of the British tanks used by the 8th Army in the desert war in North Africa. It could be unreliable, but was much respected by the enemy, having a top speed of almost 64km/h (40mph) which could be exploited at its best in desert conditions. The vehicle illustrated is a Crusader III of 6th Armoured Division at Tunis in early 1943.

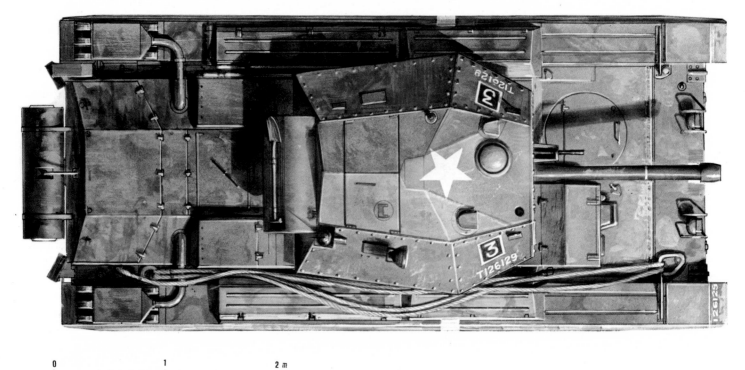

0   1   2 m

Pino dell'Orco – Nicola Pignato

Cruiser Tank Mk VI (A15) Crusader III

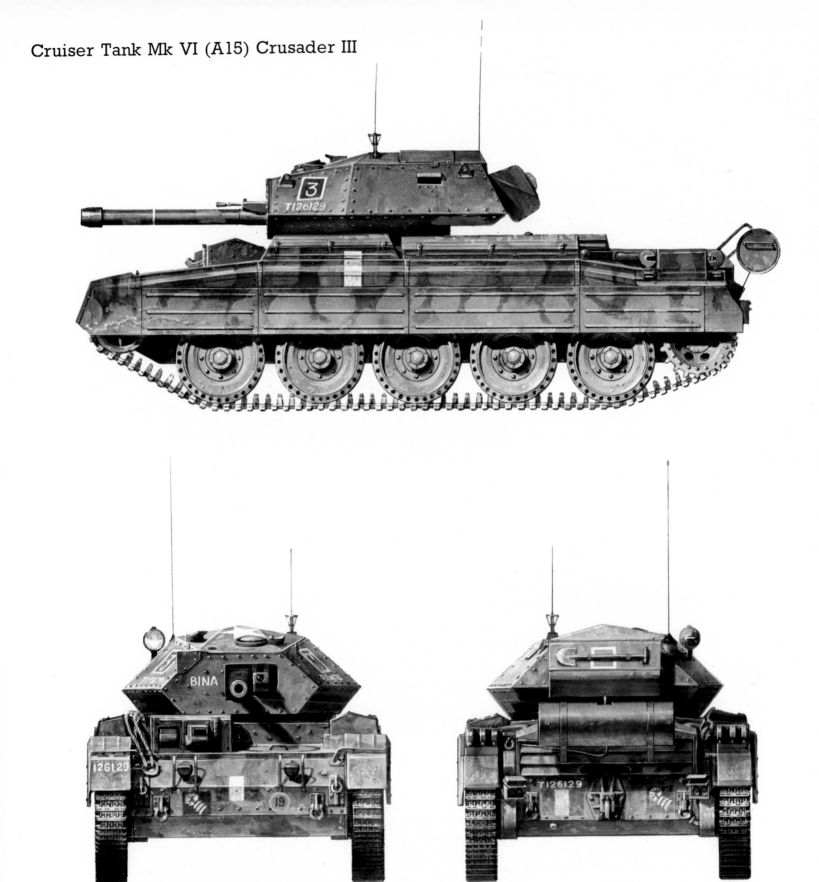

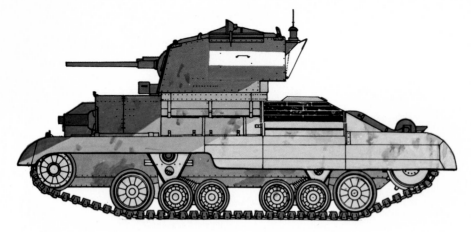

Cruiser Tank Mk I captured and used by the 63rd Tank Battalion of the Italian Army, October 1940.

Cruiser Tank MK IICS (close support) of 2nd Armoured Division, captured by Italian forces and taken to Italy for evaluation at the Central School of Motorization.

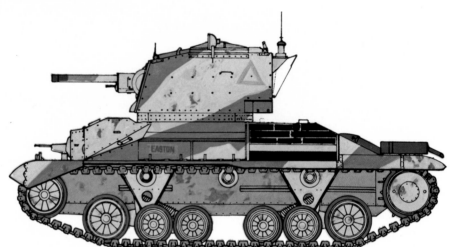

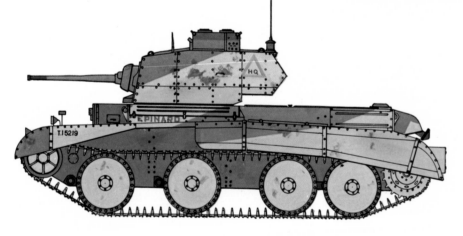

Cruiser Tank Mk IV of 2nd Armoured Division, Libya, 1941.

Cruiser Tank Mk VI, Crusader I, Bir El Gobi, December 1941. Note auxiliary front turret.

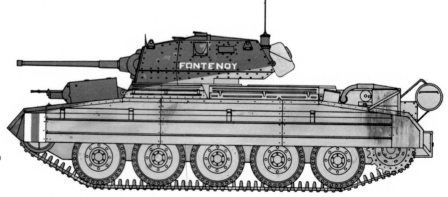

Pino dell'Orco – Nicola Pignato

Cruiser Tank A9/A15

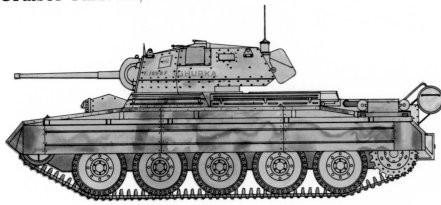

Cruiser Tank Mk VI, Crusader II, at El-Alamein, October 1942.

Cruiser Tank Mk VI, Crusader II, at Alam Halfa, August 1942.

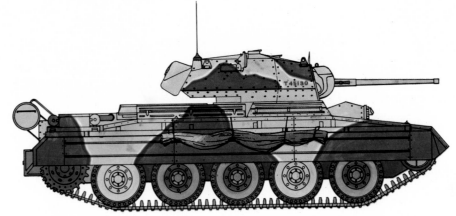

Turret of Crusader AA Mk II of 7th Armoured Division showing twin 20mm guns, Normandy, June 1944.

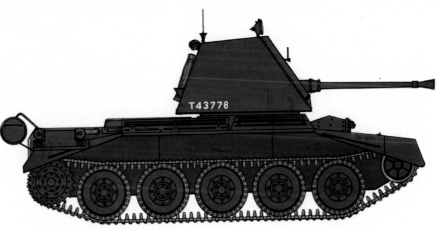

Crusader AA Mk I with 40mm Bofors gun in open turret.

Flakpanzer IV (2cm) Wirbelwind Auf Fahrgestell IV/3 was an interesting example of the series of flak vehicles based on tank chassis and produced during the final stages of the war. It carries the typical mixture of dark-green and dark-earth camouflage applied over the standard factory yellow finish at a time of almost total Allied air superiority. More tanks and other AFVs were being destroyed from the air by machines like Typhoons, P-47s and Stormoviks than were being destroyed by Allied tanks and anti-tank guns. As a result the Germans were forced to divert much effort to making AA vehicles to defend their field units, and dark colours were commonly adopted by German armoured vehicles in the last year or so of the war. Also typical of late-war practice is the absence of unit or tactical marks.

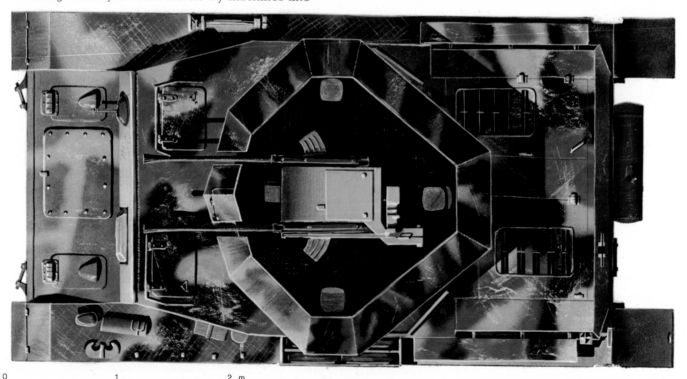

0   1   2 m

Danilo Renzulli

Flakpanzer IV (2cm) Wirbelwind auf Fahrgestell IV/3

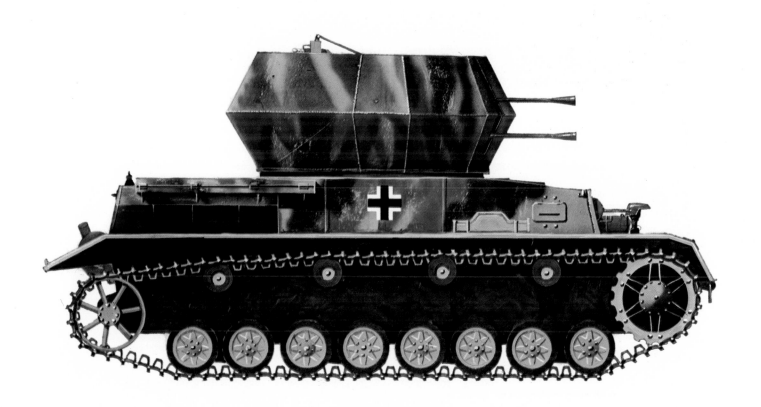

Flakpanzer IV (3·7cm) Ostwind of
an unidentified unit.

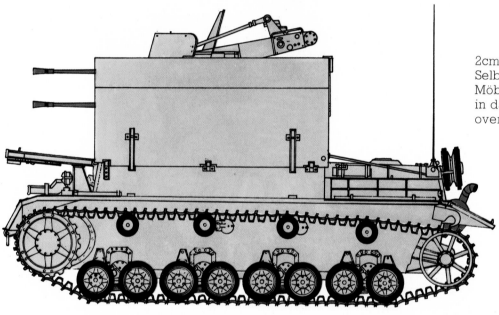

2cm Flakvierling 38 auf
Selbstfahrlafette PzKpfw IV
Möbelwagen. This is a new vehicle
in dark yellow factory finish
overall.

3·7cm Flak 43 auf Selbstfahrlafette
PzKpfw IV Möbelwagen was a
further design based on the
PzKpfw IV chassis.

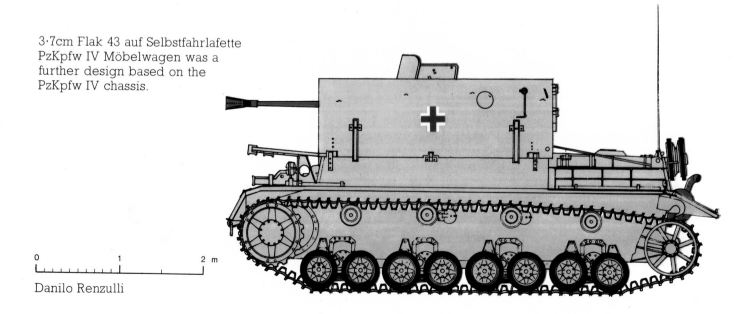

0   1   2 m

Danilo Renzulli

Flakpanzer IV and 38(t)

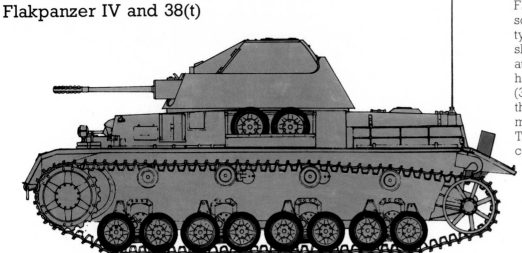

Flakpanzer IV Kügelblitz was a sophisticated AA tank with 'ball' type turret inside an armoured shield. It used the same 30mm automatic cannon with belt feed as had been developed for U-boats (3cm FlaK 103/38). It is believed that only two, and certainly no more than five, vehicles were built. The war ended before production could begin.

8·8cm Flak auf Sonderfahrgestell never went into production. It was a prototype installation of the 8·8cm FlaK 41 on a 'special chassis' – essentially a lengthened Panther tank hull. The sides folded down to form a platform for the crew when the gun went into action.

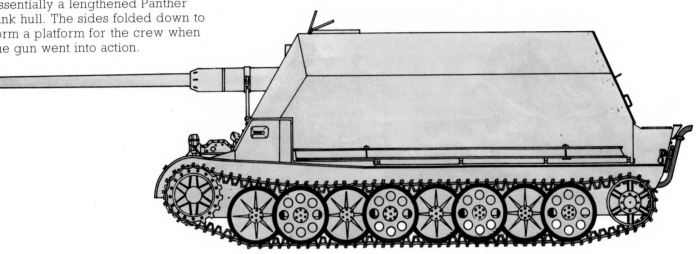

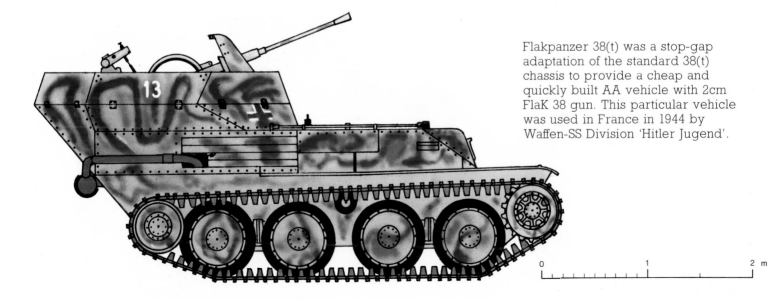

Flakpanzer 38(t) was a stop-gap adaptation of the standard 38(t) chassis to provide a cheap and quickly built AA vehicle with 2cm FlaK 38 gun. This particular vehicle was used in France in 1944 by Waffen-SS Division 'Hitler Jugend'.

0   1   2 m

Flakpanzer IV and 38(t)

As the war progressed, the ever-increasing strength of Allied air power caused grave problems for the Wehrmacht on both Eastern and Western fronts. There was therefore an urgent need to strengthen AA defence power for panzer units and a number of models were developed in the 1943–4 period.

First of these was the 3·7cm Flak auf Fahrgestell PzKpw IV (Sf) (Sd Kfz 161/3) or Möbelwagen. This was a hurried design considered to be a stop-gap while a purpose-built AA tank (the Kügelblitz) was designed and put into production. Essentially the Möbelwagen was a PzKpfw IV with the turret removed and a 3·7cm FlaK 43 mounted in its place. It was an extremely simple conversion with hand traverse and armoured shields (30mm thick) forming a 'box' around the mount. When the vehicle went into action the shields were dropped to make a larger platform on which the five-man crew could man the gun (the sixth crew member was the vehicle driver). Some 240 vehicles were produced by Krupp and the type was built from March 1944 to March 1945, being issued to the AA platoons of tank regiments.

To supplement the Möbelwagen, a second Flakpanzer IV was built with 2cm Flakvierling. Some 86 vehicles were constructed in the July–November 1944 period, using old 'war weary' PzKpfw IV tanks with their turrets removed. The 2cm Flakvierling 38 was a quad automatic mount with a high cyclic rate of fire. An open-topped, multi-faceted turret was used to protect the mount and crew. The mount was hand traversed and laid, and the turret had 16mm of angled armour. This vehicle was called the Wirbelwind (Whirlwind). Production was curtailed largely because the 2cm gun was much less effective than the 3·7cm.

As a replacement for the Wirbelwind an improved model, the Ostwind (East-wind) was designed. Fully designated Flakpanzer IV/3·7cm Flak, 43 vehicles were built by the Ostbau company between December 1944 and March 1945. Most of these were old tanks converted, but seven were built new. In fact, 100 were ordered but all German war production virtually ceased in March 1945. The turret was of similar type to the Wirbelwind but modified in shape to carry the FlaK 43 3·7cm gun as mounted in the Möbelwagen. In all these vehicles sighting was by the standard Flakvisier, a visual range-finder and sight, hand-held by the gun commander.

While these expedient types were being very quickly produced, the Rheinmetall and Daimler-Benz companies were co-operating to combine a PzKpfw IV chassis with a new, fully armoured 'ball' type turret carrying two high-performance 3cm Mk 103 Doppelflak automatic cannon of the type then being designed for new U-boats. To give fast smooth traverse the turret race was taken from the Tiger tank, and mechanical traverse was used to give elevation and traverse at 10° per second. The guns were belt fed and had a rate of fire of 650rpm. The design was finalized in November 1944 and production of 30 vehicles a month was ordered. However, because of the disruption of industry, only two vehicles were completed before the war ended.

The other flak vehicle built in the same general period was the Flakpanzer 38(t) auf St 38(t) Ausf M. This actually pre-dated the Flakpanzer IV models and was produced as a stop-gap for service until the new vehicles became available. The Selbstfahrlafette 38(t) Ausf M was a derivation of the original Czech-designed PzKpfw 38(t) tank intended as a chassis for the mounting of self-propelled guns. Since the chassis was already in production, it was a simple matter to mount a 2cm FlaK 38 in a low, open superstructure with folding sides. In the November 1943–February 1944 period some 140 vehicles were built by the Czech firm of BMM. Almost all were issued to tank units on the Western Front and were the main type in service in the Normandy campaign.

Further Flakpanzers were built but only in prototype form.

MODELS Flakpanzer IV/3·7cm Flak Ostwind I; Flakpanzer IV/2cm Vierling Wirbelwind; Leichter Flakpanzer IV/3cm Kügelblitz.

COUNTRY OF ORIGIN Germany.

WEIGHT **Ostwind:** 25 tonnes (24·6 tons); **Wirbelwind:** 22 tonnes (21·65 tons); **Kügelblitz:** 25 tonnes (24·6 tons).

LENGTH 5·92m (19ft 5in).

WIDTH 2·95m (9ft 8in).

HEIGHT 3m (9ft 10in).

GROUND CLEARANCE 0·4m (1ft 3¾in).

ARMOUR 80mm.

ENGINE Maybach HLTRM 112, gasoline.

MAXIMUM SPEED 38km/h (24mph).

RANGE 200km (124 miles).

CREW 6.

ARMAMENT **Ostwind:** 1 × 3·7cm FlaK 43/1 L/70; **Wirbelwind:** 4 × 2cm FlaK 38; **Kügelblitz:** 2 × 3cm MK 103. All versions had 1 × 7·92mm MG.

AMMUNITION **Ostwind:** 1,000 rds; **Wirbelwind:** 3,200 rds; **Kügelblitz:** 1,200 rds. MG: 1,350 rds in all versions.

TRENCH CROSSING 2·3m (7ft 6in).

TRACK WIDTH 0·38m (1ft 3in).

MAXIMUM ELEVATION **Ostwind and Wirbelwind:** 90°; **Kügelblitz:** 70°.

FORDING DEPTH 0·8m (2ft 7in).

M3 Grant/Lee

The massive US re-armament programme of 1941 included an urgent need for more than 4,000 tanks. It was decided that the only way to produce tanks in these quantities was to co-opt the expertise of the motor industry and build a special Tank Arsenal at Detroit where Chrysler was to undertake the work. The new medium tank, the M3, would be based on the existing M2A1 medium tank, but mount a 75mm gun in the hull sponson. Events moved fast, with construction of the 420m (460yd) by 150m (165yd) building beginning on a huge site outside Detroit in September 1940.

While this was being done the US Army's Rock Island Arsenal was working on the final M3 medium design with Chrysler engineers in attendance to devise plant and production equipment as design proceeded. Final M3 design work was completed in March 1941, by which time construction of the huge Arsenal building was almost finished, the whole operation taking just six months. Meanwhile the Ordnance Department had contracted with two major heavy engineering firms, American Locomotive and Baldwin Locomotive, for 685 and 533 M3 mediums respectively, also conforming with original plans. At all stages of design, Rock Island Arsenal consulted with engineers and designers from the contractors concerned and there were also informal discussions with the members of the British Tank Commission, which had arrived in USA in June 1940 to place contracts for American-built tanks for the British Army. The latter was able to suggest detail improvements in the light of combat experience in the European theatre.

The three contracting firms all produced pilot models of the M3 in April 1941, and by August full-scale production had started in all three plants, American Locomotive, Baldwin and Detroit Arsenal. Production of the M3 medium, and its variants, continued until December 1942, by which time a grand total of 6,258 M3 series vehicles had been turned out. In addition, in August 1941 Pressed Steel and Pullman each received contracts for 500 M3s from the British Tank Commission. In October 1941, when the M4 medium design was standardized, the M3 was reclassified 'substitute standard' and in April 1943 when M4s were in full service, it was declassified to 'limited standard', finally being declared obsolete in April 1944.

The Medium Tank M3 was dimensionally similar to the M2A1 medium and had the same Wright radial air-cooled gasoline engine and vertical volute suspension. The 75mm M2 gun (M3 in later models) was in a limited traverse mount in the right sponson and a 37mm gun was carried in a fully traversing turret off-set to the left. Maximum armour thickness was 56mm. Turret and sponson were cast and the rest of the hull was riveted though changes were made in subsequent variants. As originally designed the M3 had side doors and a commander's cupola, though again there were subsequent changes. Most important innovation of all, however, was the installation of gyro-stabilizers for both the 75mm and 37mm guns, allowing the vehicle to fire with accuracy while on the move. This same equipment was also fitted in the M3 series light tanks from this time (mid-1941) on. Power and hand traverse were provided for the turret, and periscope sights were fitted for both guns. Total weight of the M3 medium was 30 (short) tons.

The tanks ordered by the British Tank Commission had turrets and other fittings to suit British operational requirements. The turret was different from the US design, having a rear overhang to carry the radio and no cupola. This type in British service was known as the Grant. The original US version, with smaller turret and a cupola, was known as a Lee to the British, who had this type as well as the Grant. Canada, Australia, New Zealand, France, Italy (from 1944) and India all had M3 Lees, and this tank type was used by the British Commonwealth forces in Burma until the end of World War 2.

MODELS M3 Grant/Lee.

COUNTRY OF ORIGIN USA.

WEIGHT 27·2 tonnes (26·78 tons).

LENGTH 5·63m (18ft 6in).

WIDTH 2·72m (8ft 11in).

HEIGHT 3·12m (10ft 3in).

GROUND CLEARANCE 0·43m (1ft 5in).

ARMOUR 35–56mm.

ENGINE 9-cylinder Wright Continental R-975, 340hp, gasoline.

MAXIMUM SPEED 41·8km/h (26mph).

RANGE 192km (120 miles).

CREW 6.

ARMAMENT 1 × 75mm gun, 1 × 37mm gun, plus 3 × ·30 cal. MG (Grant), 4 × ·30 cal. MG (Lee).

AMMUNITION 75mm: 46 rds, 37mm: 178 rds, MG: 9,200 rds.

TRENCH CROSSING 1·8m (6ft).

TRACK WIDTH 0·4m (1ft 4½in).

MAXIMUM ELEVATION 75mm: 20°, 37mm: 60°.

FORDING DEPTH 1m (3ft 4in).

The Medium Tank M3 was the first US medium tank to enter production in World War 2. It was mass-produced at extremely short notice, the US automotive industry being harnessed for this work rather than the engineering industry, as was traditional. A Tank Arsenal was built at Detroit by the Chrysler Car Co. on behalf of the US government specifically to produce M3s on the flow line principle, as the best way of meeting an immediate requirement for 4,000 tanks to re-arm the US Army. With its sponson-mounted 75mm gun it was one of the most distinctive tanks. A version built with a larger turret to meet British requirements was called the Grant, but the illustration shows the version for the US Army (also later used by the British and Canadians) called the Lee. The early production M3 Lee shown was in service with the US 1st Armored Division at Fort Benning, Georgia, in April 1942.

0   1   2 m

Pino dell'Orco – Nicola Pignato

Medium Tank M3 Lee

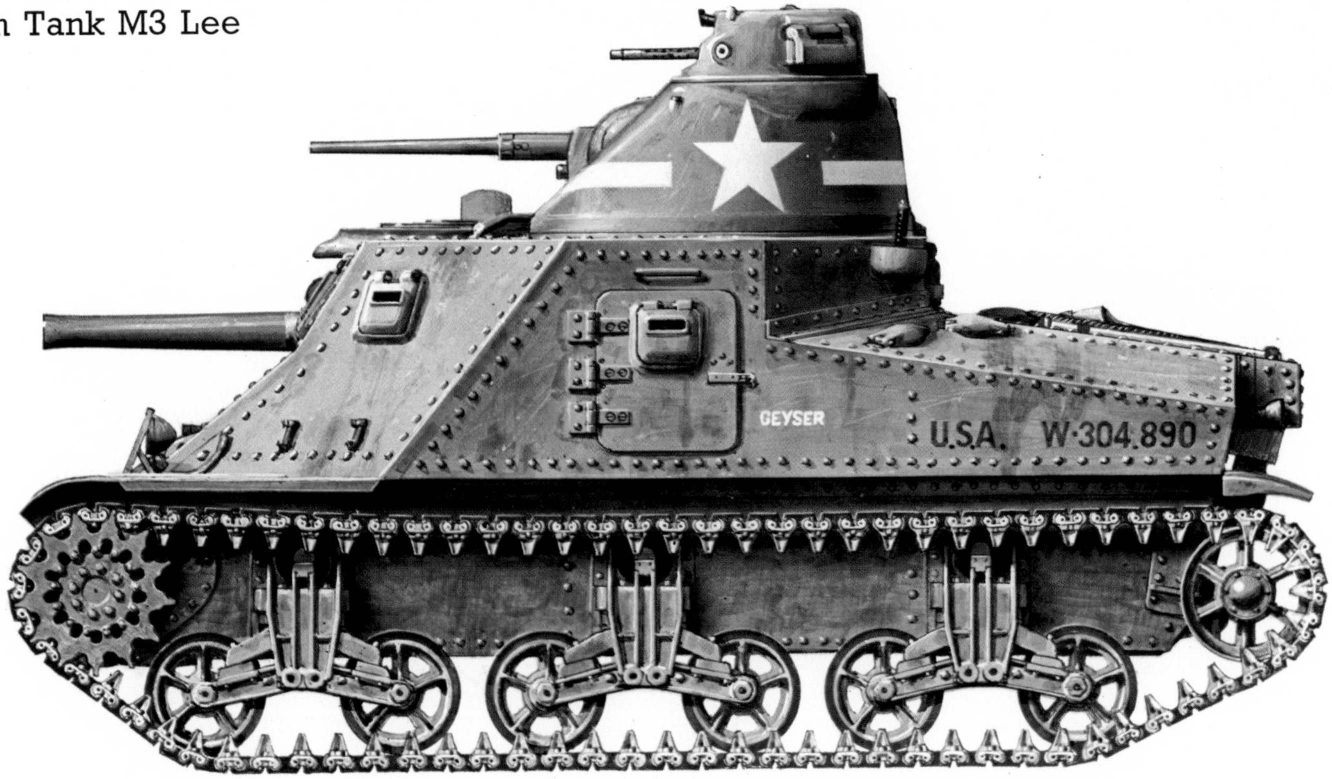
GEYSER
U.S.A. W-304.890

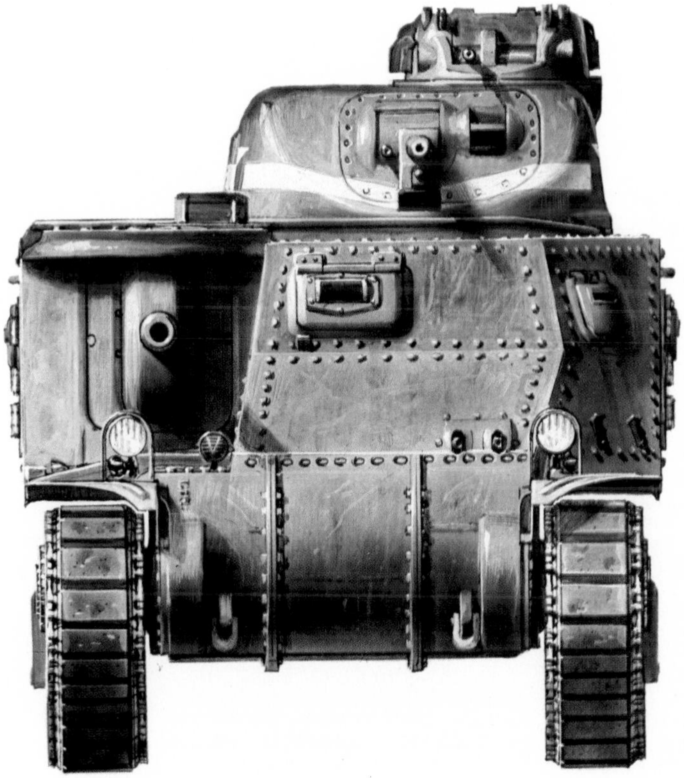

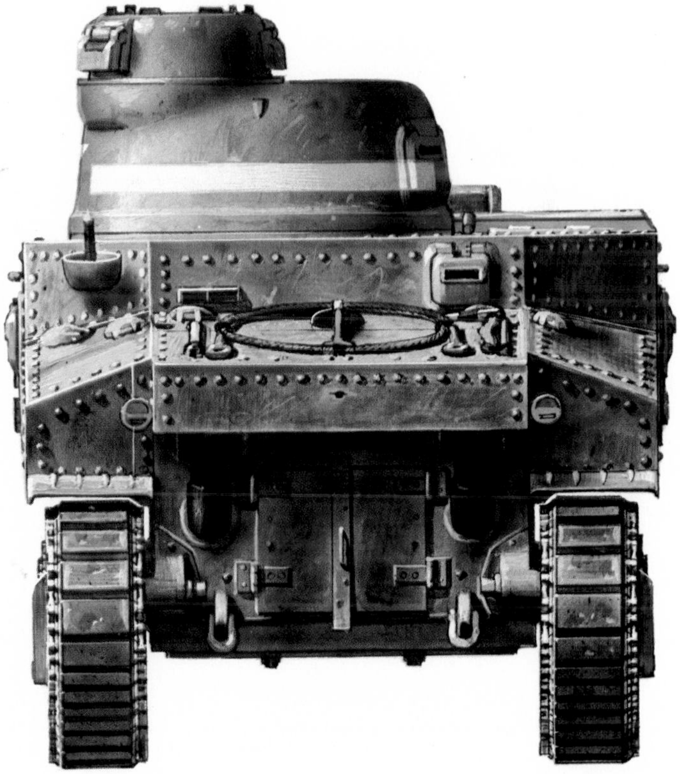

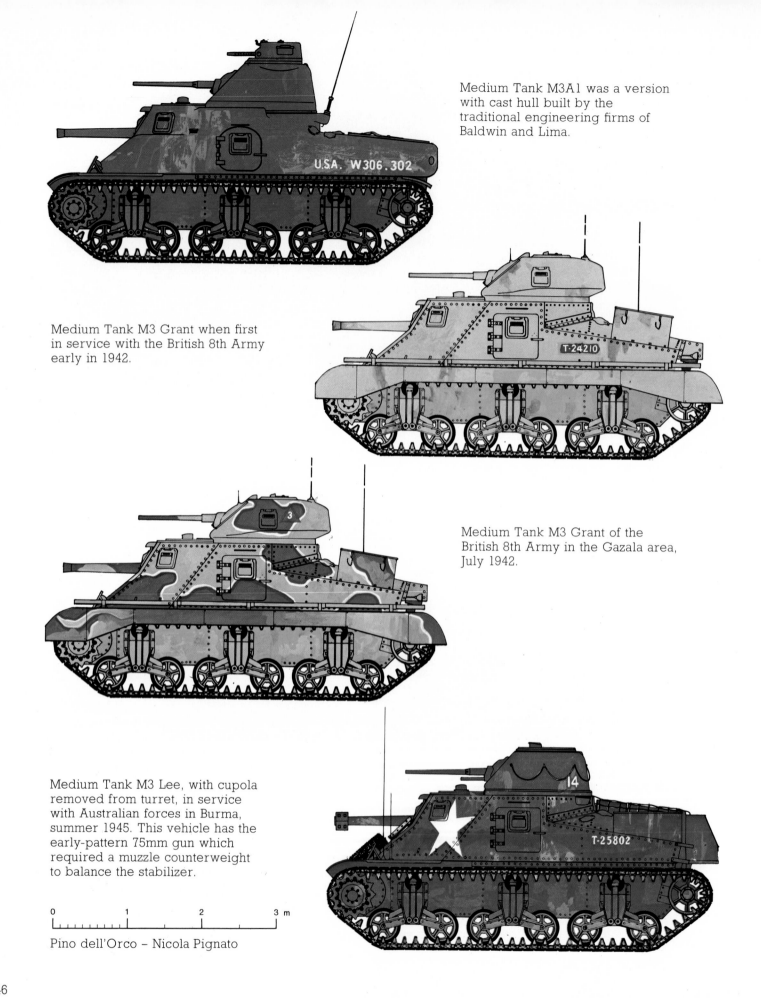

Medium Tank M3A1 was a version with cast hull built by the traditional engineering firms of Baldwin and Lima.

Medium Tank M3 Grant when first in service with the British 8th Army early in 1942.

Medium Tank M3 Grant of the British 8th Army in the Gazala area, July 1942.

Medium Tank M3 Lee, with cupola removed from turret, in service with Australian forces in Burma, summer 1945. This vehicle has the early-pattern 75mm gun which required a muzzle counterweight to balance the stabilizer.

U.S.A. W306.302

T·24210

T·25802

0 1 2 3 m

Pino dell'Orco – Nicola Pignato

M3 Grant/Lee

Medium Tank M3 Lee in Canadian service, with modifications including mud chutes for suspension, and jettisonable extra fuel tanks.

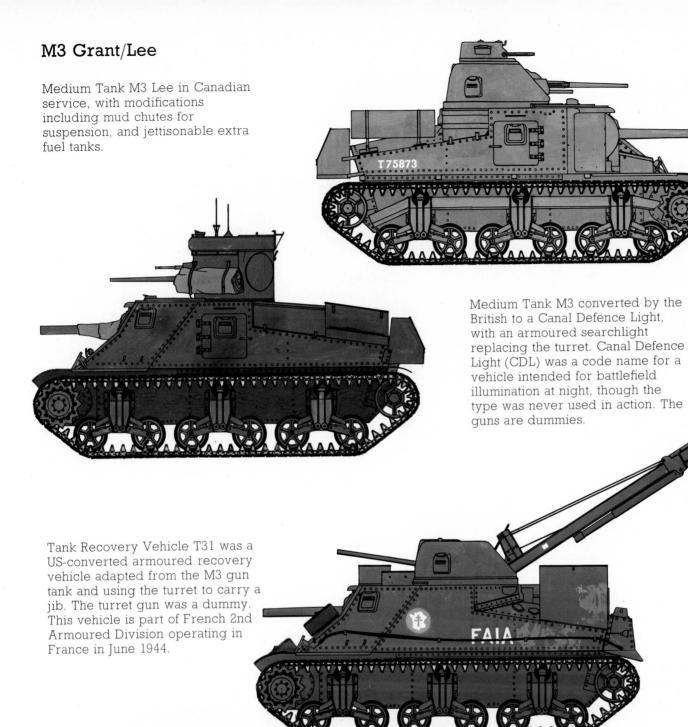

Medium Tank M3 converted by the British to a Canal Defence Light, with an armoured searchlight replacing the turret. Canal Defence Light (CDL) was a code name for a vehicle intended for battlefield illumination at night, though the type was never used in action. The guns are dummies.

Tank Recovery Vehicle T31 was a US-converted armoured recovery vehicle adapted from the M3 gun tank and using the turret to carry a jib. The turret gun was a dummy. This vehicle is part of French 2nd Armoured Division operating in France in June 1944.

Grant ARV Mk I was a British armoured recovery conversion based on an obsolete Grant tank. The turret was removed and a winch was fitted in the fighting compartment.

The illustration shows an Armored Car M8 in service with the Army of Occupation in Germany in 1948. It belongs to the 42nd Squadron of the 2nd Constabulary Regiment, a US military police unit based in Grafenwohr. The inset view shows a typical way in which these cars were camouflaged with local foliage when on reconnaissance patrol.

Apart from being manufactured as an armoured car, this same basic vehicle was produced as Armored Utility Car M20. This was simply an M8 with the gun turret removed and replaced by a gun ring for a skate-mounted MG. Internal stowage was considerably revised, however, to eliminate

ammunition racks and other fittings associated with the turret. Initially it had been proposed to develop a version for the command role and another for carrier duties, but it was found feasible to combine the two roles in one vehicle. The resulting design was standardized as Armored Utility Car M10 in April 1943, though this was changed to M20 a month later to avoid confusion with the M10 Gun Motor Carriage. The M20 was a very widely used vehicle, mainly employed as a liaison and command car by virtually all arms, and particularly as an observation and command vehicle by tank destroyer units.

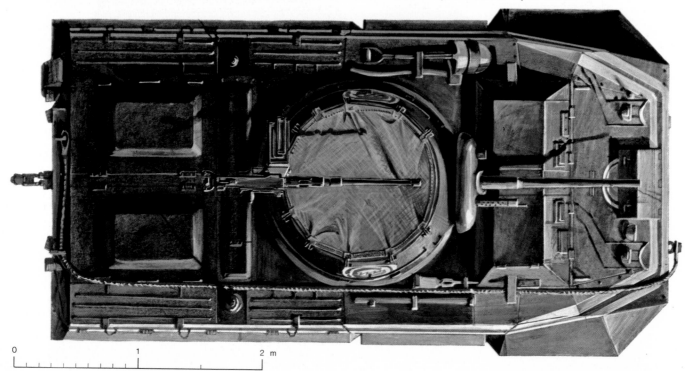

0   1   2 m

Gistudio

M8 Greyhound

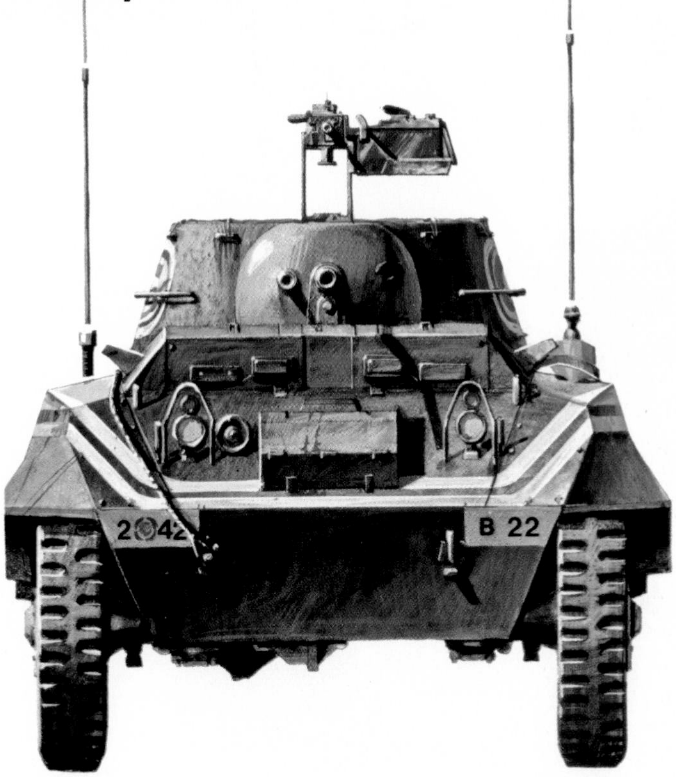
2 42
B 22

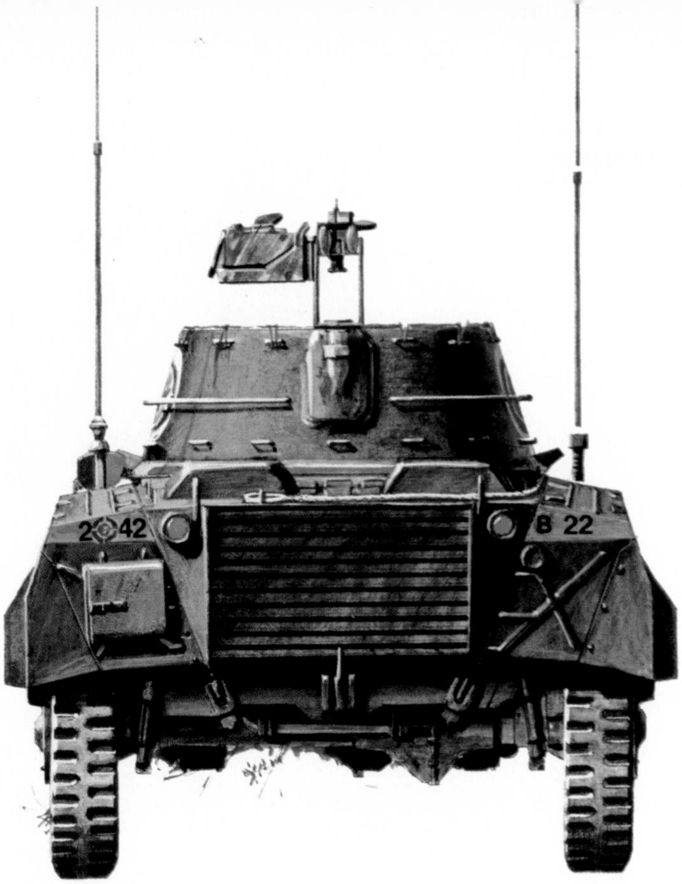
2 42
B 22

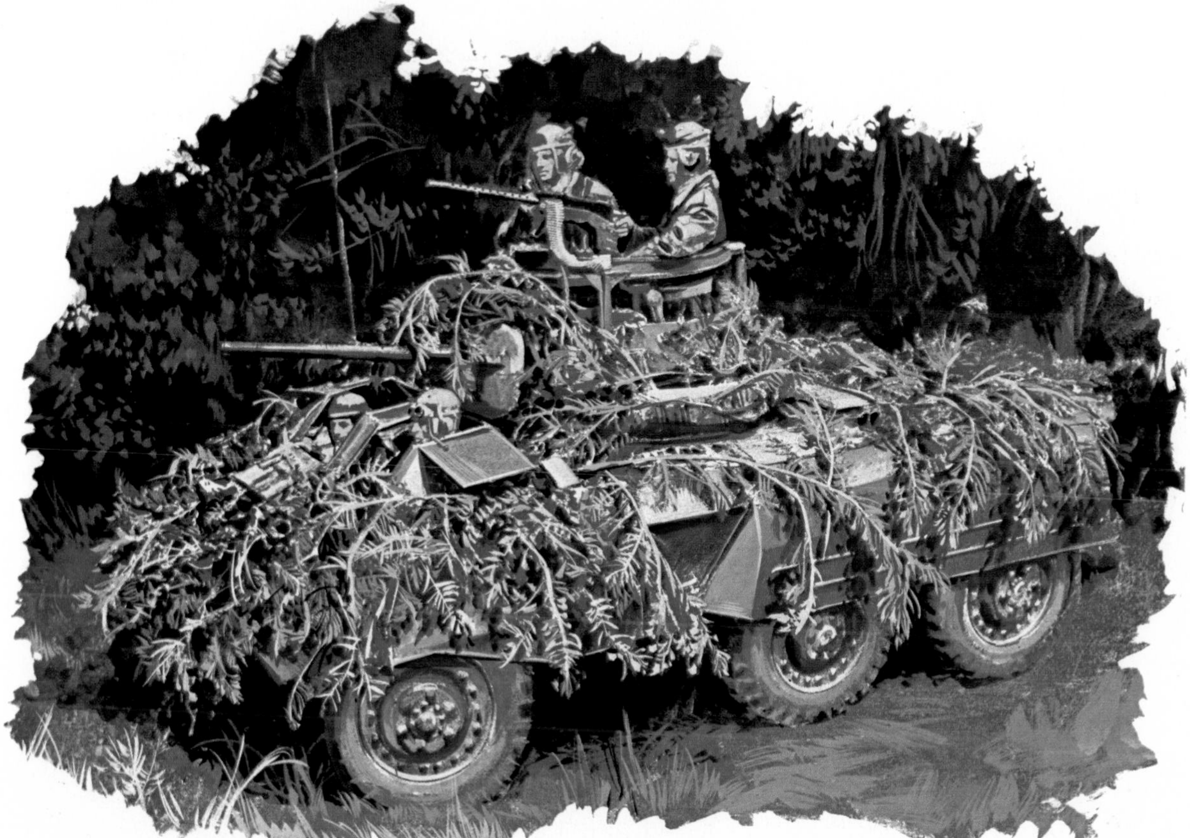

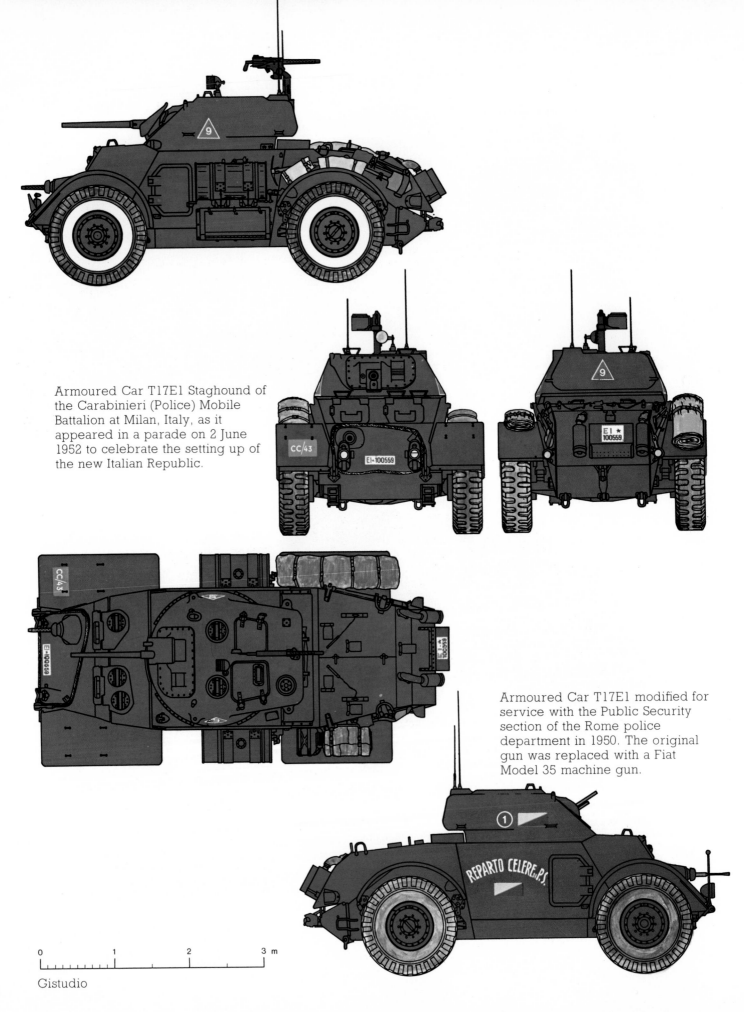

Armoured Car T17E1 Staghound of the Carabinieri (Police) Mobile Battalion at Milan, Italy, as it appeared in a parade on 2 June 1952 to celebrate the setting up of the new Italian Republic.

Armoured Car T17E1 modified for service with the Public Security section of the Rome police department in 1950. The original gun was replaced with a Fiat Model 35 machine gun.

0 1 2 3 m

Gistudio

M8 Greyhound and T17E1 Staghound

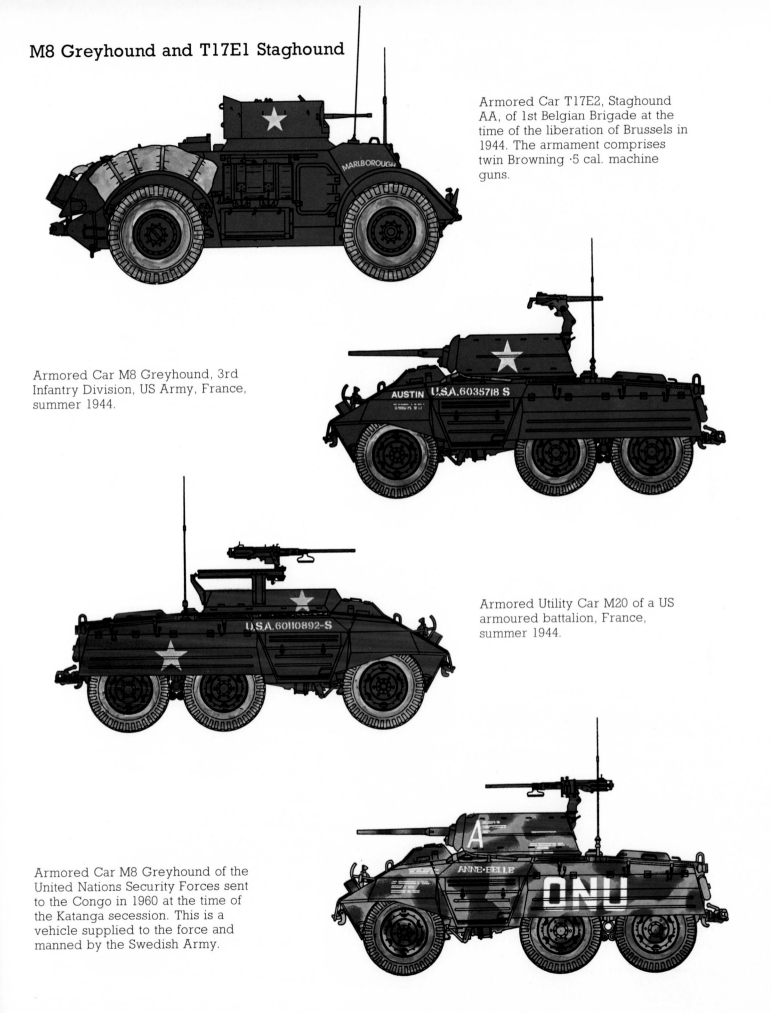

Armored Car T17E2, Staghound AA, of 1st Belgian Brigade at the time of the liberation of Brussels in 1944. The armament comprises twin Browning ·5 cal. machine guns.

Armored Car M8 Greyhound, 3rd Infantry Division, US Army, France, summer 1944.

Armored Utility Car M20 of a US armoured battalion, France, summer 1944.

Armored Car M8 Greyhound of the United Nations Security Forces sent to the Congo in 1960 at the time of the Katanga secession. This is a vehicle supplied to the force and manned by the Swedish Army.

51

M8 Greyhound and T17E1 Staghound

Influenced by the British use of armoured cars, the US Cavalry in mid-1940 began to investigate armoured car development.

The T17 was the first real attempt to produce a vehicle as a result of war experience. From mid-1940 on there was a British Tank Mission in the United States charged with the task of procuring armoured vehicles for British use, initially by purchase. The T17 series armoured cars were conceived to meet both US Armored Force and British requirements and were to be made available to Britain under Lend-Lease.

In July 1941 the Ordnance Department drew up a specification which called for a medium armoured car with all-wheel drive and a 37mm gun in a fully traversing turret. Tenders for designs with either four or six wheels were invited from the major automobile companies and a six-wheel design offered by Ford and a four-wheel design by Chevrolet were selected for production as pilot models. The Ford vehicle was designated T17 and the Chevrolet was designated T17E1.

The T17E1 weighed 14 tons and had two GMC 97hp engines, each with Hydramatic transmission. Armour maximum was 50mm. After successful trials with the pilot model, an order for 2,000 production vehicles was placed in January 1942. The British Tank Mission asked for 300 initially for delivery to Britain, the order for these being placed in March 1942, but this was increased to 1,500 for Lend-Lease purposes the following month. The first T17E1s came off the production line in October 1942 and 157 had been completed by the year's end. However, the Special Armored Vehicle Board examining existing designs at this period recommended that all orders be cancelled since the Armored Force no longer required armoured cars of this weight and size. The T17E1 was, however, liked by the British Army in whose service it was known as the Staghound. It was therefore decided to divert all production T17E1s to Britain and a total of 2,687 were produced and delivered in 1943.

Production ceased in December 1943 by which time British requirements had been fulfilled.

However, a further variant was produced for the British especially for the AA role. This had the 37mm gun and turret replaced by a Frazer-Nash power-operated, open-topped turret fitted with twin ·50 cal. Browning machine guns. A total of 1,000 was requested by the British, but only 789 of these were built and delivered when production ceased in April 1944. In its AA form it was designated T17E2 and was known as the Staghound AA to the British.

In October 1941 tenders for designs to meet US Army requirements were considered and contracts for two pilot models were awarded. One went to Ford who were to build 6×6 vehicle with integral hull/chassis under the designation 37mm Gun Motor Carriage T22. The other went to the Fargo Division of the Chrysler Corporation who were to build a 6×6 vehicle with a separate truck-type chassis, under the designation 37mm GMC T23.

Of the pilot models the T22 proved the best. Various modifications were asked for, however, including changes in the driving compartment hatches to give improved vision (protectoscopes instead of vision slits), elimination of the hull ·30 cal. machine gun, the addition of removable sand shields over the wheels, and provision of armoured stowage boxes on each side of the hull for stores and radio equipment. Thus altered, the T22 was redesignated T22E2. On 19 May 1942, it was standardized as the Light Armored Car M8, having been approved in all respects.

The M8 Greyhound became the major armoured car in production in the USA in World War 2 and, indeed, was destined to become one of the most widely used and best-known AFVs ever produced. At the time it was standardized a total production of 5,000 M8s was envisaged. This was almost immediately raised to 6,000 and in July 1942 a second order for a further 5,070 was placed. Later, however, this was revised to 2,460.

MODELS M8 Greyhound and T17E1 Staghound.

COUNTRY OF ORIGIN USA.

WEIGHT **M8:** 7·89 tonnes (7·76 tons); **T17E1:** 12·07 tonnes (11·85 tons).

LENGTH **M8:** 5m (16ft 5in); **T17E1:** 5·43m (17ft 10in).

WIDTH **M8:** 2·55m (8ft 4in); **T17E1:** 2·69m (8ft 10in).

HEIGHT **M8:** 2·24m (7ft 4½in); **T17E1:** 2·36m (7ft 9in).

GROUND CLEARANCE **M8:** 0·29m (10½in); **T17E1:** 0·38m (1ft 3in).

ARMOUR **M8:** 6·3–19mm; **T17E1:** 6·25–44mm.

ENGINES **M8:** 6-cylinder Hercules JXD, 110hp, gasoline; **T17E1:** 2×6-cylinder, GMC 270, 97hp, gasoline.

MAXIMUM SPEED **M8:** 88km/h (55mph); **T17E1:** 88km/h (55mph).

RANGE **M8:** 560km (350 miles); **T17E1:** 724km (450 miles).

CREW **M8:** 4; **T17E1:** 5.

ARMAMENT **M8:** 1×37mm gun, 1×·30 cal. MG, 1×·50 cal. MG; **T17E1:** 1×37mm gun, 3×·30 cal. MG.

AMMUNITION **M8:** 37mm: 80 rds, MG: ·30 cal.: 1,500 rds, ·50 cal.: 400 rds; **T17E1:** 37mm: 103 rds, MG: 5,250 rds.

MAXIMUM ELEVATION **M8:** 20°; **T17E1:** 40°.

FORDING DEPTH **M8:** 0·60m (2ft); **T17E1:** 0·80m (2ft 8in).

Gun Motor Carriage M7, M10 and M36

In June 1941, as soon as the M3 was in production, plans were made for mounting a 105mm howitzer on the chassis of the M3 medium tank in order to provide self-propelled artillery support for armoured divisions. Two pilot models were constructed, designated T32, based on the M3 medium chassis, but with an open-topped superstructure. The standard M1A2 105mm howitzer was installed with its complete carriage suitably modified to fit, and was offset to the right of centre. The trials vehicles were successful and the design was standardized as the M7 HMC in February 1942. Production vehicles included modified front shields and a cupola and ring for an AA machine gun. American Locomotive Co. started production in April and built 2,028 in 1942. Late production vehicles had M4-type bogies with trailing return rollers. The M7 had identical chassis and mechanical specifications to the M3 medium tank, also produced by the United States.

Meanwhile the M4 had superseded the M3 in production, and in September 1943 M7 production continued on the chassis of the M4A3 medium tank. Designated M7B1, this vehicle differed from the M7 in having a Ford GAA engine replacing the Wright Continental R-975.

In March 1942 the British Tank Mission in the United States saw the M7 pilot model and immediately requested 2,500 for British use for the end of 1942 with a further 3,000 for delivery in 1943. These demands were never met in full because American forces had to be equipped first. Due to the serious position of the 8th Army in the Western Desert in September 1942, however, 90 M7s were diverted from production intended for American troops and sent to the British.

After the successful development of the 105mm howitzer on the medium tank chassis to make the M7, plans were made in April 1942 to mount a high-velocity gun on the same chassis to provide a vehicle for the Tank Destroyer Command. Designated T35 this vehicle utilized an early production M4A2 tank chassis, then just available. It had an open-topped low sloped circular turret adapted from the turret design for the T1 Heavy Tank, and the 3in gun projected for the same vehicle. However, the Tank Destroyer Board asked for a lower silhouette and angled hull superstructure, so an improved design T35E1 was drawn up, again based on the M4A2 chassis, but incorporating these features. The T35E1 had thinner armour than the T35 and the circular turret was subsequently abandoned in favour of a five-sided welded turret. As finalized, the design was standardized in June 1942 and designated M10 GMC. In order to increase production, use of the M4A3 chassis was also authorized and vehicles built on this chassis were designated M10A1 GMC.

Some M10s and M10A1s were supplied to Britain in 1944 where they were designated '3in SP, Wolverine'. These were issued for combat service in British units in Italy and France; most were converted from late 1944 by replacement of the 3in gun with the British 17pdr weapon, producing a much more potent tank destroyer than the M10 in its original form. In its new guise the vehicle was designated '17pdr SP, Achilles Mk IC'.

In October 1942 it was decided to try adapting the 90mm AA gun as a high-velocity anti-tank gun for mounting in American tanks and SP vehicles. In early 1943 a 90mm gun was installed in the turret of the M10, but the gun proved too long and heavy for the turret which was, in any case, not entirely adequate for the 3in gun. In March 1943, therefore, work began on designing a new large turret to fit the M10 and take the 90mm gun. The modified vehicle was very satisfactory and an initial 'limited procurement' order of 500 vehicles was placed under the designation T71 GMC. In June 1944, the vehicle was standardized as the M36 GMC and entered service in NW Europe in late 1944, where it proved most successful. M36B1 was a variant based on a standard M4A3 tank chassis.

MODELS HMC M7, GMC M10 and GMC M36.

COUNTRY OF ORIGIN USA.

WEIGHT **M7:** 22·96 tonnes (22·6 tons); **M10:** 30 tonnes (29·5 tons); **M36:** 28·18 tonnes (27·7 tons).

LENGTH **M7:** 6m (19ft 9in); **M10:** 6·83m (22ft 5in); **M36:** 7·96m (26ft 1½in).

WIDTH **M7:** 2·53m (8ft 4in); **M10:** 3·05m (10ft); **M36:** 3·05m (10ft).

HEIGHT **M7:** 2·86m (9ft 5¼in); **M10:** 2·56m (8ft 5in); **M36:** 2·67m (8ft 10in).

GROUND CLEARANCE **M7:** 0·43m (1ft 5in); **M10:** 0·48m (1ft 7in); **M36:** 0·48m (1ft 7in).

ARMOUR **M7:** 12–62mm; **M10:** 13–57mm; **M36:** 13–50mm.

ENGINES **M7:** Continental R-975 radial, air-cooled, 400hp, gasoline; **M10:** 2 × GM 6046D, 375hp, diesel; **M36:** Ford GAA V8, 500hp, gasoline.

MAXIMUM SPEED **M7:** 41km/h (26mph); **M10:** 52km/h (32mph); **M36:** 48km/h (30mph).

RANGE **M7:** 136–200km (85–125 miles); **M10:** 322km (200 miles); **M36:** 241km (150 miles).

CREW **M7:** 7; **M10:** 5; **M36:** 5.

ARMAMENT **M7:** 1 × 105mm howitzer, 1 × ·50 cal. MG; **M10:** 1 × 3in gun, 1 × ·50 cal. MG; **M36:** 1 × 90mm gun, 1 × ·50 cal. MG.

AMMUNITION **M7:** 105mm: 69 rds, MG: 300 rds; **M10:** 3in: 40 rds, MG: 400 rds; **M36:** 90mm: 47 rds, MG: 100 rds.

TRENCH CROSSING **M7:** 2·28m (7ft 6in); **M10:** 2·44m (8ft); **M36:** 2·44m (8ft).

TRACK WIDTH **M7:** 0·4m (1ft 4½in); **M10:** 0·4m (1ft 4½in); **M36:** 0·4m (1ft 4½in).

MAXIMUM ELEVATION **M7:** 35°; **M10:** 19°; **M36:** 20°.

FORDING DEPTH **M7:** 1·2m (4ft); **M10:** 1·2m (4ft); **M36:** 1·2m (4ft).

The Gun Motor Carriage M10 was a very successful adaptation of the basic Sherman tank design to give a powerful tank destroyer mounting a 76mm gun. The superstructure was a redesign of the original M4 superstructure to make it more suitable for carrying the heavy counterweighted turret. The ·5 cal. heavy Browning machine gun on the turret was for AA defence. The illustration shows the M10A1 version which was based on the running gear and engine of the Medium Tank M4A3, and was the model most widely used by the US Army. This vehicle, 'Spirit of Atlanta', was used at Bastogne during the Ardennes offensive, winter 1944–5.

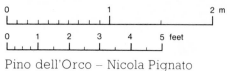

Pino dell'Orco – Nicola Pignato

3 inch Gun Motor Carriage M10A1

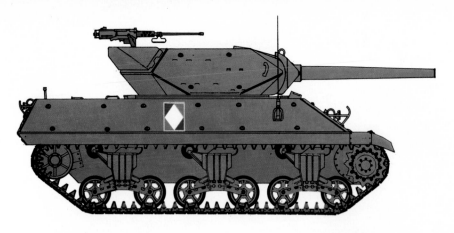

Gun Motor Carriage M10 used by the French 2nd Armoured Division (Free French forces) in France, 1944–5.

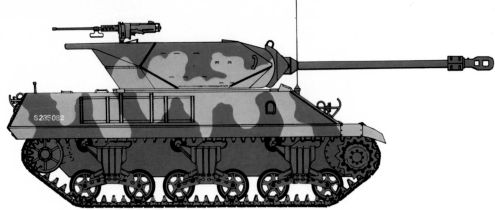

Some of the M10s supplied under Lend-Lease to the British Army had the 76mm gun replaced by a British 17pdr weapon to make them into a much more powerful type of vehicle, the 17pdr being then the best Allied anti-tank gun. The conversions were designated SP 17pdr Achilles, and were in service in 1944 and for some years after the war.

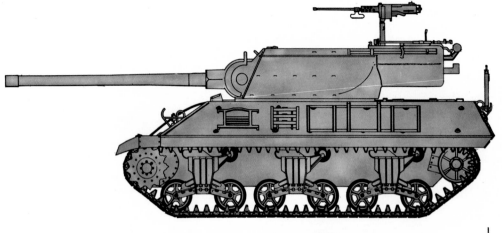

Gun Motor Carriage M36 had a larger turret mounting a 90mm gun on the same chassis as the M10. This example was operating in the Ardennes sector in December 1944.

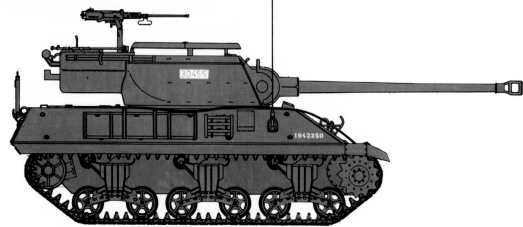

Gun Motor Carriage M36B2 was a similar conversion to the M36 but used the M10A1 chassis as a basis. On this model an armoured roof was added above the open turret. Turkish army.

0   1   2   3 m

Pino dell'Orco – Nicola Pignato

Gun Motor Carriage M7, M10 and M36

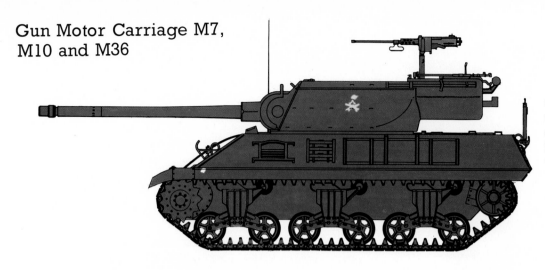

Gun Motor Carriage M36 of XXI Gruppo, Italian armoured artillery, at Milan, 1957–60. In Italian service it was designated Semoventi Controcarro da 90/50.

Howitzer Motor Carriage M7, an early example of the type, which was based on the Medium Tank M3 chassis, used in the recapture of Luzon, Philippines, 1945.

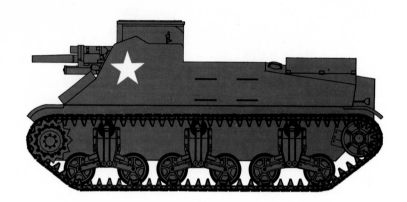

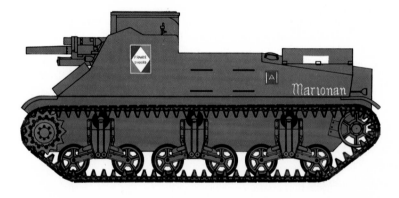

Howitzer Motor Carriage M7 of French 2nd Armoured Division, France, 1944.

Howitzer Motor Carriage M7B1 in Italian Army service in the post-war years and modified to carry an Italian 105/34 gun. It was designated Semovente da 105/34.

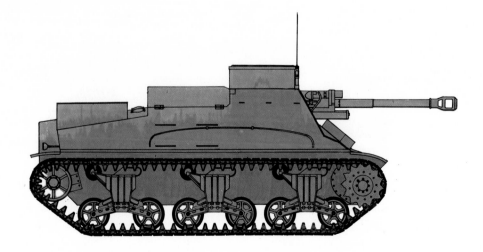

The vehicle illustrated is a Half-track Personnel Carrier M3A1 of the HQ company, 46th Infantry Battalion, US Army, at Normandy, June 1944. The M3 and M3A1 were the most widely used half-tracks in the US Army. Each was a personnel carrier model with seats for 10 men (a rifle squad) in the rear and room for three in the cab. The body was about 25cm (10in) longer than the earlier M2 and had an access door in the rear. Because of this, there was no skate rail, and a pedestal mount for a ·30 cal. MG was fitted to the floor of the rear compartment. The Half-track Personnel Carrier M3A1 was the developed M3 design with ring mount and 'pulpit' for the AA machine gun.

Pino dell'Orco – Nicola Pignato

APC Half-track M3A1

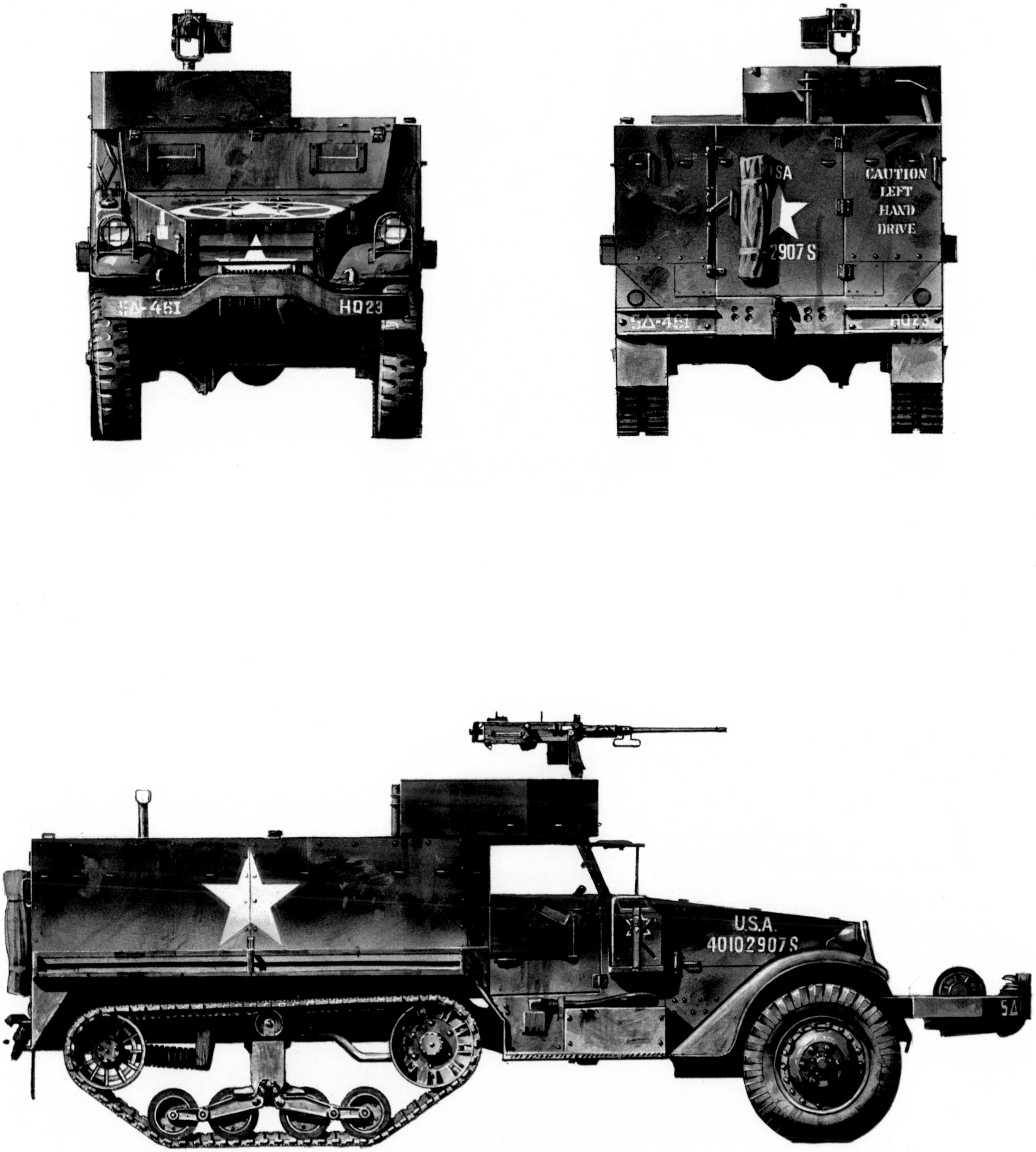
5Δ-461
HQ23
CAUTION
LEFT
HAND
DRIVE
2907 S
U.S.A.
40102907 S

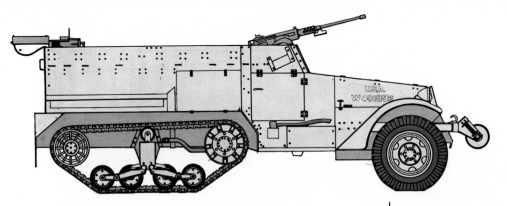

Half-track Car M2 was the basic artillery prime mover for the 105mm howitzer (on field carriage) in artillery battalions. It had seats for 10 men (full gun crew) and room in the cab for the driver, assistant driver and commander. There was no rear door and the body was shorter than that of the M3. There were two ammunition lockers on each side of the interior behind the driving cab, with doors to these from outside the vehicle. A skate rail for machine guns ran round the edge of the superstructure.

81mm Mortar Carrier M4A1 was a purpose-built version of the M2 half-track. This vehicle could carry crew, mortar and ammunition. Seating capacity in the rear was reduced to three, the remaining space being taken up by ammunition racks and stowage for the mortar. In the M4 there was no provision for firing the mortar from the vehicle, though this could be done in emergency situations. Some 572 M4s were built by early 1942 when the model was replaced by an improved design, M4A1, which had a reinforced floor and mounts for firing from the vehicle. Both vehicles shown above were used by the US 1st Armored Division at Tunis, 1943.

Gun Motor Carriage M3 was a tank destroyer conversion with 75mm gun. This example was used by the British 3rd Dragoon Guards in Italy in 1944.

Half-track Car M9A1 was the variant produced by International Harvester, corresponding to the M2A1, for the gun tower role. However, unlike the M2A1 half-track, it had a rear access door and body length matching the M5. Some 3,433 were built, making this a major production type. This vehicle was used by the French 1st Armoured Division in 1944–5.

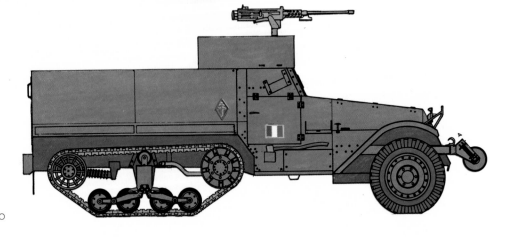

Pino dell'Orco – Nicola Pignato

M3 Half-track

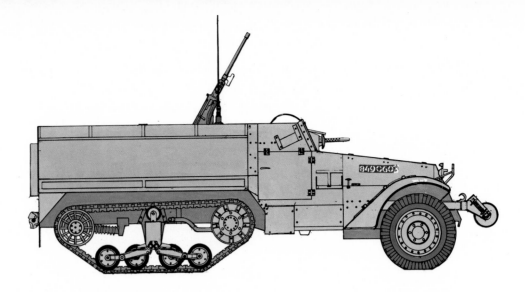

The Israeli Army was the largest post-war user of half-tracks. This is an M3 used in the Yom Kippur war of 1973 and the previous 1967 war. It carries a Browning ·5 cal. machine gun on a pivot mount and a 7·6mm machine gun in the front of the cab.

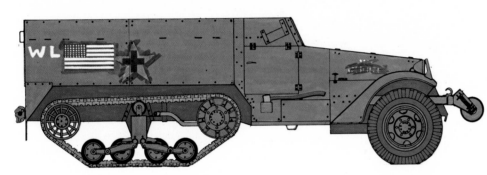

Half-track Personnel Carrier M3 captured from the US 1st Armored Division in Tunis in 1943 and used by a Luftwaffe parachute unit.

Multiple Gun Motor Carriage M16 with Maxson turret and four ·5 cal. machine guns was widely used for AA defence in American divisions in the 1944–5 period. The example shown was used by the 32nd Infantry Division at Luzon in 1945.

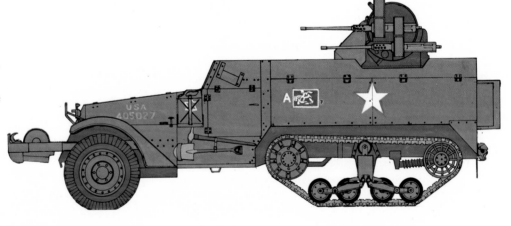

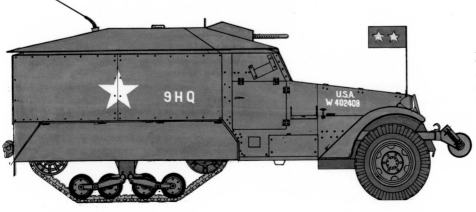

Half-track Personnel Carrier M3 specially modified to act as mobile command post for General Patton in Tunis and Italy, 1943.

M3 Half-track

In 1925 the US Army bought two Citroën-Kegresse semi-tracked open vehicles from France, and another was purchased in 1931. US firms then undertook development work for the Ordnance Department and the first new design, the TI Half-track, was built by Cunningham of Rochester, NY, in 1932. By 1939–40 Half-track Personnel Carrier T14 had been produced and became the prototype of all other half-track types used by the US in World War 2. In September 1940 the T14 was standardized as the Half-track M2 and, modified to transport personnel, it became the Half-track Personnel Carrier M3.

The M2 and M3 were similar in design and all major assemblies were interchangeable. The chassis and drive units were commercial components. The armoured hull was 6mm thick and included armoured shutters over the radiator, while armoured shields 13mm thick were provided for the cab windscreen and side windows. Vehicles were built with either an unditching roller mounted ahead of the front fender (though this was sometimes removed), or else with a winch. Later production vehicles also had stowage racks on the hull sides.

The M2 was a gun tractor with ammunition stowage facilities, and the M3 was a personnel carrier with slightly longer hull and bench seating. Production was started by White and Autocar (M2) and Diamond T (M3) in September 1940. White had produced the Scout Car M2A1, one of which had been converted to a half-track during development work leading to the T14 prototype. Thus the Scout Car M2A1 and the half-track had similar superstructures.

M2 deliveries started in May 1941 and a total of 11,415 was built. M3 half-track production reached 12,499. For AA protection, the M2 had a track running round the inner edge of the superstructure, on which were mounted skates for ·30 and ·50 cal. MGs, while the M3 had a pedestal mount instead. Changes in 1943 led to the removal of these types of gun mounts in favour of a 'pulpit' with circular gun mount just behind the cab.

Three pintles were provided, also for AA machine guns. With these new features, the vehicles were redesignated M2A1 and M3A1 respectively. These replaced the earlier models from October 1943, and when production ceased in March 1944 2,862 M3A1s and 1,643 M2A1s, all incorporating a White engine, had been delivered.

Further variants based on the M2A1, but designated separately, were built as mortar carriers. In 1942, when there was an increased requirement for half-tracks, International Harvester was also brought into the production group and built models with minor detail improvements and International, instead of White, engines. Designated Half-tracks M9 and M5, these corresponded to the M2 and M3 respectively. With the later production improvements came the M9A1 and M5A1; these correspond to the M2A1 and M3A1 produced by the White/Autocar/Diamond T plants.

In April 1943, it was decided to standardize the half-track design to produce a 'universal' vehicle with common body features suitable as a gun tower/mortar carrier or a personnel carrier. This led to the M3A2 and M5A2 types from White/Autocar/Diamond T and International Harvester Co. respectively. By now US Army interest in the half-track was beginning to wane and production of this type of vehicle tailed off completely in mid-1944 – after a total run of 41,169 units, though half-tracks remained in wide service. For artillery use half-tracks were to be replaced as gun towers by full-tracks and in other service arms there was a growing preference for full-track utility vehicles or trucks.

While the half-track was initially conceived as a fast reconnaissance vehicle protected against small arms fire and with a good cross-country ability for infantry and artillery use, it was also widely employed by other arms and its large size gave it good development potential as a gun carriage. For the Armored Force, the Ordnance Department produced a number of designs of gun motor carriage.

MODEL M3 Half-track.

COUNTRY OF ORIGIN USA.

WEIGHT 10·2 tonnes (10 tons).

LENGTH 6·35m (20ft 9⅝in).

WIDTH 2·22m (7ft 3½in).

HEIGHT 2·25m (7ft 5in).

GROUND CLEARANCE 0·28m (11¼in).

ARMOUR 6–12mm.

ENGINE White 160AX, 144hp, gasoline.

MAXIMUM SPEED 72km/h (45mph).

RANGE 290–345km (180–215 miles).

CREW 13.

ARMAMENT 1 × ·30 cal. Browning MG.

AMMUNITION 4,000 rds.

TRACK WIDTH 0·305m (1ft).

FORDING DEPTH 0·90m (2ft 11in).

M18 Hellcat and M39 Armored Utility Vehicle

Beginnings of the M18 GMC and other vehicles on the same chassis go back to December 1941 when the Ordnance Department recommended the development of a fast tank destroyer with 37mm gun on a chassis utilizing Christie suspension and a Wright Continental R-975 engine. Two pilot models were started and the first was completed in mid-1942, designated T49 GMC. Changes in the original requirements included the substitution of the M1 57mm gun for the 37mm (mainly because of the need for more hitting power) and the adoption of torsion bar, instead of Christie, suspension.

The T49 was tested in July 1942, but the Tank Destroyer Command demanded an even heavier gun and asked the Ordnance Department to complete the second pilot model with a 75mm M3 gun (as mounted in the M4 medium tank). The T49 project was accordingly cancelled in December 1942 in favour of the up-gunned version, and the pilot model as completed was designated T67 GMC. It had a rounded, sloped, open-topped turret similar to that which had been produced for the T35 GMC. It was tested successfully by the Armored Vehicle Board, and, because of its comparatively light weight (under 20 tons) and powerful engine, it proved to have a fast performance, and was recommended for standardization.

In February 1943, however, Tank Destroyer Command again requested a more powerful gun, this time suggesting the 76mm M1 gun which was being developed for fitting to the M4 medium tank series. Six more pilot models were built, all similar to the T67 but with the new gun. These were designated T70 GMC. As a result of trials a few detail changes were made, including a modified and simplified shape for the hull front, and a new turret which included a bustle for the counter-weight and stowage box. Essentially, however, the T70 design was excellent, needing little further modification for production, which started in July 1943 at the Buick factory. The vehicle was standardized in February 1944 as the M18 GMC, later

being popularly called 'Hellcat'. When production ended in October 1944 2,507 M18s had been built.

The M18 was one of the finest tank destroyers of any nation in World War 2, and by virtue of its excellent power-to-weight ratio it was also the fastest tracked AFV to appear in that period. It had other virtues too, such as a low silhouette, well-shaped armour protection, good reliability and strong suspension. In both Italy and NW Europe, 1944–5, the 'hit and run' tactics possible with the superior performance allowed them to knock out a large number of enemy tanks with relatively few losses. Their versatility in the field made them extremely popular with the American tank destroyer battalions.

Following the success of the M18 in service, the Ordnance Department suggested in August 1944 the development of a similar vehicle mounting the 105mm T12 howitzer. A pilot model was completed in December 1944, identical in all respects to the M18 except for the gun and sighting arrangements. Designated T88, the project was cancelled at the end of the war in August 1945 while still under test.

In June 1944 it was proposed to use the high speed/low silhouette characteristics of the M18 to produce a utility armoured vehicle capable of acting as a prime mover for the 3in M6 anti-tank gun (wheeled) or as a reconnaissance vehicle and troop carrier. Two M18s were modified by removal of the turret and revised internal layout. In prime mover form the vehicle was designated T41 while the reconnaissance variant was designated T41E1. The only difference was in the internal seating/stowage arrangements. A ring for a ·50 cal. Browning AA machine gun was fitted at the front end of the fighting compartment. Ordered as a 'limited procurement' item in June 1944, it was standardized as the M39 in early 1945. It carried a crew of two, but also accommodated a full gun crew of seven. Because of the ending of the war in the summer of 1945 relatively few of these armoured utility vehicles were ever completed.

MODELS GMC M18 Hellcat and Utility Carrier M39.

COUNTRY OF ORIGIN USA.

WEIGHT **M18:** 17·03 tonnes (16·7 tons); **M39:** 15·9 tonnes (15·65 tons).

LENGTH **M18:** 5·43m (17ft 10in); **M39:** 5·28m (17ft 4in).

WIDTH 2·86m (9ft 5in).

HEIGHT **M18:** 2·36m (7ft 9in); **M39:** 1·8m (5ft 11in).

GROUND CLEARANCE 0·37m (1ft 2½in).

ARMOUR 6–25mm.

ENGINES Continental R-975 C1 340hp or C4 400hp.

MAXIMUM SPEED 89km/h (55mph).

RANGE 169km (105 miles).

CREW **M18:** 5; **M39:** 2 (plus 7 passengers).

ARMAMENT **M18:** 1 × 76mm gun, 1 × ·50 cal. Browning AA; **M39:** 1 × ·50 cal. Browning AA.

AMMUNITION **M18:** 76mm: 45 rds, ·50 cal.: 800 rds; **M39:** ·50 cal.: 800 rds.

TRENCH CROSSING 1·88m (6ft 2in).

TRACK WIDTH 36·5cm (14·38in).

MAXIMUM ELEVATION 19½°.

FORDING DEPTH 1·2m (4ft).

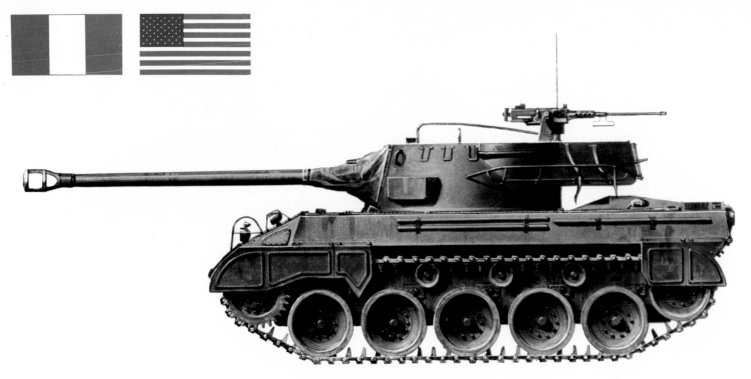

Fastest production AFV of World War 2 was the Gun Motor Carriage M18 Hellcat, over 2,500 of which were built as tank destroyers. They proved extremely useful and potent because of their high speed and 76mm gun. They were able to 'hit and run' in highly mobile fashion. At the end of the war a number were supplied to the Italian and Yugoslav Armies. The vehicle illustrated served with the Italian Army School of Artillery at Bracciano. The Italian designation was M18 Hellcat Cannone Semovente da 77/52.

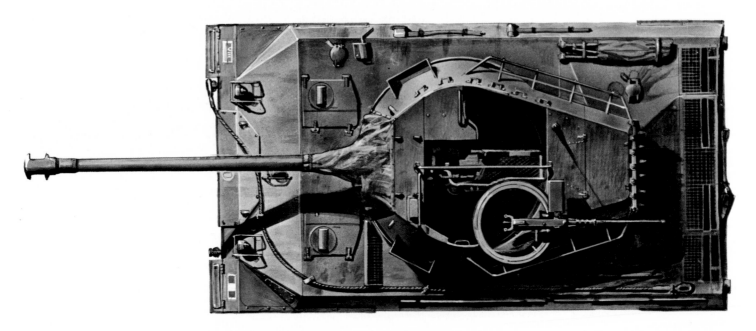

0   1   2 m

Pino dell'Orco – Nicola Pignato

Gun Motor Carriage M18 Hellcat

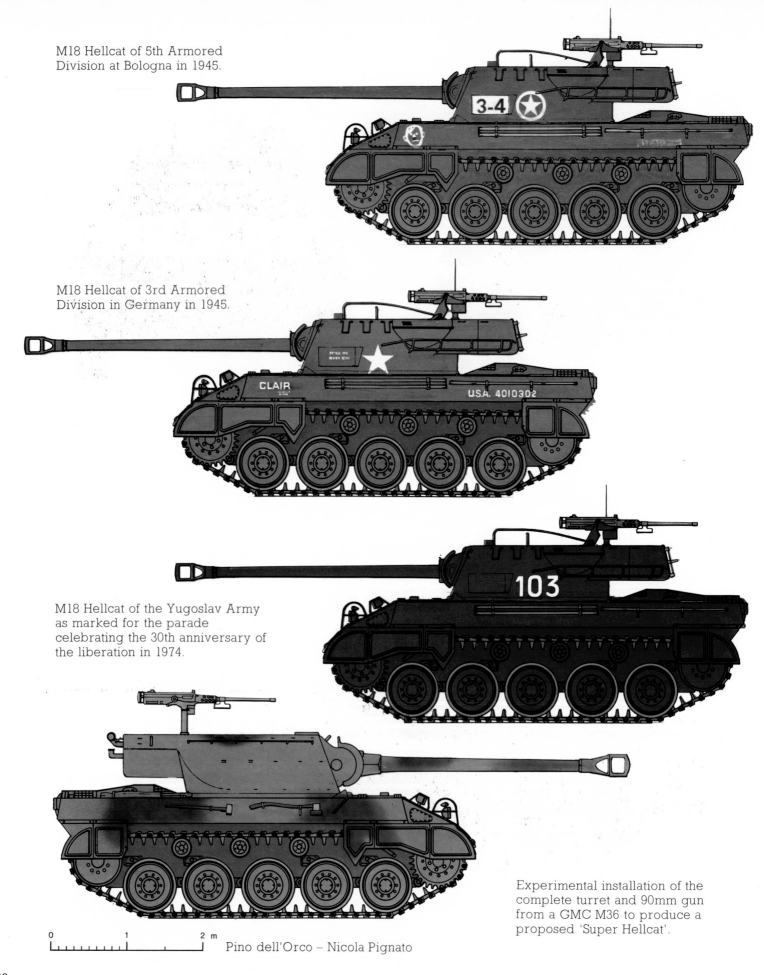

M18 Hellcat of 5th Armored
Division at Bologna in 1945.

M18 Hellcat of 3rd Armored
Division in Germany in 1945.

M18 Hellcat of the Yugoslav Army
as marked for the parade
celebrating the 30th anniversary of
the liberation in 1974.

Experimental installation of the
complete turret and 90mm gun
from a GMC M36 to produce a
proposed 'Super Hellcat'.

0   1   2 m

Pino dell'Orco – Nicola Pignato

66

M18 Hellcat and M39 Armored Utility Vehicle

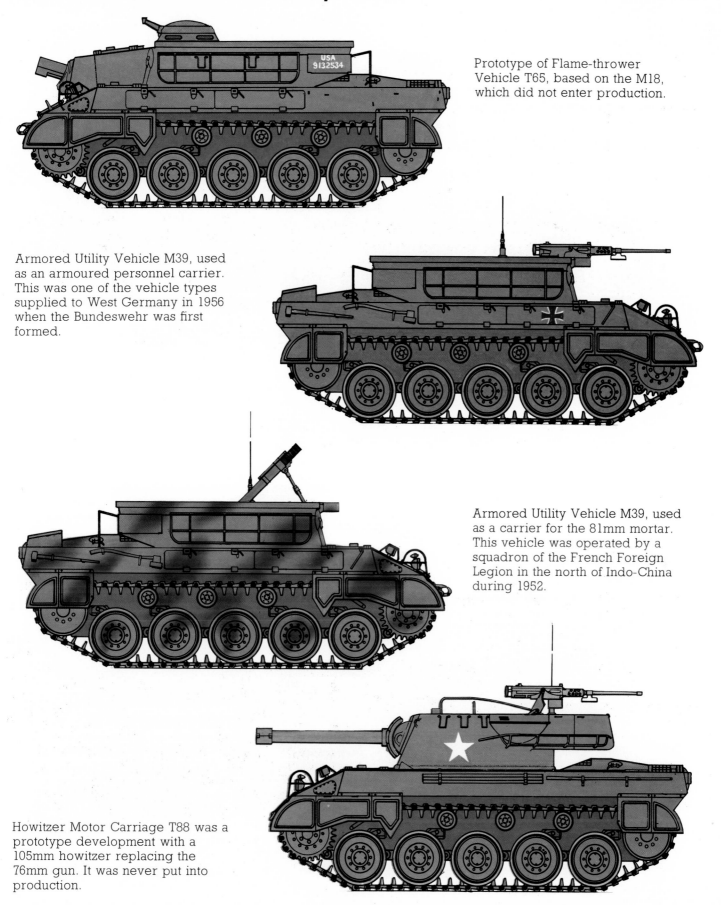

Prototype of Flame-thrower Vehicle T65, based on the M18, which did not enter production.

Armored Utility Vehicle M39, used as an armoured personnel carrier. This was one of the vehicle types supplied to West Germany in 1956 when the Bundeswehr was first formed.

Armored Utility Vehicle M39, used as a carrier for the 81mm mortar. This vehicle was operated by a squadron of the French Foreign Legion in the north of Indo-China during 1952.

Howitzer Motor Carriage T88 was a prototype development with a 105mm howitzer replacing the 76mm gun. It was never put into production.

Gw III/IV Selbstfahrlafette für 15cm Haubitze –
carrier for 15cm howitzer. The Hummel was one
of the biggest and most impressive of German
self-propelled weapons. It used the basic chassis
which had originally been designed to serve as a
rationalized combined design of the PzKpfw III and
PzKpfw IV tanks. The road wheels came from the
PzKpfw IV and the sprockets from the PzKpfw III.
The vehicle illustrated is from Waffen-SS Division
'Das Reich', and the final drawing shows the
munitions carrier version, with gun removed,
from the same unit.

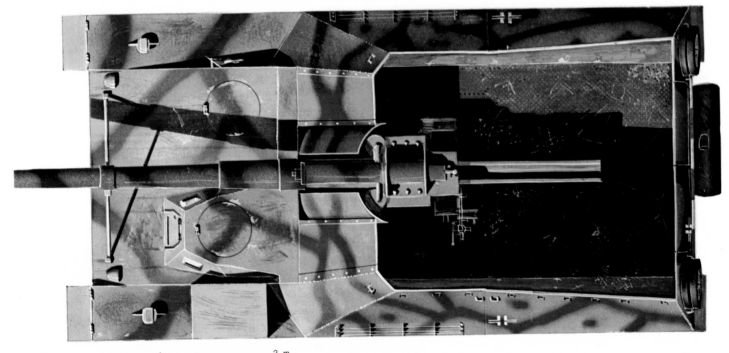

0   1   2 m

Danilo Renzulli

Gw III/IV Sfl für 15cm Haubitze Hummel

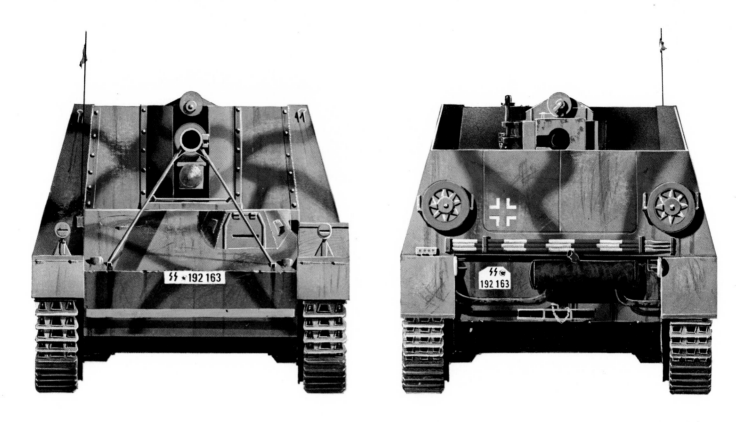

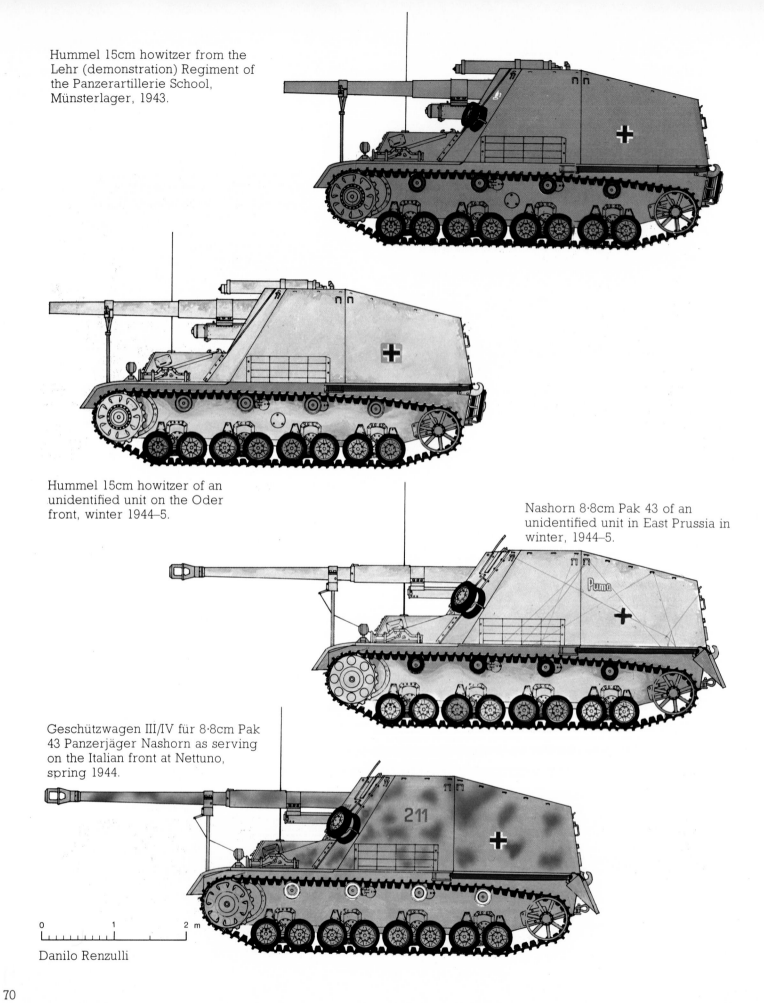

Hummel 15cm howitzer from the Lehr (demonstration) Regiment of the Panzerartillerie School, Münsterlager, 1943.

Hummel 15cm howitzer of an unidentified unit on the Oder front, winter 1944–5.

Nashorn 8·8cm Pak 43 of an unidentified unit in East Prussia in winter, 1944–5.

Geschützwagen III/IV für 8·8cm Pak 43 Panzerjäger Nashorn as serving on the Italian front at Nettuno, spring 1944.

0   1   2 m

Danilo Renzulli

Hummel, Nashorn and variants

Geschützwagen III/IV für 10·5cm leichte Feldhaubitze 18/40 was an experimental vehicle on a shortened chassis, with a traversing turret. It did not go into full production.

Geschützwagen III/IV für 10·5cm, Feldkanone K18 was another experimental vehicle on the Gw III/IV chassis. It did not enter production but the prototypes were used on the Russian Front.

Waffenträger für 10·5cm leichte Feldhaubitze 18/40 Grille 10 was one of a series of Waffenträger (weapons carrier) designs, where the gun was intended to be unshipped and emplaced for action, being recovered by the vehicle later. Only prototypes were built.

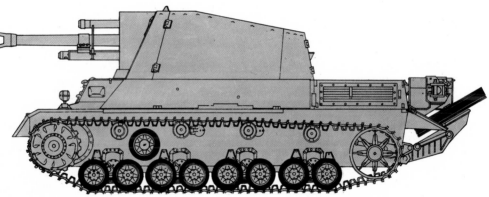

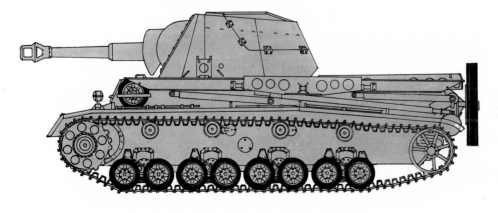

Waffenträger für 10·5cm leichte Feldhaubitze 18/40 Heuschrecke was another weapons carrier design of the experimental Waffenträger series. It carried a collapsible gantry to allow the gun to be lifted off and emplaced.

Hummel, Nashorn and variants

During 1941 rationalization of the PzKpfw III and PzKpfw IV production programme into one basic design was proposed in the interests of simplicity, and ease of building and maintenance. A design was drawn up combining the best features of the two into a single chassis type designated PzKpfw III/IV.

In the event this vehicle never went into production in tank form, but the basic chassis design was used for a heavy assault gun conversion which became one of the best-known German SPs. The III/IV chassis was a lengthened PzKpfw IV type with PzKpfw IV bogies and PzKpfw III sprocket and drive parts. For the SP model the engine was moved from the back to the middle, leaving a rear space for the gun. The Alkett firm started design work in July 1942 and the prototype was approved for production the following October. Though quite an elaborate and thorough design the Hummel (Bumble Bee), as it was called, was intended as a stop-gap until a better vehicle was produced. A total of 100 Hummels was ordered, to be ready in May 1943 in time for summer operations on the Eastern Front. In addition, there were 157 unarmed ammunition carriers to transport the shells for the armed vehicles. The gun carried in the Hummel was the 15cm sFH 18/1 model, a very large and powerful piece. The full designation of the vehicle was 15cm Schwere Panzerhaubitze auf Fahrgestell PzKpfw III/IV (Sf), Hummel. The Hummel gun carrier had a separate front compartment for the driver and radio operator, and the rest of the six-man crew rode in the rear gun compartment. The gun traversed 15° on either side. The Hummel munitions carrier lacked the gun and had the front embrasure plated in.

Hummels were big and powerful SP artillery pieces organized in batteries of six and allocated to the heavy batteries of leading panzer divisions' armoured artillery units. They were first used in action in the big Kursk offensive in the summer of 1943. Early models had a sloped front to the driving compartment while later vehicles had a roomier square-fronted structure.

Following on from the Hummel came another imposing type based on the same PzKpfw III/IV chassis. Once the Hummel design was approved by Hitler in October 1942 it was decided to fit the 8·8cm Pak 43 on the same chassis to produce an equivalent size vehicle for the tank destroyer role. This was designated 8·8cm Pak 43/1 (L/71) auf Fahrgestell PzKpfw III/IV (Sf) Hornisse. This vehicle, built by Deutsche-Eisenwerke, was known both as the Hornisse (Hornet) and Nashorn (Rhinoceros). When the Hummel was ordered, 100 Hornisses were also put in hand for delivery in May 1943. Total orders later reached 500, and by the end of the war 494 of these had been built. At the time of their introduction they were the most powerful tank destroyers available to the Wehrmacht, though the Jagdpanther of 1944 was a greatly superior vehicle mounting the same gun. In service the Hornisse or Nashorn was issued to heavy tank destroyer units, these being corps troops rather than divisional troops, and they were then deployed where most needed on a section of front. Six such units formed in 1943 saw service in the East and West, and when carefully used, the Hornisse proved to be a most formidable weapon.

Prior to the appearance of the Hummel, the biggest SP vehicles in service were the 10·5cm K18 auf Panzer Selbstfahrlafette IVa, which were built early in 1941. Only two vehicles were made as prototypes, based on the PzKpfw IV Ausf D chassis. It was planned as a heavy tank destroyer able to take on any big gun tank produced by Britain or Russia. A second design was projected but not built, in which a 12·8cm gun replaced the 10·5cm weapon. Production was planned for 1942, but by this time the Germans were fighting in Russia and the need then was for smaller less elaborate vehicles. So the two prototypes were the only ones to see service where they were used both against tanks and fortified positions.

MODELS 15cm sFH auf Fahrgestell PzKpfw III/IV (Hummel); 8·8cm Pak 43/1 (L/71) auf Fahrgestell PzKpfw III/IV (Nashorn).

COUNTRY OF ORIGIN Germany.

WEIGHT 23·5 tonnes (23·13 tons).

LENGTH **Hummel:** 7·17m (23ft 6in); **Nashorn:** 8·44m (27ft 8in).

WIDTH **Hummel:** 2·92m (9ft 7¼in); **Nashorn:** 2·86m (9ft 4in).

HEIGHT **Hummel:** 2·79m (9ft 2in); **Nashorn:** 2·65m (8ft 8in).

GROUND CLEARANCE 0·40m (1ft 3½in).

ARMOUR 10–30mm.

ENGINE Maybach HL 120 TRM, 300hp, gasoline.

MAXIMUM SPEED 42km/h (26mph).

RANGE 215km (133 miles).

CREW **Hummel:** 6; **Nashorn:** 4.

ARMAMENT **Hummel:** 1 × 15cm sFH 18/1 L/30; **Nashorn:** 1 × 8·8cm Pak 43/1 L/71, 1 × 7·92mm MG.

AMMUNITION **Hummel:** 15cm: 18 rds; **Nashorn:** 8·8cm: 40 rds, MG: 600 rds.

TRENCH CROSSING 2·3m (7ft 6in).

TRACK WIDTH 0·4m (1ft 4in).

MAXIMUM ELEVATION **Hummel:** 42°; **Nashorn:** 20°.

FORDING DEPTH 1m (3ft 3in).

IS-1, IS-2, ISU-152, IS-3 and T-10

In order for the Russians to counter the increasing use of heavy (88mm) tank and anti-tank guns by the Germans, better speed and manoeuvrability were necessary, as well as a heavier tank gun than the existing 76·2mm and 85mm weapons. The best answer – since it could be produced in minimum time – was a much modified version of the KV-85.

Known as the IS-85 (IS = Iosef Stalin), a small number were produced in late 1943. To improve the firepower a 100mm gun was fitted next (IS-100), but the design was finalized in mid-1944 with a new 122mm gun. This was the IS-122, later called the IS-1. The Stalin differed from the KV in having its sprocket and idler heights lowered to give a greater depth of superstructure; in turn this allowed the superstructure to be carried out over the tracks and so allow a bigger turret. The Stalin also had a cast-formed nose section which gave a greatly improved ballistic shape. The hull rear was sloped as in the T-34.

First IS-1s were in service at the end of 1943, and an improved model, the IS-2, followed in early 1944. The IS-2 had a cast sloping hull front of 'turtle back' shape, quite distinctive from the front of the IS-1 and ballistically much superior. Lastly came the IS-3 which was revolutionary in every sense. It was designed in late 1944 by Kotin and associates. It had fully sloped armour and the glacis plate was in the form of a shallow inverted 'V'. The 122mm L/43 gun was the biggest and most powerful ever mounted in any production gun tank (as opposed to SPs) and the turret was of 'inverted frying-pan' form. First IS-3s were in service January 1945 but full production started later and the type's first public appearance was in the Berlin Victory Parade of September 1945, where it astonished Western observers by its advanced conception.

For years the IS-3 was to remain the yardstick by which new designs were measured by the Western Powers, and it remained in service (and saw further development) in the post-war years. To its crews the IS-3 was known as the 'Pike' because of its menacing pointed nose. To update the IS-3 in the early 1950s, the gun was provided with a fume extractor, armoured skirts were added to cover the top run of the track, the suspension was strengthened, internal stowage was modified and the engine was uprated to 690hp. In this form the vehicle was redesignated IS-4.

Last of the Stalin tank line, and directly descended from the basic IS-3 design, was the T-10. This appeared in 1953 and was also known as the Lenin tank. It had a longer chassis of essentially the same type as the IS-3 with one extra road bogie each side. The angled front armour had an equivalent value of 150mm thickness at 60° incline and the 122mm gun was given a new stabilizer which enabled it to be fired on the move. The longer hull allowed the limited round capacity of 28 to be increased to 50. The T-10 saw wide service and was followed in 1957 by the last of the line, the T-10M, which had a modified nose shape, superior sights, infra-red night-fighting equipment, and a multi-baffle muzzle brake.

The original KV chassis was used to produce the mighty SU-152. This consisted of the big 152mm Model 1937 corps gun/howitzer mounted in a low, heavily armoured superstructure on the chassis of the KV. This type went into production in February 1943 and was first used in numbers in the Kursk offensive later the same year. The gun had 17,300m (19,000yd) range and high velocity (1,900fps). With massive frontal armour and low silhouette, it was known as 'Zveroboy' (conquering beast) to its crews. Later, when the Stalin replaced the KV in production, it was built on the IS chassis and these vehicles were designated ISU-152.

In late 1943 the SU-122 appeared, identical to the SU-152/ISU-152 except that it mounted the long barrel Model 1937 122mm gun. Whereas the SU-152 was a true assault gun, the SU-122 was a tank destroyer first and foremost. Only 35 were built on the KV chassis, after which the IS chassis was used as a basis for these vehicles.

MODELS IS-3 and T-10M.

COUNTRY OF ORIGIN USSR.

WEIGHT **IS-3:** 46·54 tonnes (45·8 tons); **T-10M:** 46 tonnes (45 tons).

LENGTH **IS-3:** 9·9m (32ft 9in); **T-10M:** 10·3m (33ft 10in).

WIDTH **IS-3:** 3·17m (10ft 6in); **T-10M:** 3·5m (11ft 6in).

HEIGHT **IS-3:** 2·71m (8ft 11in); **T-10M:** 2·41m (7ft 11in).

GROUND CLEARANCE **IS-3:** 0·45m (1ft 6in); **T-10M:** 0·45m (1ft 6in).

ARMOUR **IS-3:** 20–230mm; **T-10M:** 20–273mm.

ENGINES 12-cylinder V-2-IS, water-cooled, diesel, 513hp (**IS-3**), 690hp (**T-10M**).

MAXIMUM SPEED **IS-3:** 35km/h (22mph); **T-10M:** 50km/h (31mph).

RANGE **IS-3:** 170km (106 miles); **T-10M:** 298km (185 miles).

CREW 4.

ARMAMENT 1 × 122mm D-25 M1943 dual-purpose gun, 2 × 14·5mm MG.

AMMUNITION **IS-3:** 122mm: 28 rds, MG: 1,000 rds; **T-10M:** 122mm: 50 rds, MG: 1,000 rds.

TRENCH CROSSING 3m (9ft 10in).

TRACK WIDTH **IS-3:** 0·65m (2ft 1½in); **T-10M:** 0·72m (2ft 4½in).

MAXIMUM ELEVATION **IS-3:** 20 ; **T-10M:** 17°.

FORDING DEPTH 1·29m (4ft 3in).

In early 1945 the most formidably armed heavy tank in the world was the IS-2 (Iosef Stalin 2), the Red Army's principal heavy tank. Its massive 122mm gun was bigger and more powerful than those mounted in any other conventional tank. Because of the size of the rounds, however, ammunition stowage was limited and the interior of the vehicle was cramped. This particular example belonged to a squadron of 11th Armoured Corps of the Red Army and was used in the final attack on and occupation of Berlin in April 1945. The red-star panel shown inset was carried on the rear decking of the tank (where indicated) as an aerial recognition sign.

Pino dell'Orco – Nicola Pignato

IS-2 (Iosef Stalin II)

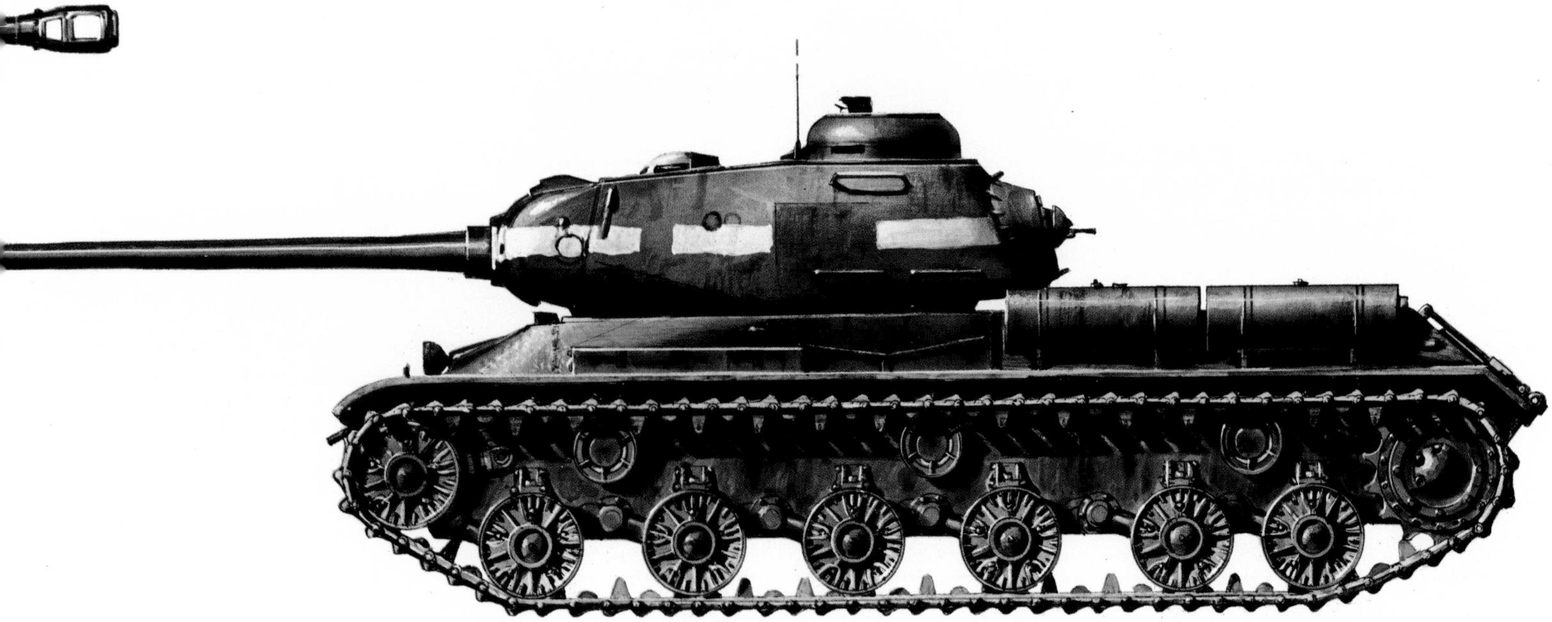

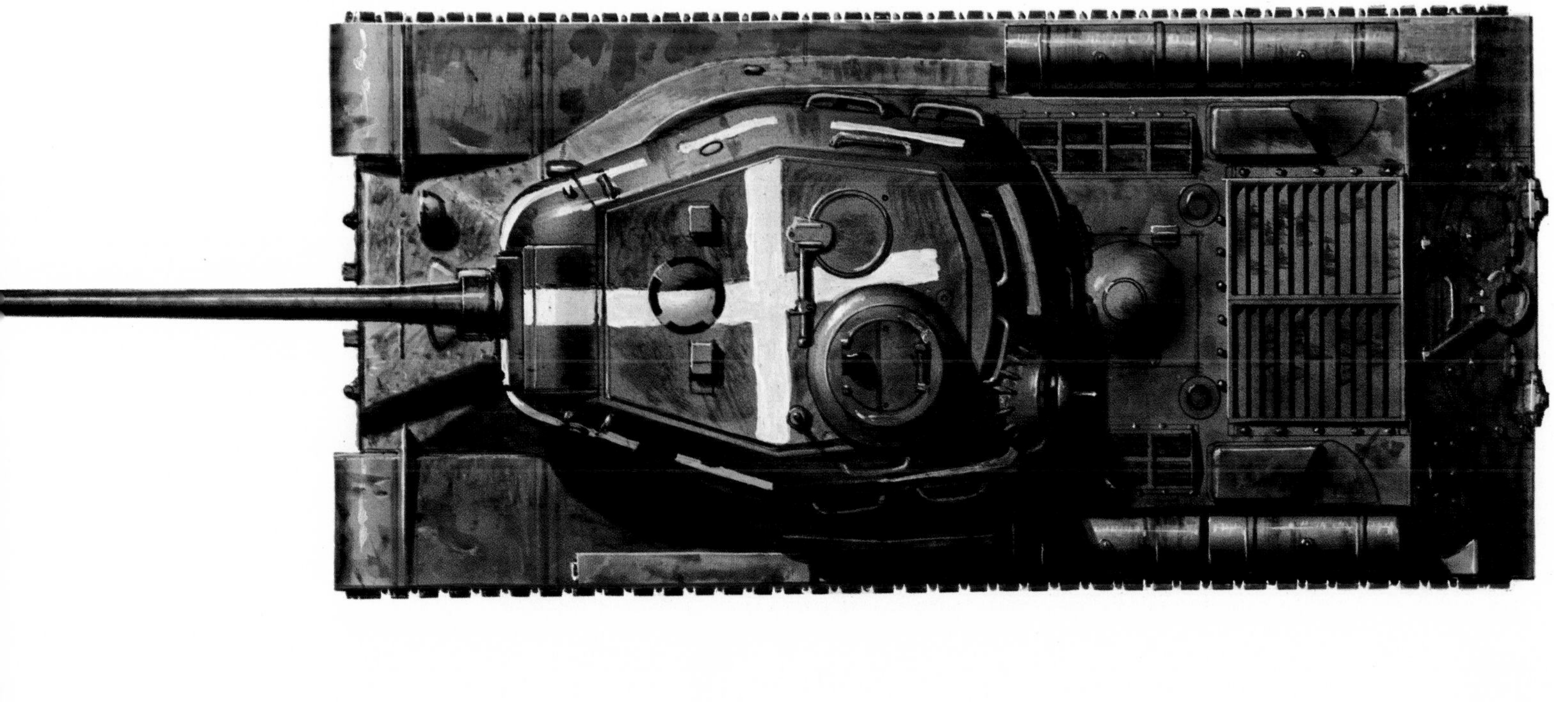

ISU-152 of General Koniev's
Armoured Corps during the battle
for Berlin, April 1945.

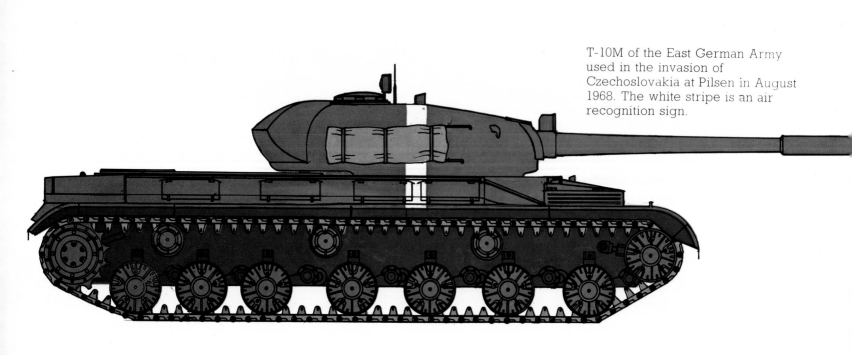

T-10M of the East German Army
used in the invasion of
Czechoslovakia at Pilsen in August
1968. The white stripe is an air
recognition sign.

IS-1, ISU-152, IS-3 and T-10

IS-1 of an unidentified Russian unit
in the Ukraine, early in 1944.

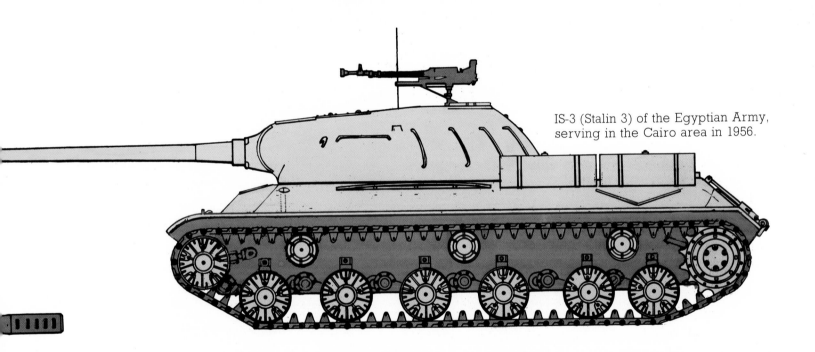

IS-3 (Stalin 3) of the Egyptian Army,
serving in the Cairo area in 1956.

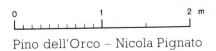

0   1   2 m

Pino dell'Orco – Nicola Pignato

Air recognition flag of the Red Army.

The KV-1C was the most widely used of the Klimenti Voroshilov family. The drawing represents the 1942 production model with the inscription 'for the fatherland' on the turret side. The drawing (opposite below) shows the KV-8, a lightened model with 45mm gun converted from a KV-1A of 1941.

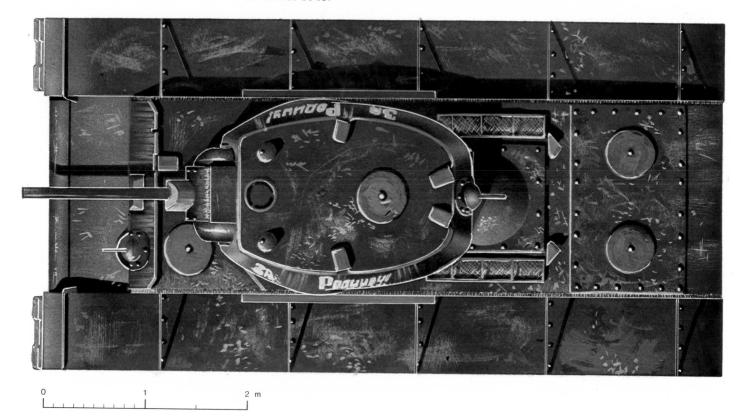

0   1   2 m

Danilo Renzulli

Klimenti Vorishilov KV-IC

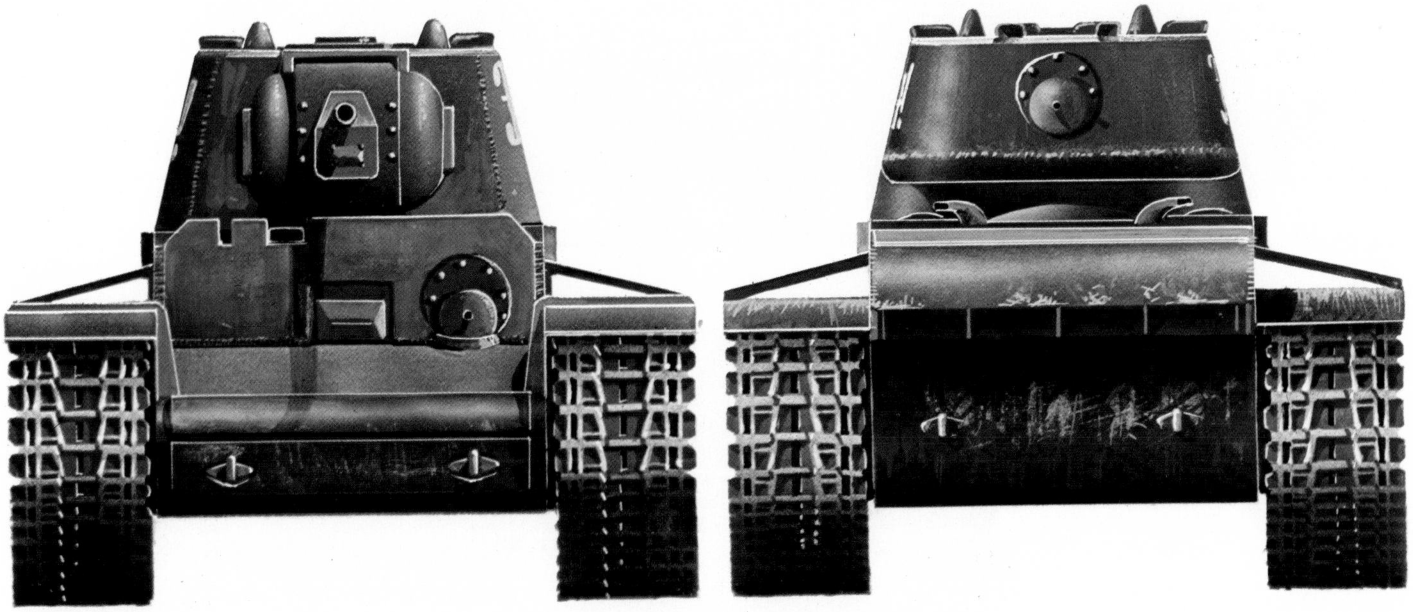

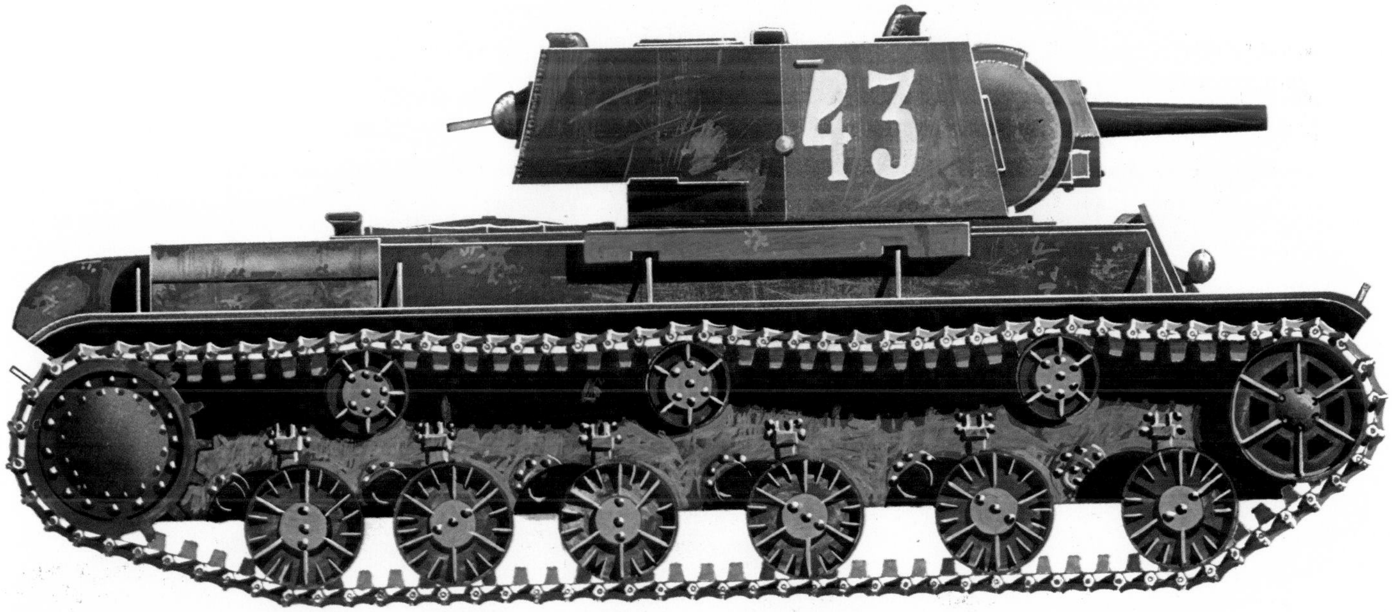
43

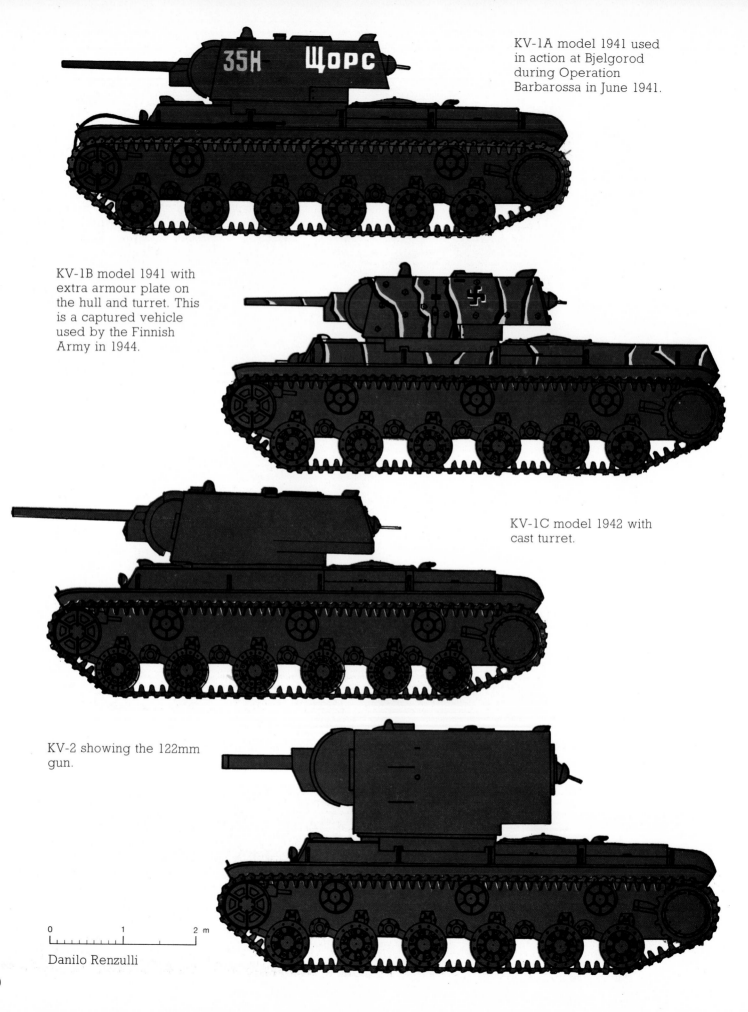

KV-1A model 1941 used in action at Bjelgorod during Operation Barbarossa in June 1941.

KV-1B model 1941 with extra armour plate on the hull and turret. This is a captured vehicle used by the Finnish Army in 1944.

KV-1C model 1942 with cast turret.

KV-2 showing the 122mm gun.

0   1   2 m

Danilo Renzulli

Klimenti Vorishilov

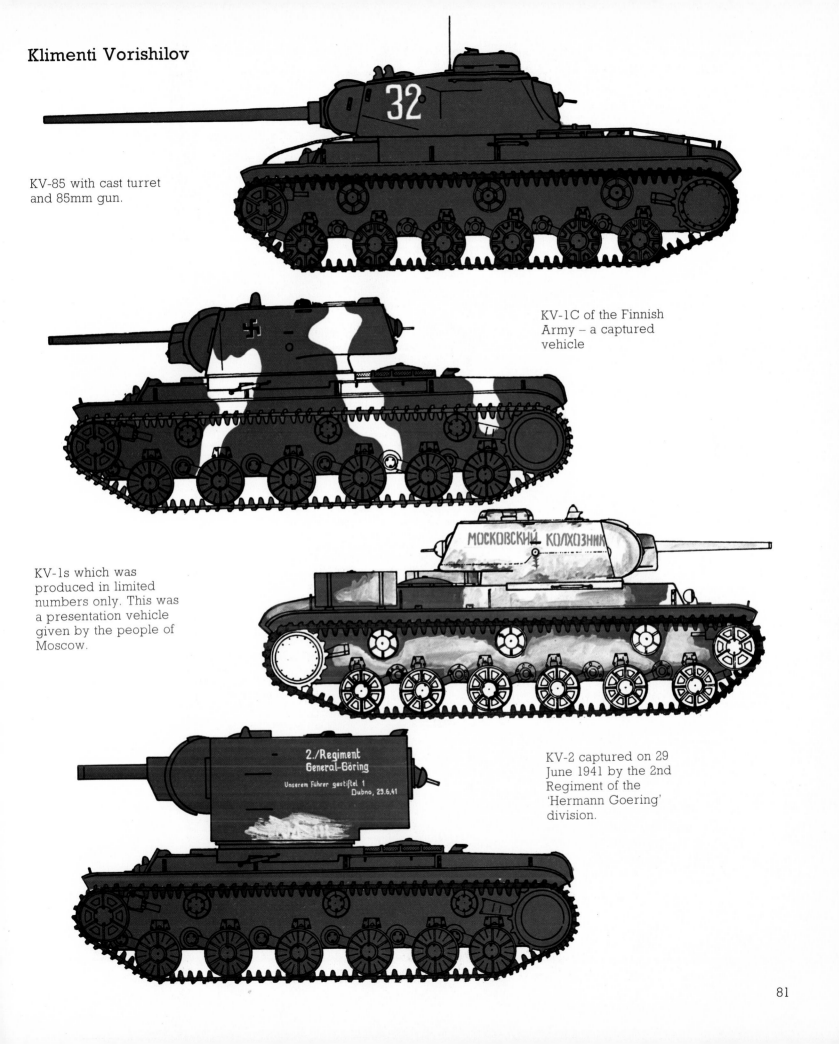

KV-85 with cast turret
and 85mm gun.

KV-1C of the Finnish
Army – a captured
vehicle

KV-1s which was
produced in limited
numbers only. This was
a presentation vehicle
given by the people of
Moscow.

КV-2 captured on 29
June 1941 by the 2nd
Regiment of the
'Hermann Goering'
division.

Klimenti Vorishilov

The Russian SMK (short for Sergius Mironovitch Kirov) and T-100 were two almost identical vehicles designed in 1938 under Z. Kotin, chief engineer of the Kirov-Zavod tank factory, Leningrad. They were intended as replacements for the multi-turreted T-35 and were of similar size and bulk. The original project featured three turrets, but one was eliminated in the design stage in favour of increased armour. The vehicles were virtually identical externally, but the SMK had noticeably wider tracks and stronger suspension. It also had thicker armour, however, and was the heavier vehicle at 56 tons. The front turret featured a 45mm gun.

Both the T-100 and SMK were built as prototypes only for trials, but they were tested in action in the Russo-Finnish War and found unsuitable, being too bulky and too complicated.

Largely at Stalin's suggestion, Kotin modified the over-large T-100 design by removing the smaller front turret and utilizing the weight and length thus saved to produce a more compact vehicle with single turret and armour basis increased to 75mm. Originally called the Kotin-Stalin, it was soon officially named the Klementi Vorishilov (KV) after the famous Soviet general. The prototype KV-1 appeared in September 1939 and production commenced in December. The following KV models subsequently appeared:

KV-2 was a special support version with a massive 152mm howitzer in a greatly enlarged turret. It proved to be exceedingly cumbersome and the big turret made the vehicle unstable. By the time production ceased just after the German invasion in June 1941, two production variants had appeared, the KV-2A on the original KV-1 chassis, and the KV-2B on the KV-1A chassis.

KV-1A was an improved version of the KV-1 built in 1940. It had new pattern all-steel bogie wheels, a hull MG, the longer L/41·5 76·2mm gun, and a new cast cradle and mantlet.

KV-1B was the designation given to up-armoured, re-worked models of the KV-1. Appliqué armour was bolted on the turret sides and sometimes on the hull sides, and welded on the front. This appeared in spring 1941 and 25–35mm armour was added to bring the basis up to about 100mm. Hull MG was added to vehicles formerly lacking this.

KV-1B (cast turret) was an improved model of the KV-1A with a new, thicker cast turret and appliqué armour welded on the hull front and sides to bring the basis up to about 100mm. It appeared in 1941.

KV-1C was the 1942 production model with cast turret of improved shape and slightly thicker at the bottom. It also had thicker appliqué armour with a maximum thickness of 120–130mm.

KV-1s (Russian designation) was a 'fast' KV model produced in small numbers during late 1942; armour thickness was reduced to 60mm and slight mechanical changes made so that a speed of 40km/h (25mph) could be attained to allow the vehicle to operate with T-34s. A vision cupola was added to the turret of the tank.

KV-85 was the final version, produced in early 1943, and was an up-gunned variant of the KV-1C with a new enlarged cast turret mounting the M1943 85mm tank gun, an adaptation of an existing AA gun. It featured a cupola for the commander and a ball-mounted MG in the rear face. The turret was subsequently adapted for the T-34.

KV-8 was a flame-thrower version built in very small numbers with 45mm gun and co-axial flame projector replacing the 76·2mm gun.

At the time of its first appearance in 1939, the KV was a remarkable technical achievement which heralded the Soviet preference for simple but robust designs of great effectiveness. When it was designed it was far in advance of any other large tank of the time, and surpassed anything even the Germans were then contemplating. Its development was quick and the secret of its building was well kept. The priority for Kotin the designer was to produce a completely shell-proof tank – and, in the context of the 1939 period, he succeeded.

MODELS KV-1 and KV-2.

COUNTRY OF ORIGIN USSR.

WEIGHT **KV-1:** 47 tonnes (46·35 tons); **KV-2:** 53 tonnes (52·15 tons).

LENGTH 6·88m (22ft 7in).

WIDTH 3·25m (10ft 8in).

HEIGHT **KV-1:** 2·66m (8ft 9in); **KV-2:** 3·6m (12ft).

GROUND CLEARANCE 0·45m (1ft 6in).

ARMOUR **KV-1:** 35–78mm; **KV-2:** 35–100mm.

ENGINE V-2K, 550hp, diesel.

MAXIMUM SPEED **KV-1:** 35·4km/h (22mph); **KV-2:** 25·75km/h (16mph).

RANGE **KV-1:** 225km (140 miles); **KV-2:** 161km (100 miles).

CREW **KV-1:** 5; **KV-2:** 6.

ARMAMENT **KV-1:** 1 × 76·2mm dual-purpose gun, 3 × 7·62 MG; **KV-2:** 1 × 152mm howitzer, 2 × 7·62 MG.

AMMUNITION **KV-1:** 76·2mm: 111 rds, MG: 3,024 rds; **KV-2:** 152mm: 36 rds, MG: 3,087 rds.

TRENCH CROSSING 2·69m (8ft 10in).

TRACK WIDTH 0·7m (2ft 3½in).

MAXIMUM ELEVATION 24·5°.

FORDING DEPTH 1·44m (4ft 9in).

LVT 1-4

LVT stood for 'Landing Vehicle Tracked', and all US World War 2 LVTs stemmed from the Alligator design of Donald Roebling Jr, who had produced a lightweight tracked amphibious vehicle in 1935 for rescue work in the swamps of the Florida Everglades. In 1940 Roebling redesigned this vehicle to suit US Marine requirements. The first order, for 200 vehicles, designated LVT 1, was placed in November 1940, and in August 1941 the first USMC amphibian tractor battalions were formed with these types. A larger improved version was designated LVT 2, and both were intended as cargo carriers for ship-to-shore supply operations. They were made of mild steel and had the valuable ability to run directly up a beach.

In November 1943, LVT 2s were used to carry troops ashore at Tarawa and it was realized that the LVT, suitably altered, could be used to provide fire support for amphibious operations. What was virtually a floating tank was therefore developed, simply by building an LVT 2 in armour plate instead of mild steel, decking in the cargo space and adding the turret and 37mm gun from the M3 light tank. This became the LVT(A)1, (A for armoured). Developments from then on included the following:

Designed at the end of 1943, the LVT(A)1 was in service in 1944 and proved most successful. In addition to the turret, two machine gun positions were cut in the rear decking with ·30 cal. Brownings mounted on Scarff rings and fitted with shield and coamings. There was a six-man crew.

Next followed the LVT(A)2 built to US Army requirements at the same time as the LVT(A)1. This vehicle was identical to the original mild steel LVT 2 in appearance but was constructed of armour plate like the LVT(A)1. Turret, guns and decking were omitted so that it could be used as an armoured troop/store carrier for assault landings to transport troops over the beach and inland for disembarkation. The idea for this came after the Tarawa landings at the end of 1943, when the original LVT 2 had been given extemporized armour protection from bolted on plating. These LVTs were called 'Water Buffalo' by the American forces.

In March 1944, when the need for armament heavier than the 37mm gun had been appreciated, the LVT(A)1 was further modified by the fitting of the complete turret and 75mm howitzer from the M8 GMC. Designated LVT(A)4, this variant proved a most useful and successful vehicle in the many amphibious assault landings of the Pacific war. It suffered, however, by having only hand traverse and no stabilization of the gun. LVT(A)5 remedied these shortcomings by the addition of power traverse and a gyro-stabilizer in the turret. Designed in 1945, it did not come into service, however, until after the war.

A disadvantage of the original LVT 1 and 2 designs had been the rear mounted engine and central cargo space. Their siting meant that troops and stores were loaded over the side of the vehicle and there were consequent limitations on the sort of item which could be loaded. The LVT 4 was basically the LVT(A)2 modified by having its engine moved forward and resited immediately behind the driving compartment. The transom was then replaced by a ramp operated by a hand winch. This allowed troops and stores to be loaded through the stern of the vehicle. It could carry 30 troops (compared with 18 in the LVT 2) and light vehicles (such as a Jeep) or field guns. The LVT 4 was first used at Saipan in mid-1944, and was also used in Italy and NW Europe in 1944–5. The LVT 4 was also operated by the British Army, under the designation 'LVT, Buffalo'. In British service it was fitted with a Polsten 20mm cannon and two ·30 cal. Browning MGs. In American service it carried a mount on each side for either ·30 cal. or ·50 cal. machine gun. The major operation in NW Europe in which the LVT 4 featured was the Rhine crossing in 1945 where troops and equipment were ferried in large numbers.

MODELS LVT 1 and LVT(A)1.

COUNTRY OF ORIGIN USA.

WEIGHT Empty 7·84 tonnes (7·72 tons).

LENGTH **LVT 1:** 6·55m (21ft 6in); **LVT(A)1:** 7·94m (26ft 1in).

WIDTH **LVT 1:** 3m (9ft 10in); **LVT(A)1:** 3·25m (10ft 8in).

HEIGHT **LVT 1:** 2·47m (8ft 1½in); **LVT(A)1:** 2·35m (7ft 8in).

GROUND CLEARANCE 0·43m (1ft 6in).

ARMOUR **LVT 1:** Not armoured; **LVT(A)1:** Light bolt-on armour.

ENGINES **LVT 1:** 6-cylinder Hercules, 150hp, gasoline; **LVT(A)1:** 7-cylinder Continental, 250hp, gasoline.

MAXIMUM SPEED **LVT 1:** land: 19·3km/h (12mph), water: 9·6km/h (6mph); **LVT(A)1:** land: 32km/h (20mph), water: 12km/h (7·5mph).

RANGE **LVT 1:** land: 240km (150 miles), water: 96km (60 miles); **LVT(A)1:** land: 240km (150 miles), water: 120·6km (75 miles).

CREW **LVT 1:** 2–3; **LVT(A)1:** 5.

ARMAMENT **LVT 1:** 2 × ·30 cal. MG; **LVT(A)1:** 1 × 37mm gun, 2 × ·50 cal. MG.

AMMUNITION **LVT 1:** 6,000 rds; **LVT(A)1:** 37mm: 104 rds, ·50 cal.: 6,000 rds.

TRACK WIDTH **LVT 1:** 0·26m (10¼in); **LVT(A)1:** 0·36m (1ft 2¼in).

The main illustration shows an LVT(A)1 of the
708th Battalion, US Army, as used at Saipan in the
Marianas on 15 June 1944. This is the version
armed with a 3·7cm gun. The illustration (opposite
below) shows the unarmoured LVT 2. This
example was used by the 2nd Division, US Marine
Corps, at Tarawa on 20 November 1943. All LVT
types were propelled in the water by cup-shaped
grousers which formed an integral part of the
track shoe. Suspension was achieved by rubber
cushioning of the bogie wheel axles.

0   1   2   3 m

Gistudio

Landing Vehicle Tracked LVT(A)1 and LVT 2

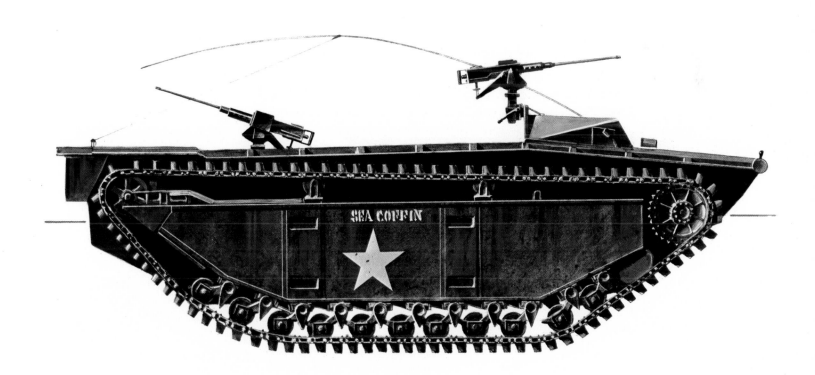

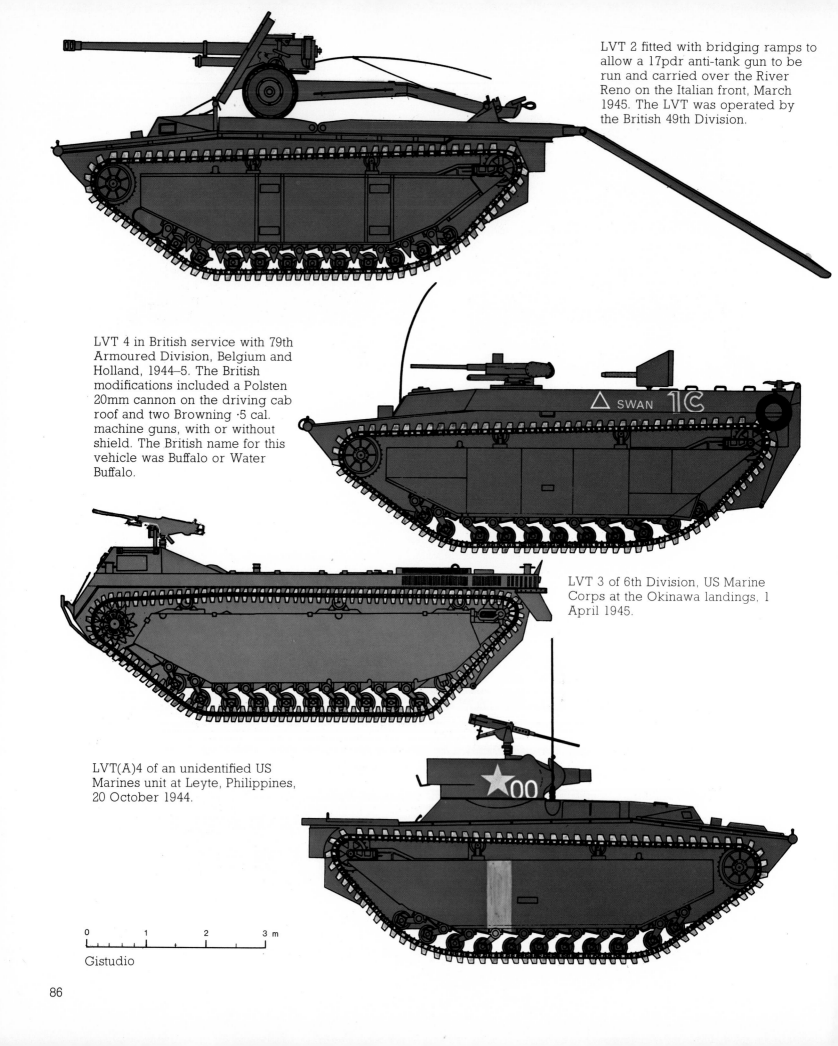

LVT 2 fitted with bridging ramps to allow a 17pdr anti-tank gun to be run and carried over the River Reno on the Italian front, March 1945. The LVT was operated by the British 49th Division.

LVT 4 in British service with 79th Armoured Division, Belgium and Holland, 1944–5. The British modifications included a Polsten 20mm cannon on the driving cab roof and two Browning ·5 cal. machine guns, with or without shield. The British name for this vehicle was Buffalo or Water Buffalo.

LVT 3 of 6th Division, US Marine Corps at the Okinawa landings, 1 April 1945.

LVT(A)4 of an unidentified US Marines unit at Leyte, Philippines, 20 October 1944.

0   1   2   3 m

Gistudio

LVT 2-4

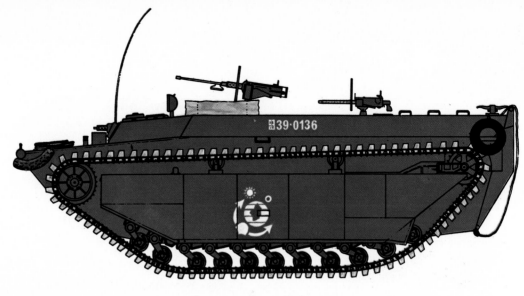

LVT 4 of the Chinese Nationalist forces on Formosa in the 1950s.

The LVT 3 was a vehicle developed by Borg Warner which was similar in external appearance to the LVT 4, complete with stern ramp but which had a single Cadillac 125hp engine mounted in each side pontoon and the Hydramatic automatic transmission used in the M5 light tank. This produced a vehicle of superior performance more efficient than the Continental-engined designs. Called the Bushmaster, it was produced in 1944 and first used in action at Okinawa. The example shown was used by the US Marines in Korea.

LVT 4 of the Italian Army. This particular vehicle was used in the early 1960s by Reggimento di Fanteria.

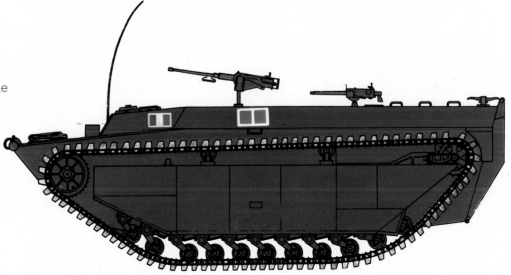

The improved model of the M13/40 in production in 1942 was designated M14/42, and one of these vehicles is shown here. It was increased in weight to 14 tons as a result of improvements which included a more powerful engine and thicker armour, as well as other minor technical changes. The vehicle here is from the 1st Company of the 13th Battalion of medium tanks of the Ariete Division. It was in action at the Battle of El-Alamein in October 1942 where it was captured by British forces after being abandoned by its crew. It is now on display in the Royal Armoured Corps Tank Museum, Bovington, Dorset, England. Note the addition of sandbags across the vehicle front to give a measure of extra protection; tanks of this series were inadequately armoured by the standards of the day

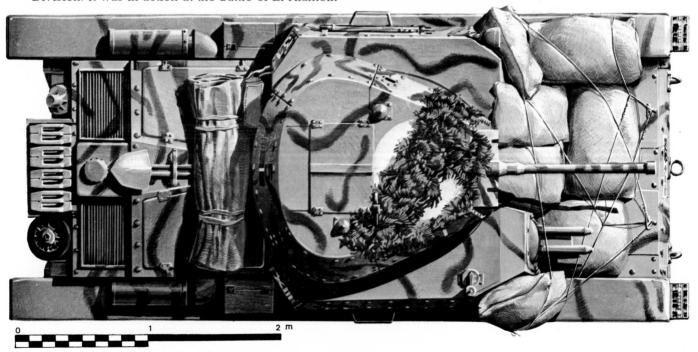

Gistudio – Claudio Tatangelo

Carro Armato M14/42

Inset: Mantlet of a M13/40 of the 41st Battalion of medium tanks in the Littorio Division with the motto 'A Colpo Sicuro' ('Safe from Blows'). Note the wide sighting-ports which were a serious bullet splash hazard. The M14/42 had narrower ports as a result.

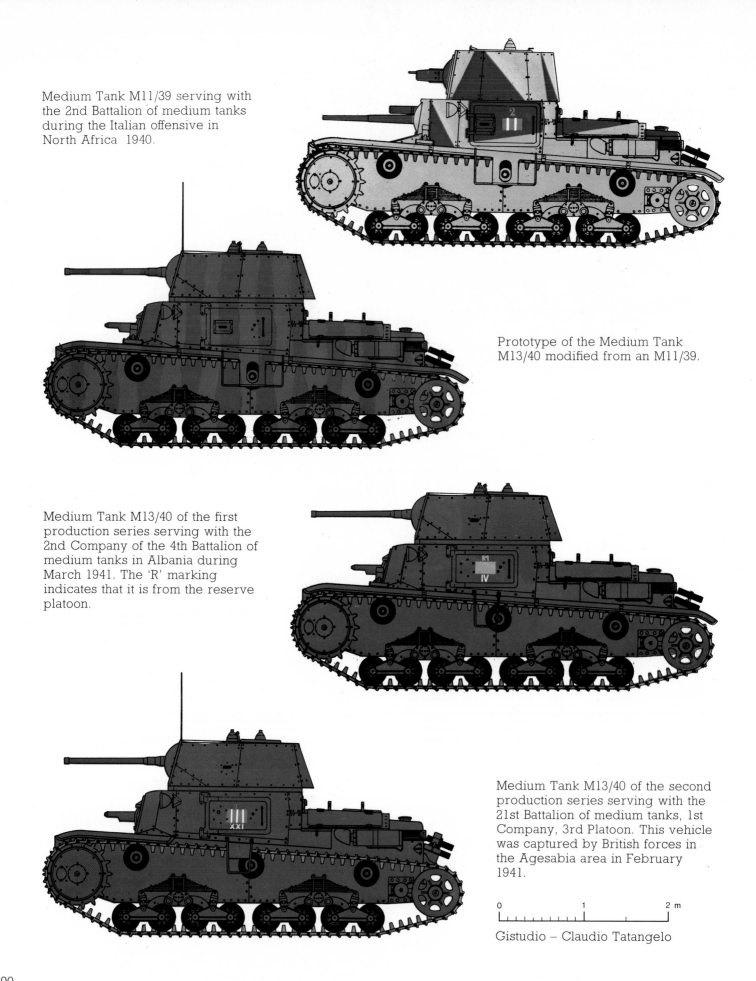

Medium Tank M11/39 serving with the 2nd Battalion of medium tanks during the Italian offensive in North Africa 1940.

Prototype of the Medium Tank M13/40 modified from an M11/39.

Medium Tank M13/40 of the first production series serving with the 2nd Company of the 4th Battalion of medium tanks in Albania during March 1941. The 'R' marking indicates that it is from the reserve platoon.

Medium Tank M13/40 of the second production series serving with the 21st Battalion of medium tanks, 1st Company, 3rd Platoon. This vehicle was captured by British forces in the Agesabia area in February 1941.

0   1   2 m

Gistudio – Claudio Tatangelo

M13/40

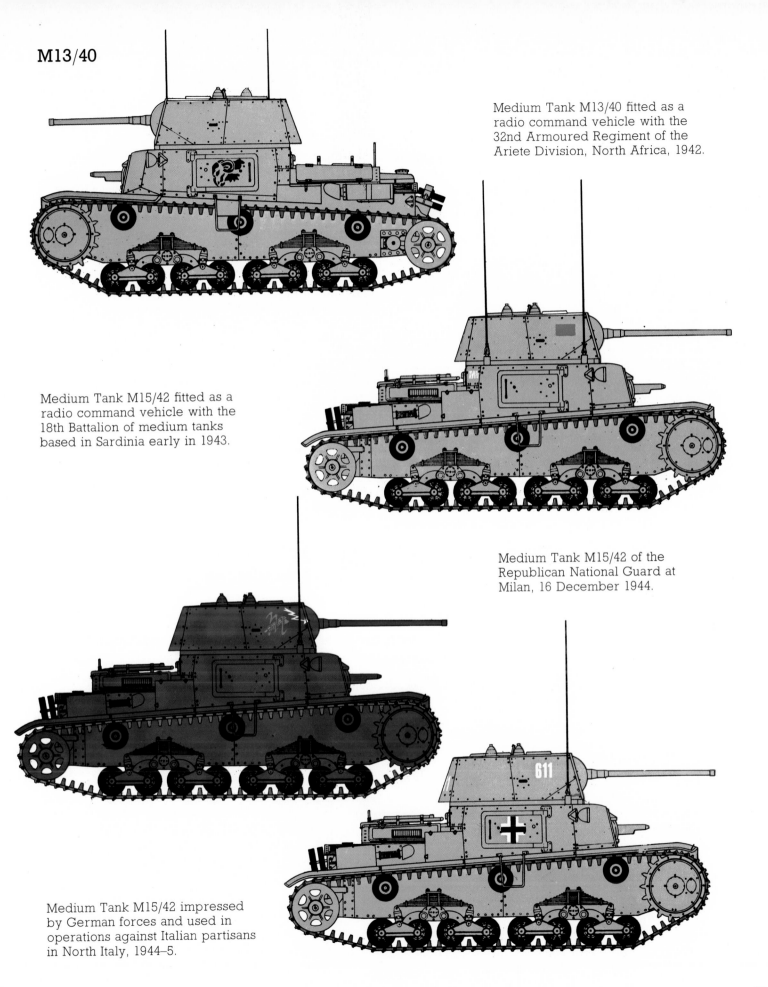

Medium Tank M13/40 fitted as a radio command vehicle with the 32nd Armoured Regiment of the Ariete Division, North Africa, 1942.

Medium Tank M15/42 fitted as a radio command vehicle with the 18th Battalion of medium tanks based in Sardinia early in 1943.

Medium Tank M15/42 of the Republican National Guard at Milan, 16 December 1944.

Medium Tank M15/42 impressed by German forces and used in operations against Italian partisans in North Italy, 1944–5.

M13/40

Until 1938 the Italian Army's most numerously available AFV was the tiny CV 3/33 tankette, developed from the original British Carden-Loyd tankette design of the 1920s. While this had been developed into a number of models adequate for police work in Italy's North African colonies, and had been used with success (against negligible opposition) in the invasion of Abyssinia in 1935, the CV was by no stretch of the imagination suitable for use in a full-scale war. In 1939 General Caracciolo di Feroleto became head of the newly created Inspectorate of Technical Services, charged with the quick procurement of new weapons. With the possibility of war there was an urgent need for an Italian tank to match those of other major powers.

Development of a medium tank started with the M11/39 which went into production in 1939. This vehicle used as its starting point a Fiat-Ansaldo prototype for a 'breakthrough tank' – *Carro di rottura* – which had been built for trials in 1935. The *Carro di rottura* was somewhat ahead of its time – a robust chassis with a fixed superstructure and a front-mounted howitzer in a limited traverse mount. It was, in short, what became known as an assault gun in World War 2 when similar types of vehicle were developed. The *Carro di rottura* had a long chassis with twin bogie assemblies each carried on semi-elliptic leaf springs, making for ease of production and maintenance.

Studies in 1937 suggested that mounting a small turret on the superstructure would combine the facility of the fixed forward-firing gun with the ability to give traversing fire against infantry by machine gun. A new design, essentially a modification of the *Carro di rottura* layout, incorporated a lower superstructure mounting a 37mm high velocity gun in the right-hand front of the superstructure and a small round turret with twin 8mm machine guns on top. This configuration was rushed into production as the new medium tank M11/39 with an order placed for one hundred vehicles.

It was seen almost at once that it would be more desirable to have the main gun in the traversing turret rather than in the front hull, and General Caracciolo personally supervised the changes necessary to get the design revised, having to overcome bureaucratic inertia in the process. Fifteen production vehicles were ready by July 1940 and the first 250 had been completed by the year's end. This was none too soon, for Italy declared war on Britain and France in June 1940, and started military operations on the Libya-Egypt border in August–September. The new model was designated M13/40 and the first vehicles were in service in Libya in October 1940.

The M13/40 had a four-man crew – commander/gunner, loader, driver and front machine gunner/radio operator. The 37mm gun of the M11/39 had been replaced by a 47mm weapon in the turret, while twin 8mm machine guns were carried in the front superstructure in a cast housing. There was a V8 diesel engine, liquid cooled with drive and transmission to the front sprockets via reduction gear and gearbox inside the nose.

Construction was all riveted over a conventional girder frame, with 25mm armour plate. The turret was hand traversed, though there was a simple oleo-dynamic traverse system as an alternative. Telescopes, periscopes and simple slits provided external vision. A Breda 38 AA machine gun could be mounted on the roof. The gun mantlet was fixed, with the 47mm gun and its co-axial machine gun elevating and depressing vertically from inside the turret. The slots for the gun provided a vulnerable access for bullet splash, and, because the tank was small, it was cramped and difficult to evacuate in a hurry.

In service the M13/40 proved barely adequate. Because there was no heavier tank available (though one was planned), M13/40s had to be used for all roles.

They were not reliable mechanically and experienced more than their fair share of breakdowns in desert service.

MODEL M13/40.

COUNTRY OF ORIGIN Italy.

WEIGHT 14·2 tonnes (14 tons).

LENGTH 4·93m (16ft 2in).

WIDTH 2·23m (7ft 4in).

HEIGHT 2·36m (7ft 9½in).

GROUND CLEARANCE 0·38m (1ft 3in).

ARMOUR 9–30mm.

ENGINE Spa 8 TM40 V8, 105hp, diesel.

MAXIMUM SPEED 33km/h (21mph).

RANGE 200km (124 miles).

CREW 4.

ARMAMENT 1 × 47mm gun, 2 × 8mm MG.

AMMUNITION 47mm: 104 rds, MG: 3,048 rds.

TRENCH CROSSING 2·10m (6ft 11in).

TRACK WIDTH 26cm (10¼in).

MAXIMUM ELEVATION 30°.

FORDING DEPTH 1m (3ft 3in).

Marder and Hetzer

To supplement tanks on the Eastern Front, the Germans placed captured Russian 7.62cm anti-tank guns on PzKpfw 38(t) tank chassis. The new vehicle was designated Panzerjäger 38(t) für 7·62cm Pak 36(r) and was given the name Marder III (Marder = Martin). A first production order late in December 1941 called for 17 such vehicles a month, but this was soon increased to 30. Nearly 350 were eventually built in the April–October 1942 period, and a few more were converted from old PzKpfw 38(t) tanks in 1943. So that German ammunition could be used, the 7·62cm gun was rechambered.

Following early experience it was decided to divert all further PzKpfw 38(t) production for conversion to self-propelled carriages. The engine was removed from the rear and repositioned in the middle where the fighting compartment of the tank was sited. This meant that the gun could now be positioned at the rear of the chassis with a corresponding lower centre of gravity and much better weight distribution. The altered design was ready by February 1943 and the Czech BMM company was asked to produce the new type forthwith at a rate of 150 per month. Accordingly in the April 1943–May 1944 period a total of 975 vehicles was produced. In this modified design the German 7·5cm Pak 40 gun was used, and the type was officially designated Panzerjäger 38(t) mit 7·5cm Pak 40/3 Ausf M – and still called Marder III.

To supplement these vehicles based on the PzKpfw 38(t) chassis, it was decided to convert many PzKpfw II tanks to SP guns since they had become less suitable as combat tanks by 1942. Among the conversions were 650 PzKpfw II Ausf F converted to Marder standard and named 7·5cm Pak 40/2 auf Fahrgestell PzKpfw II – Marder II.

Famo, MAN and Daimler-Benz were brought in to carry out the conversions, over a period from June 1942–June 1943. All had the German Pak 40 7·5cm gun, and the PzKpfw II Ausf F was used for most of these conversions, though some other models were used too.

Concurrently with these Marder II vehicles some 200 PzKpfw II Ausf D models were converted in a similar style to the original Marder III on the PzKpfw 38(t) chassis. The PzKpfw II Ausf D had Christie suspension and was the least successful of the PzKpfw II series. The conversions were designated Pz Sf für 7·62cm Pak 36(r) auf Fg PzKpfw II Ausf D. The gun, as can be seen from the designation, was the rechambered captured Russian anti-tank gun. Though this vehicle was built to standards similar to those of the Marder II, it was never officially called a Marder. (A Marder appears on page 111.)

In 1943, Guderian, Inspector General of Armoured Forces, suggested the urgent need for a light tank destroyer with fully enclosed armoured hull and, above all, a low silhouette (something the extemporized vehicles lacked). A design was drawn up based on a slightly widened PzKpfw 38(t) chassis with 7·5cm Pak 39 armament in a limited traverse front mount. Following successful prototype trials it was decided to switch all new tank destroyer production on the PzKpfw 38(t) hull to the new design which was designated Jagdpanzer 38(t) Hetzer (= Baiter).

The Hetzer proved to be an exceptionally fine vehicle of great mechanical reliability though its small fighting compartment was very cramped. There was a roof-mounted machine gun for close-in fighting and this was remotely controlled from inside the vehicle. The Hetzer was rushed into production in the Czech BMM and Skoda works in April 1944. By the time that output ceased in May 1945 some 2,584 had been made. It was used for some years post-war by the Czech Army, and was also purchased by the Swiss Army in 1946. There were two notable variants, a Flammpanzer 38(t) Hetzer flamethrower with gun replaced by a projector, and an unarmed recovery vehicle, Bergepanzer 38(t) Hetzer. Other SP guns used by the Germans included the Bison and Lorraine Schlepper (see page 97).

MODELS 7·5cm Pak 40/2 auf Sfl II Marder II and Jagdpanzer 38(t) Hetzer.

COUNTRY OF ORIGIN Germany.

WEIGHT **Marder:** 10·8 tonnes (10·63 tons); **Hetzer:** 16·2 tonnes (16 tons).

LENGTH **Marder:** 6·18m (20ft 3in); **Hetzer:** 4·87m (16ft).

WIDTH **Marder:** 2·31m (7ft 7in); **Hetzer:** 2·63m (8ft 8in).

HEIGHT **Marder:** 2·27m (7ft 5in); **Hetzer:** 2·1m (6ft 10in).

GROUND CLEARANCE **Marder:** 0·34m (1ft 1½in); **Hetzer:** 0·38m (1ft 3in).

ARMOUR **Marder:** 5–20mm; **Hetzer:** 8–60mm.

ENGINES **Marder:** 6-cylinder Maybach HL62TRM, 140hp, gasoline; **Hetzer:** 6-cylinder Praga, 150hp, gasoline.

MAXIMUM SPEED 40km/h (25mph).

RANGE **Marder:** 190km (118 miles); **Hetzer:** 180km (112 miles).

CREW **Marder:** 3; **Hetzer:** 4.

ARMAMENT 1 × 7·5cm gun, 1 × 7·92mm MG

AMMUNITION **Marder:** 7·5cm: 37 rds, MG: 600 rds; **Hetzer:** 7·5cm: 40 rds, MG: 600 rds.

TRENCH CROSSING **Marder:** 1·7m (5ft 7in); **Hetzer:** 1·3m (4ft 3in).

TRACK WIDTH **Marder:** 0·3m (11¾in); **Hetzer:** 0·35m (1ft 2in).

MAXIMUM ELEVATION **Marder:** 10°; **Hetzer:** 12°.

FORDING DEPTH **Marder:** 0·92m (3ft 0¼in); **Hetzer:** 0·9m (2ft 11in).

One of the last of the German tank destroyers was the little Jagdpanzer 38(t) Hetzer with 7·5cm Pak 39 gun. It was one of the best adaptations of the highly reliable Czech chassis. This chassis formed the basis of so many other SP vehicles in German service after it had become outmoded in its original tank form. With a widened hull and well-sloped low superstructure it was a very cramped vehicle for the crew but was easy to build and very reliable. The example illustrated is typical of late-1944 types used on the Western Front. The 'dapple' colour scheme, popularly called an 'ambush scheme', blended well in the autumn woods where the Jagdpanzer could hide and pick

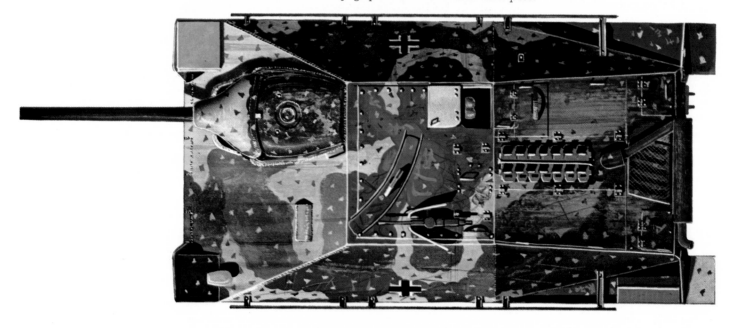

0   1   2 m

Danilo Renzulli

Jagdpanzer 38(t) Hetzer

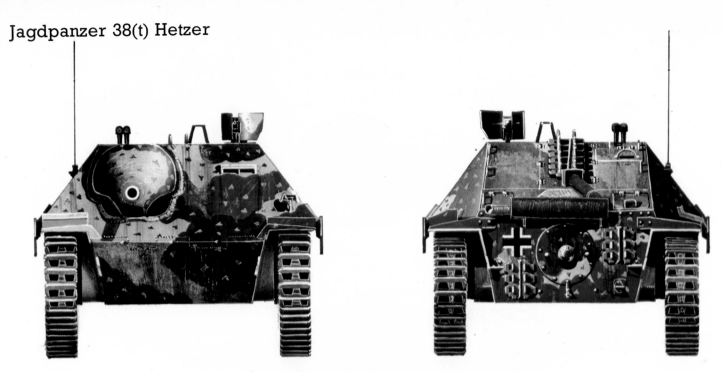

off approaching Allied armour. The particular vehicle with this colour scheme was, however, knocked out and captured by the crew of an American Sherman tank. Visible in the drawing is the Sfl ZF1 1a periscope sight used by the gunner, and the remote-control machine gun on the roof operated by the commander. The drawing (below) shows the unarmed Bergepanzer 38(t) Hetzer, 64 of which were built and issued to Hetzer units from October 1944. The superstructure of this vehicle was open at the top and slightly lower than in the armed version. A winch was fitted, together with a derrick, carried 'knocked down' on the superstructure side rack.

Jagdpanzer 38(t) Hetzer on the
Eastern Front, autumn 1944.

Jagdpanzer 38(t) Hetzer, Cologne
Germany, 1945.

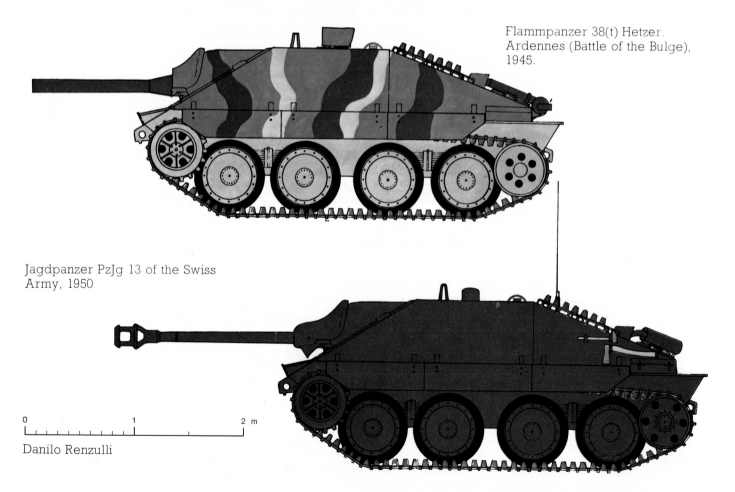

Flammpanzer 38(t) Hetzer,
Ardennes (Battle of the Bulge),
1945.

Jagdpanzer PzJg 13 of the Swiss
Army, 1950

0   1   2 m

Danilo Renzulli

Hetzer, Bison and Lorraine Schlepper

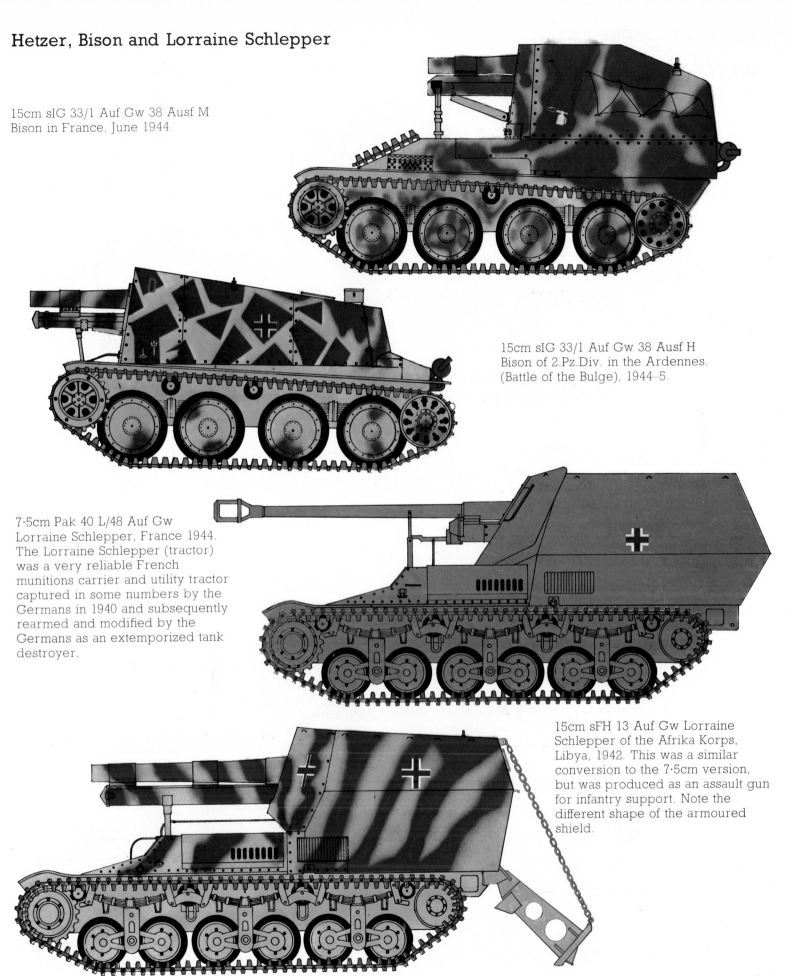

15cm sIG 33/1 Auf Gw 38 Ausf M
Bison in France, June 1944.

15cm sIG 33/1 Auf Gw 38 Ausf H
Bison of 2.Pz.Div. in the Ardennes.
(Battle of the Bulge), 1944–5.

7·5cm Pak 40 L/48 Auf Gw
Lorraine Schlepper, France 1944.
The Lorraine Schlepper (tractor)
was a very reliable French
munitions carrier and utility tractor
captured in some numbers by the
Germans in 1940 and subsequently
rearmed and modified by the
Germans as an extemporized tank
destroyer.

15cm sFH 13 Auf Gw Lorraine
Schlepper of the Afrika Korps,
Libya, 1942. This was a similar
conversion to the 7·5cm version,
but was produced as an assault gun
for infantry support. Note the
different shape of the armoured
shield.

Infantry Tank Mk II, Matilda II, of 42nd Royal Tank Regiment, 1st Army Tank Brigade, in North Africa, June 1941. At this time, the Matilda had been the most successful of British tanks in the desert war, and its armour was impregnable to all anti-tank guns until the Germans started using the FlaK 88 in the anti-tank role in mid-1941. The drawing opposite shows Matilda tank crew men 'brewing up' their tea on a 'desert cooker' made from petrol-soaked sand in an old fuel tin.

0   1   2m

Infantry Tank Mark II, Matilda II

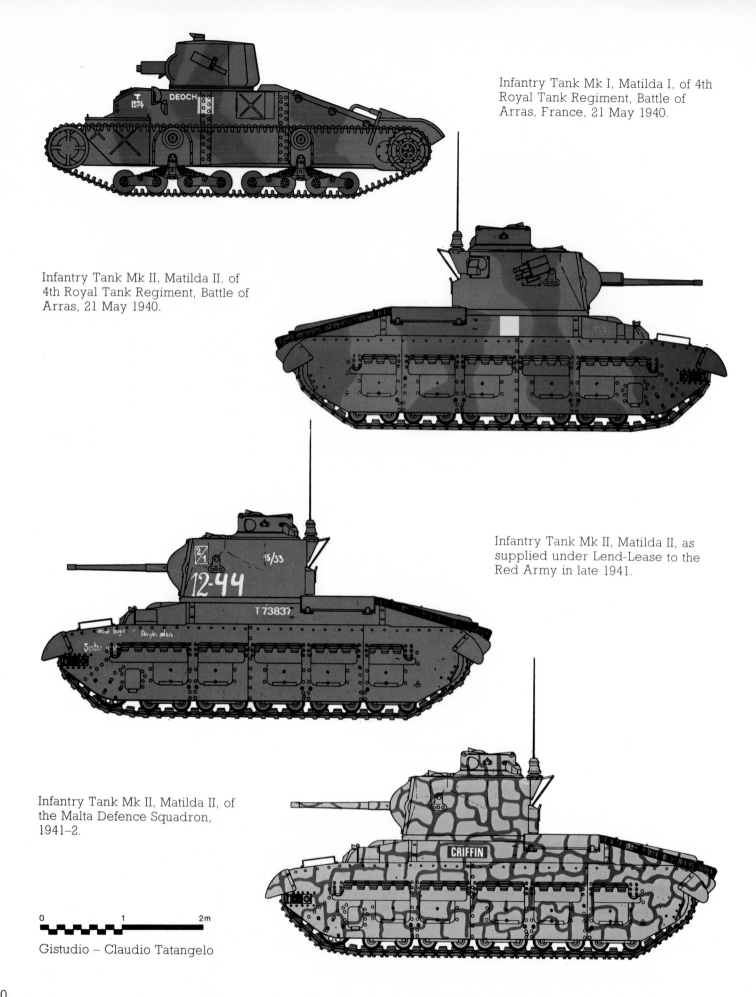

Infantry Tank Mk I, Matilda I, of 4th Royal Tank Regiment, Battle of Arras, France, 21 May 1940.

Infantry Tank Mk II, Matilda II, of 4th Royal Tank Regiment, Battle of Arras, 21 May 1940.

Infantry Tank Mk II, Matilda II, as supplied under Lend-Lease to the Red Army in late 1941.

Infantry Tank Mk II, Matilda II, of the Malta Defence Squadron, 1941–2.

0   1   2m

Gistudio – Claudio Tatangelo

Matilda Mk I and II

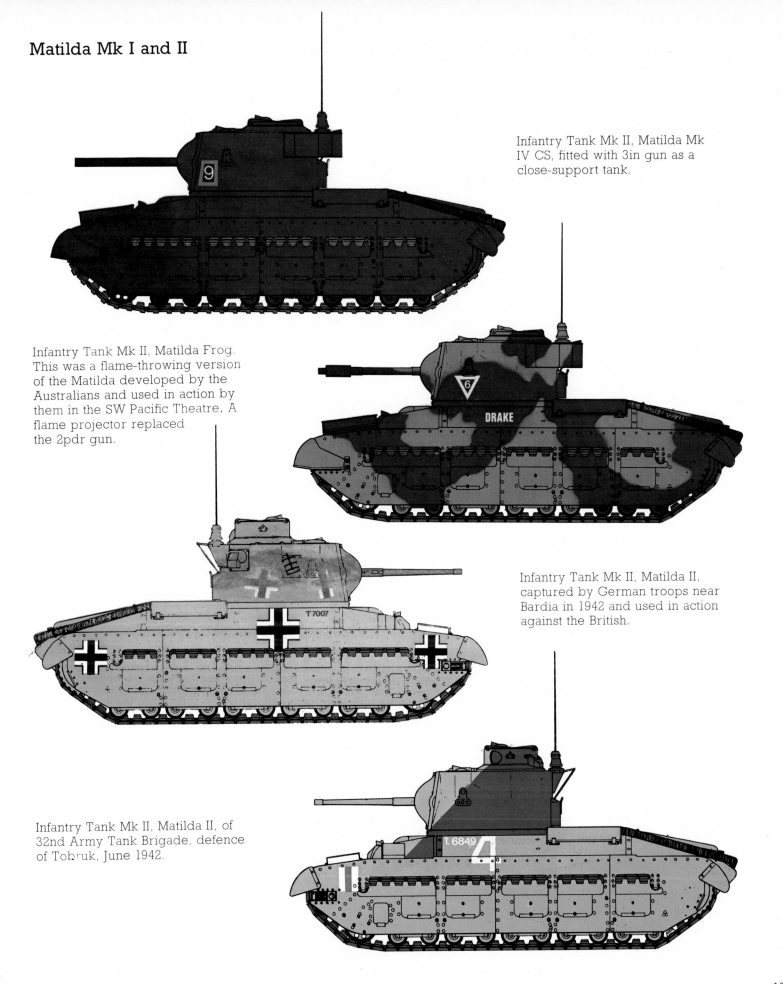

Infantry Tank Mk II, Matilda Mk IV CS, fitted with 3in gun as a close-support tank.

Infantry Tank Mk II, Matilda Frog. This was a flame-throwing version of the Matilda developed by the Australians and used in action by them in the SW Pacific Theatre. A flame projector replaced the 2pdr gun.

Infantry Tank Mk II, Matilda II, captured by German troops near Bardia in 1942 and used in action against the British.

Infantry Tank Mk II, Matilda II, of 32nd Army Tank Brigade, defence of Tobruk, June 1942.

Matilda Mk I and II

The idea of what became known as the 'infantry tank' dates back to April 1934 when the British General Staff discussed a proposal put by General Elles of the Royal Tank Corps for the future requirements of the tank arm. A major priority was for a tank to cooperate with the infantry in an advance – in essence a restatement of the original tank concept of World War 1.

Two alternatives were considered: a very small low vehicle, heavily armoured, armed with machine guns, and available in some numbers; or a bigger vehicle with a larger calibre gun and heavier armour, able to engage enemy weapons and carrying machine guns for defence against enemy infantry. The vehicle was only required to move at walking pace, or infantry speed.

For the second alternative, with a 2pdr gun as main armament, and a minimum armour thickness of 2·5cm (1in), Vickers designed the A9. They suggested to Elles that they could also design and build a prototype infantry tank to the 'small' size specification but with increased armour, proof against any known calibre of anti-tank gun. Designated A11, the pilot model was delivered to the army for trials in September 1936.

To keep down costs, the A11 (later called Matilda I) was very simple. A commercial Ford V8 engine and transmission were used, with steering, brake and clutches adapted from the type used in the Vickers light tanks. The simple suspension was adapted from that used on the Vickers Dragon gun tractors but alterations were necessary. A production order for 60 vehicles (later to be increased) was placed in April 1937. Some 140 of these vehicles had been delivered by August 1940 when production ceased.

The limitations of the machine gun armament were soon realized and design of the A12 Infantry Tank Mk II was initiated in November 1936, the A11 being regarded as an interim type. A completely new design was called for and was drawn up with 60mm armour thickness, a commercial type AEC

diesel engine and heavy side skirts to protect the suspension. The vehicle was designated A12 Infantry Tank Mk II and was also known as Matilda II.

In November 1936 Vulcan Foundry of Warrington was given contracts to produce wooden mock-ups and two mild steel pilot models of the A12 design. The mock-up was ready by April 1937, when it was decided to use twin AEC diesel engines coupled together and a Wilson epicyclic gearbox. Provision was made for mounting a 3in howitzer in close support versions. The pilot model was held up by delays in the delivery of the gearbox and other components, and the vehicle was not ready until April 1938. Meanwhile an order for 65 vehicles was given in December 1937, soon increased to 165. Trials were generally good but some small modifications were made to the gearbox and suspension. Cooling was also improved and air cleaners were fitted.

By this time re-armament was under way. In June 1938 contracts for further vehicles were placed with Fowler, Ruston and Hornsby, and later LMS, Harland and Wolff and North British Locomotive Co. For the later marks Leyland was brought in (in 1940) to make engines. Total output of A12s was 2,987 and production ceased in August 1943.

The A12 was not easy to mass-produce due to the size and shape of the armour castings used in the design. There was particular difficulty in making the one-piece armour side skirts. At the outbreak of war with Germany in September 1939 there were only two A12s in service, though a number had been issued to the 7th Royal Tank Regiment in France by early 1940. There they were used with success in the Battle of Arras just prior to the Dunkirk evacuation.

The Matilda played an important part in the early Western Desert campaigns. In Libya in 1940 it was virtually immune to any Italian anti-tank gun or tank, and Matildas reigned supreme until the appearance in mid-1941 of the German 88mm Flak gun in the anti-tank role.

MODELS Matilda I and II.

COUNTRY OF ORIGIN Great Britain.

WEIGHT I: 11·18 tonnes (11 tons); II: 26·9 tonnes (26·5 tons).

LENGTH I: 4·69m (15ft 4in); II: 5·6m (18ft 5in).

WIDTH I: 2·33m (7ft 8in); II: 2·59m (8ft 6in).

HEIGHT I: 1·84m (6ft 1½in); II: 2·51m (8ft 3in).

GROUND CLEARANCE I: 0·38m (1ft 3¼in); II: 0·40m (1ft 4in).

ARMOUR I: 10–65mm; II: 25–78mm.

ENGINES I: Ford V8, 70hp, gasoline; II: 2 × Leyland E 148, 95hp, gasoline.

MAXIMUM SPEED I: 12·9km/h (8mph); II: 24km/h (15mph).

RANGE I: 129km (80 miles); II: 256km (160 miles).

CREW I: 2; II: 4.

ARMAMENT I: 1 × Vickers ·50 cal. MG; II: 1 × 2pdr, 1 × Besa MG.

AMMUNITION I: 4,000 rds; II: 2 pdr: 93 rds, Besa MG: 2,925 rds.

TRENCH CROSSING I: 1·98m (6ft 6in); II: 2·13m (7ft).

TRACK WIDTH I: 0·29m (11½in); II: 0·35m (1ft 2in).

MAXIMUM ELEVATION I: 25°; II: 20°.

FORDING DEPTH I: 0·60m (2ft); II: 0·91m (3ft).

Panzerkampfwagen I

In 1932 a Carden Loyd Mk IV tankette chassis was bought from Vickers (England) by the German Army Weapons Office (Heereswaffenamt) who wanted to assess its suitability as a carrier for a 2cm anti-aircraft gun. They concluded that this type of vehicle would make a good light training tank, even with only a machine gun as armament. From the specification for a 5-ton vehicle with twin machine guns and fully traversing turret, the chassis design by Krupp (influenced by the Carden Loyd) was selected out of the five submitted for development, and the order was given to Kassel for construction of three running prototypes in December 1933. The responsibility for the superstructure and turret was given to Daimler-Benz. The work was divided among several firms to give each the opportunity of becoming familiar with the design.

Following successful trials after completion of the vehicles in February 1934, Krupp was given the order to produce 150 tanks. In order to conceal their true purpose, these production vehicles were designated 'Landwirtschaftlicher Schlepper', which was abbreviated to La S, and when in full service became the '1A La S Krupp'. While the prototype LKA1 had four road wheels supported on coil springs, and three return rollers, the production vehicles had an external girder, connecting the idler and the second road wheel, with suspension provided by quarter elliptic springs. Soon after the vehicles were in service, it became apparent that one or two improvements were necessary, and subsequent productions ('1B La S May') were given a more powerful engine, with a longer hull, and lengthened suspension (one extra road wheel each side).

This full-track two-man vehicle with a fully traversing turret (offset to the right) carried twin MG 13 machine guns. The turret was similar to the auxiliary ones which were used on the NbFz heavy tanks. For test purposes, some vehicles were fitted with a Krupp M601 air-cooled diesel engine, but this was not used for service versions, as it did not prove powerful enough. The engine in the 1A La S was an air-cooled Krupp M 305 3·5-litre, four-cylinder, horizontally opposed and mounted at the rear.

The drive was taken via a dryplate clutch to a ZF Aphon FG 35 five-speed gearbox, and the steering was of the clutch and brake type. However, in the 1B La S vehicle, this was replaced by a water-cooled Maybach NL 38 TR 100hp (at 3,000rpm) engine, along with improved transmission. The track was skeletal, with dry-pins and twin-guide horns. The armour was 15mm thick.

These new La S vehicles aroused considerable interest in the press when they participated in a military display at Doberitz in July 1935, and in October of that year the first three panzer divisions were officially formed. In February 1938 these tanks were named Panzerkampfwagen I, and, although they were only meant as training vehicles originally, there were 1,445 still being used when Poland was invaded on 1 September 1939. Panzerkampfwagen Is therefore proved their ability not only for training, but also as useful and versatile fighting vehicles against the somewhat disorganized opposition of the early years of World War 2. The early model was fully designated PzKpfw I Ausf A, and the later model with longer suspension was the PzKpfw I Ausf B.

Despite their inadequacy of firepower and armour protection, there were still over 800 in service in July 1941, shortly after which they were reallocated for training, or converted to self-propelled gun carriages. There were further variants of some importance. The first was a command vehicle with the turret replaced by a fixed superstructure for the use of a unit commander and his staff. This was designated Kleine Panzerbefehlswagen 1. Next came a Panzerjäger I, an SP conversion with 4·7cm gun and another SP – 15cm sIG 33 on the PzKpfw I chassis. These two types were in service for the battle of France in May 1940.

MODELS Panzerkampfwagen I Ausf A and B.

COUNTRY OF ORIGIN Germany.

WEIGHT **Model A:** 5·48 tonnes (5·4 tons); **Model B:** 5·89 tonnes (5·8 tons).

LENGTH **Model A:** 4·02m (13ft 2½in); **Model B:** 4·42m (14ft 6in).

WIDTH 2·05m (6ft 9½in).

HEIGHT 1·7m (5ft 7in).

GROUND CLEARANCE 0·29m (11½in).

ARMOUR 7–15mm.

ENGINES **Model A:** 60hp Krupp M305, gasoline; **Model B:** 100hp Maybach NL 38, gasoline.

MAXIMUM SPEED **Model A:** 37km/h (22·9mph); **Model B:** 40km/h (25mph).

RANGE **Model A:** 145km (90 miles); **Model B:** 140 km (87 miles).

CREW 2.

ARMAMENT 2 × 7·92mm MG.

AMMUNITION 1,525 rds.

TRENCH CROSSING 1·4m (4ft 7in).

TRACK WIDTH 0·28m (11in).

MAXIMUM ELEVATION 45°.

FORDING DEPTH 0·58m (1ft 11in).

The PzKpfw I was the first of the German panzers and was intended as a small tank for training purposes. In the event it was also extensively used in combat in the early part of World War 2, in the Polish, French, Norwegian, Balkan and African campaigns, being mainly employed in the reconnaissance role. The example shown, a PzKpfw I Ausf B, is from 1.SS.Pz.Div. – Leibstandarte Adolf Hitler – the premier Waffen-SS division, and took part in the Paris Victory Parade in June 1940 after France capitulated.

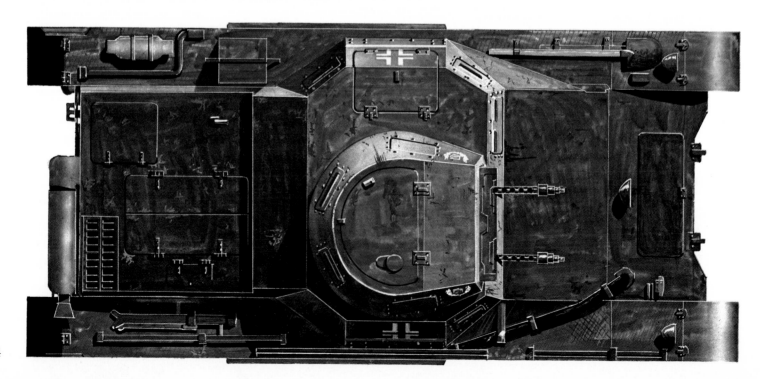

Panzerkampfwagen I Ausf B

Claudio Tatangelo

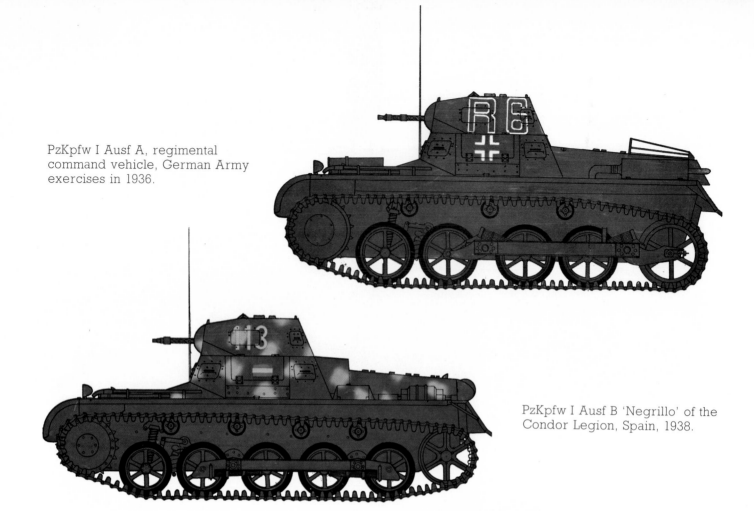

PzKpfw I Ausf A, regimental command vehicle, German Army exercises in 1936.

PzKpfw I Ausf B 'Negrillo' of the Condor Legion, Spain, 1938.

Panzerbefehlswagen I Ausf B of 1.Pz.Rgt., 2.Pz.Div., Poland, September 1939. This was the command vehicle version with enlarged superstructure and no turret.

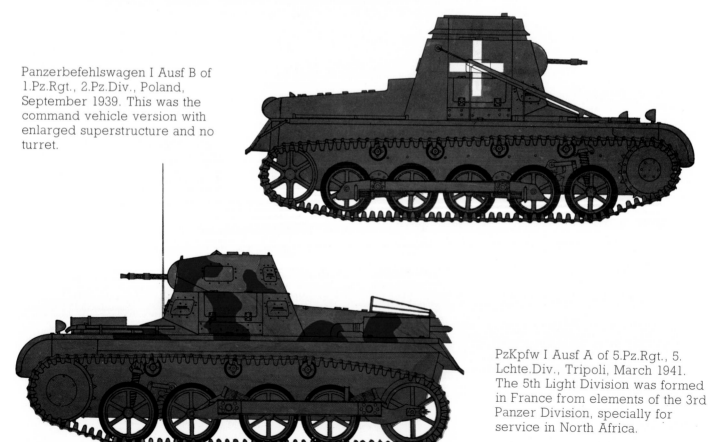

PzKpfw I Ausf A of 5.Pz.Rgt., 5. Lchte.Div., Tripoli, March 1941. The 5th Light Division was formed in France from elements of the 3rd Panzer Division, specially for service in North Africa.

Panzerkampfwagen I

Panzerjäger I Ausf B of
5.Lchte.Div., Tripoli, March 1941.
This was the tank hunter
conversion of the PzKpfw I made
by fitting a captured Czech 4·7cm
anti-tank gun.

Panzerbefehlswagen I Ausf B of
21.Pz.Div. at El-Alamein,
September 1942.

Numerous old PzKpfw I vehicles
after withdrawal from service had
the superstructure removed for
use by NSKK units or Army tank
schools as driver school vehicles
(Fahrerschulewagen I). NSKK was
the National Socialist Motor Corps,
a pre-military service organization.
Other vehicles had only their
turrets removed for use as
munitions carriers or tractors.

15cm sIG 33 auf PzKpfw I Ausf B.
This was one of the earliest of the
German self-propelled gun
conversions, with a 15cm infantry
gun mounted on the chassis of a
PzKpfw I Ausf B. It was used widely
in the Polish and French campaigns
of 1939–40.

Claudio Tatangelo

The Panzerkampfwagen II was the second of the new types of tank designed for the German Army in the early 1930s. It was, like the PzKpfw I, deliberately made simply and inexpensively as a training vehicle, but when the war came it was in extensive use and saw service in various forms throughout the war, the chassis being in production for SP guns until 1944. It was mainly used in the reconnaissance role as a tank. The vehicle illustrated is a PzKpfw II Ausf F of 15.Pz. Div., Afrika Korps. The turret markings indicate that it is from the HQ company of the second battalion of an armoured regiment, as shown by the prefix II – for second battalion.

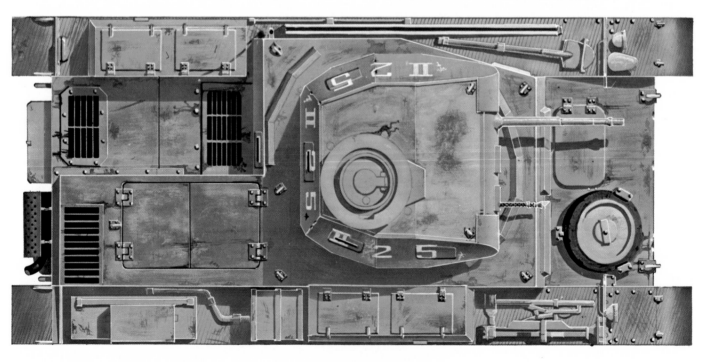

0   1   2   3 m

Danilo Renzulli

Panzerkampfwagen II Ausf F

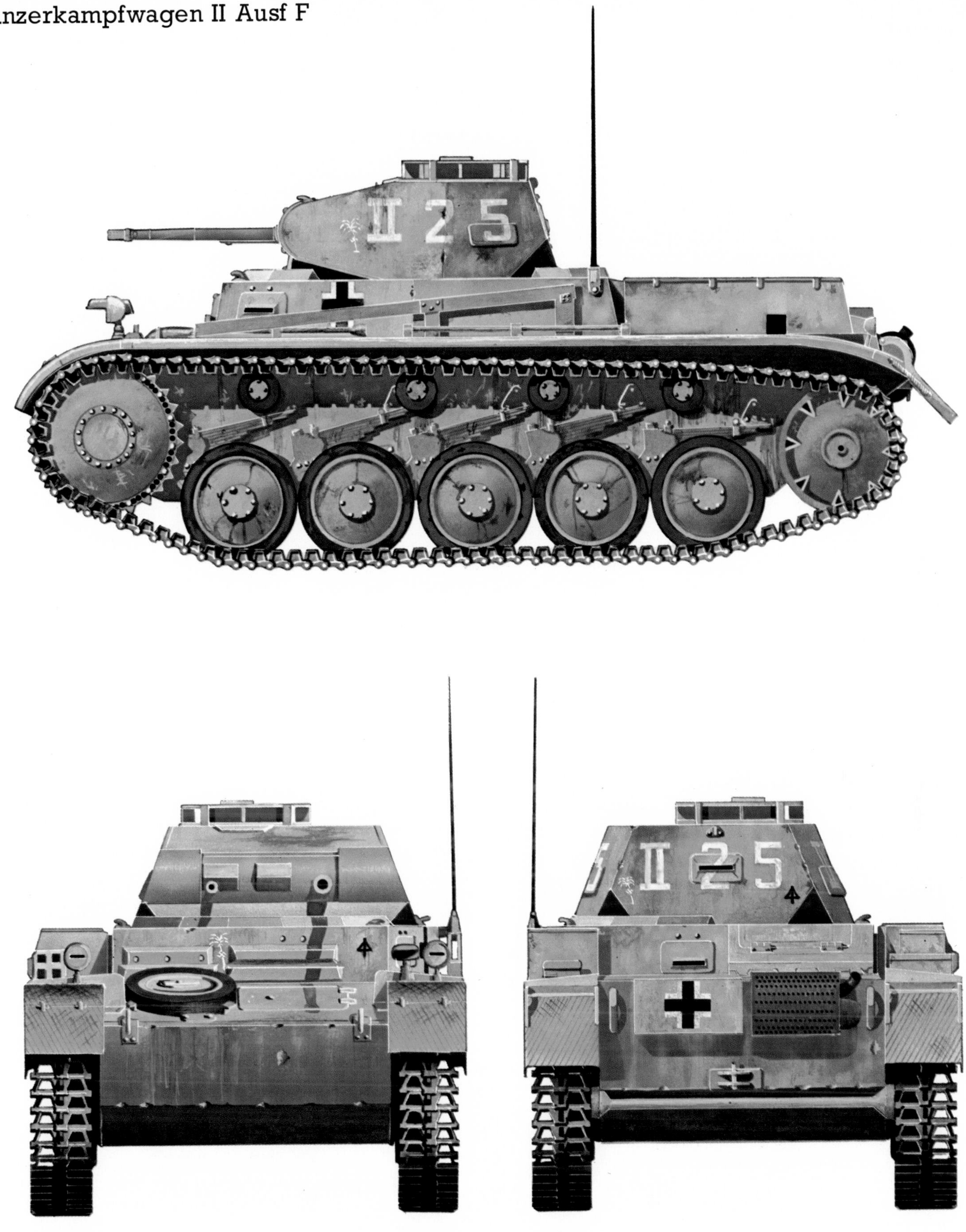

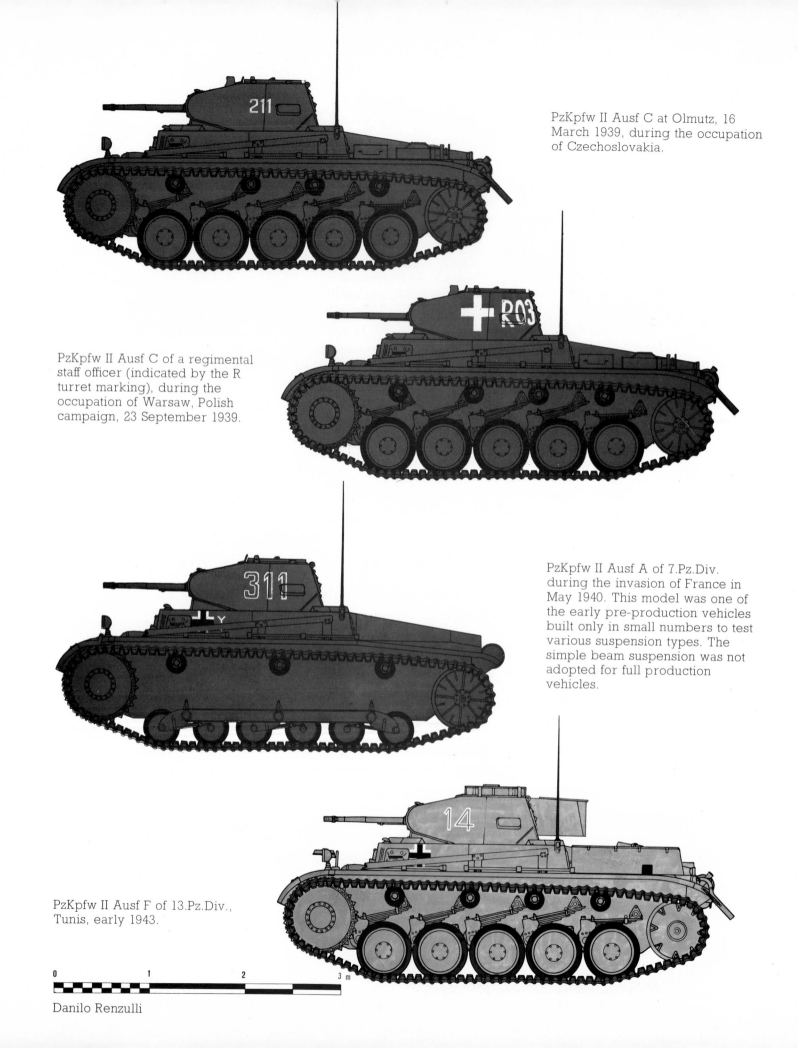

PzKpfw II Ausf C at Olmutz, 16 March 1939, during the occupation of Czechoslovakia.

PzKpfw II Ausf C of a regimental staff officer (indicated by the R turret marking), during the occupation of Warsaw, Polish campaign, 23 September 1939.

PzKpfw II Ausf A of 7.Pz.Div. during the invasion of France in May 1940. This model was one of the early pre-production vehicles built only in small numbers to test various suspension types. The simple beam suspension was not adopted for full production vehicles.

PzKpfw II Ausf F of 13.Pz.Div., Tunis, early 1943.

0   1   2   3 m

Danilo Renzulli

Panzerkampfwagen II

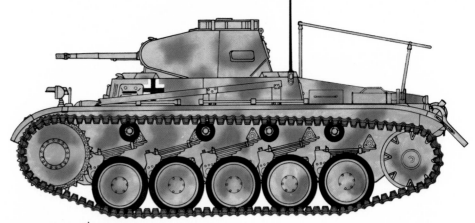

Beobachtungswagen II Ausf C, Russian Front, spring 1943. This was a conversion (with dummy gun) to provide an observation post/command vehicle for assault gun batteries. The turret was fixed and extra radio was fitted with a rail type aerial around the rear decking.

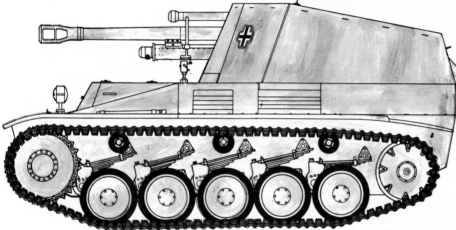

Leichte Panzerhaubitze 10·5cm Wespe auf Gw PzKpfw II, Russian Front, winter 1942–3. This was one of the most successful and widely used of self-propelled gun conversions. On some later vehicles the chassis was extended to the rear to give a more stable gun platform. The weapon was the standard 10·5cm field piece and the engines were moved to the centre of the vehicle when the conversion work was carried out.

7·5cm Pak 40 Panzerjäger Marder II Auf Gw PzKpfw II. This was one of the earliest of the tank destroyer conversions, with a Pak 40 anti-tank gun mounted directly on top of a PzKpfw II chassis which was otherwise unaltered. It was an expedient design which was got quickly into service. This example was used by a parachute battalion in the defence of Rome, 8 September 1943 (Marder=Martin). For more details of the Marder, see page 93.

PzKpfw II Ausf L Luchs was the final model in the PzKpfw II series and was produced specifically as a fast reconnaissance vehicle with high performance and improved interleaved suspension to give a better ride. These vehicles were in use until the war's end (Luchs=Lynx).

Panzerkampfwagen II

In July 1934 the German Army Weapons Office invited three manufacturers to submit designs for a 10-ton vehicle with 2cm KwK 30 and a co-axial machine gun in a fully traversing turret, having realized that it would take longer to develop the main tanks needed for the panzer divisions than was at first anticipated. The design by MAN was preferred to the Krupp prototype as it had a longer, lower superstructure. When the prototypes were being tested, these vehicles were given a 'camouflage' designation, La S 100 (Landwirtschaftlicher Schlepper 100). A number of pre-production series were used extensively, and it became obvious that a few modifications were necessary; the suspension system underwent a major change, and there were alterations to the layout of the engine, and the thickness of the armour. Then in 1938 the vehicles were officially designated Panzerkampfwagen II, as it was felt the need for secrecy was now over.

The first model had a Maybach six-cylinder, 130hp engine with a six-speed gearbox, although a 140hp Maybach HL62 was used in later models, and each track had clutch and brake steering. The layout was conventional, with driver in the hull front and commander and gunner in the turret. In later models the turret was equipped with vision ports, periscopes, a stowage box on the rear, and a hatch for the commander. Though it proved reliable and effective, the Panzerkampfwagen II, like the Panzerkampfwagen I, was not originally intended for combat use. Since it proved so useful, however, it remained in increasing production, and, during the successful campaigns in Poland and France of 1939 and 1940, the Panzerkampfwagen IIs were the most numerous German-built tanks in service with the panzer divisions.

In 1937, the 3/La S 100/PzKpfw II underwent fundamental design changes, mainly to the suspension, where large disc road wheels suspended on quarter-elliptic springs replaced the girder and small bogies. This modification remained on all the subsequent models of Panzerkampfwagen II. At this time other manufacturers were brought in: Famo, MIAG, Wegmann and Henschel. Mass production started on a larger scale with the 4/La S, but it was the 5/La S that was brought widely into service in the early campaigns of World War 2.

In 1938, Daimler-Benz developed the 'SchnellKampfwagen', a faster vehicle with torsion bar suspension and larger road wheels. The design incorporated a completely new hull, and the hatches, decking, engine covers and other details were virtually scaled down items from the Daimler-Benz designed PzKpfw III. The vehicle was fitted with a Maybach Variorex VG 102/28H gearbox with pre-selector, allowing seven forward and three reverse speeds, and the crew was increased from three to four men. When France was invaded in May 1940, there were still some 950 PzKpfw IIs in service, and production continued until 1942, when over 800 were being used. Following the campaign in Poland in the winter of 1939–40, the major existing production types were refitted, with armour increased to 35mm (20mm plates were included on the 15mm frontal surfaces).

In its later years, the PzKpfw II was used in the reconnaissance role, and models were adapted to improve their reconnaissance qualities in the light of experience. The front armour was increased to a basic 35mm, and the side armour to 20mm. Hence the weight increased to 9·5 tons, with a consequent loss in speed, but, because of the improved protection this was deemed acceptable. Production started in 1941, and these vehicles were used in the Western Desert and in Russia up to 1942, though their lack of HE capability meant that they were really outmoded in 1940. Though they served well against light opposition, on the Russian Front during 1941–2 losses were heavy. However, they were kept in production to provide enough tanks for the armour force which had been increased to 36 divisions.

MODELS Panzerkampfwagen II Ausf F-J.

COUNTRY OF ORIGIN Germany.

WEIGHT 9·5 tonnes (9·34 tons).

LENGTH 4·8m (15ft 9½in).

WIDTH 2·6m (8ft 7in).

HEIGHT 2·05m (6ft 9in).

GROUND CLEARANCE 0·34m (1ft 1in).

ARMOUR 14·5mm.

ENGINE 130hp Maybach HL 62 (140hp on later models), gasoline.

MAXIMUM SPEED 40km/h (25mph).

RANGE 200km (124 miles).

CREW 3.

ARMAMENT 1 × 2cm gun, 1 × 7·92mm MG.

AMMUNITION 2cm: 180 rds, MG: 2,550 rds.

TRENCH CROSSING 2·44m (8ft).

TRACK WIDTH 0·3m (11·8in).

MAXIMUM ELEVATION 40°.

FORDING DEPTH 0·92m (3ft).

Panzerkampfwagen III

Although the Panzerkampfwagen I and II were extensively used, the panzer divisions were originally intended to be fully equipped with vehicles designed in accordance with Lutz and Guderian's original plans. The principal combat tanks of the panzer divisions were to have a 5cm armour-piercing gun, a co-axial turret machine gun and a front hull machine gun. These would be used by the three light companies of a tank battalion. The specification put out by the Army Weapons Office in 1935 was for a vehicle with a maximum weight of 24 tons (due to German bridge load restrictions). The actual requirement was for a 15-ton tank, with a top speed of 40km/h (25mph), a five-man crew (driver, radio operator/hull gunner, commander, gunner and loader), and a main gun with co-axial machine gun and bow machine gun. The commander was to have an all-round vision cupola and be stationed in the turret. All vehicles were to have a radio fitted (throat microphones were to be used – a big advance in communications for that time). A camouflage designation of Zugführerwagen (platoon commander's vehicle) was given.

Five firms were invited to submit designs, and three prototypes were produced. The order was given to Daimler-Benz (from a specification including the best points of all three prototypes). The motorized troops accepted the 3·7cm gun, which was already in production, for use by the infantry anti-tank companies in the field, providing the design allowed for a turret and turret ring which would accept a 5cm gun if necessary.

By 1939 these tanks were in such short supply that contracts, either for manufacture or assembly or both, were given to many firms (such as Alkett, FAMO, Henschel, MAN, MIAB, Wegmann and MNH), who formed a Panzerkampfwagen III production group. Guns were made by Karges Hammer and Garnh, and major sub-assemblies were manufactured by Deutsche Edelstahlwerke. The vehicle was broken down into four major sub-assemblies: hull, turret, front superstructure and rear superstructure.

It was fortunate that the design allowed for mass-production, even though this had not been originally intended; for although the target for production fixed in November 1940 was 108 vehicles per month, after the invasion of Russia and the decision to expand the armoured forces to 36 panzer divisions, it was decided that 7,992 vehicles were required. The target was never met, and the total produced was 5,664. The Panzerkampfwagen III was a fairly straightforward model; the gearbox and steering mechanism were in the forward hull compartment, with access doors in the nose. The engine was situated in the rear, and the drive from the engine was taken via a cardan shaft forward through the fighting compartment, under a false floor, to the steering and transmission compartment.

The driver had a vision block in the superstructure front, and he and the radio-operator/hull gunner sat in the front of the fighting compartment. The two forward crew-members had side visors with vision blocks, and there were also side escape doors low in the hull, although these were omitted after model L to simplify the production. There were three crew-members in the turret, which had no cage, but the commander and gunner had seats attached to the turret walls. There was a bulkhead separating the engine from the fighting compartment, and the engine was set in the centre.

The gunner had to traverse the turret by hand, but for the loader an auxiliary traverse was provided, allowing the turret to be moved more quickly when both were used. The commander and gunner had turret and target indicators.

Production models ran from PzKpfw III Ausf E (with 3·7cm gun) to PzKpfw III Ausf L (with 5cm long gun) and PzKpfw III Ausf N (with 7·5cm low velocity gun). PzKpfw III Ausf A-Ds were development models with varying suspension types.

MODELS Panzerkampfwagen III Ausf A-N.

COUNTRY OF ORIGIN Germany.

WEIGHT **A-D:** 15·2 tonnes (15 tons); **E:** 19·5 tonnes (19·18 tons); **F, G:** 20·3 tonnes (19·97 tons); **H:** 21·6 tonnes (21·25 tons); **J-N:** 22·3 tonnes (21·9 tons).

LENGTH 5·69m (18ft 8in).

WIDTH 2·8m (9ft 4in).

HEIGHT 2·36m (7ft 9in).

GROUND CLEARANCE 0·37m (1ft 3in).

ARMOUR 10–70mm.

ENGINES **A-D:** HL 108 TR 230hp, gasoline; **E-N:** Maybach HL 120 TRM 300hp, gasoline.

MAXIMUM SPEED **A-D:** 32km/h (20mph); **E-N:** 40km/h (25mph).

RANGE 150km (93 miles).

CREW 5.

ARMAMENT $3 \times 7·92$mm MG plus **A-E:** $1 \times 3·7$cm KwK L/45 gun; **F-H:** 1×5cm KwK L/42 gun; **J-L:** 1×5cm KwK L/60 gun; **M-N:** $1 \times 7·5$cm KwK L/24 gun.

AMMUNITION MG: 2,550 rds, 3·7cm (**A-E**): 150 rds, 5cm L/42 (**F-H**): 99 rds, 5cm L/60 (**J-L**): 78 rds, 7·5cm (**M-N**): 64 rds.

TRENCH CROSSING 2·6m (8ft 7in).

TRACK WIDTH 0·36m (1ft 2in).

MAXIMUM ELEVATION 35°.

FORDING DEPTH 0·8m (2ft 9in).

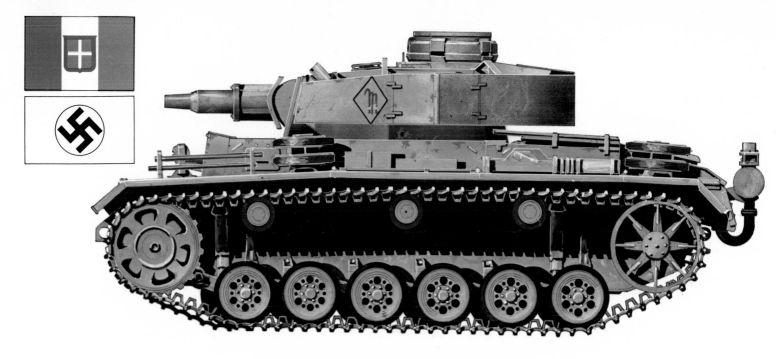

The last production model of the PzKpfw III was the Ausf N which was essentially a Model L or M fitted with the short 7·5cm gun from the early PzKpfw IV. In this form it was used as a close-support tank. In 1943 a number of these vehicles were supplied to the Italian 1st Armoured Division 'Camicie Nere'.

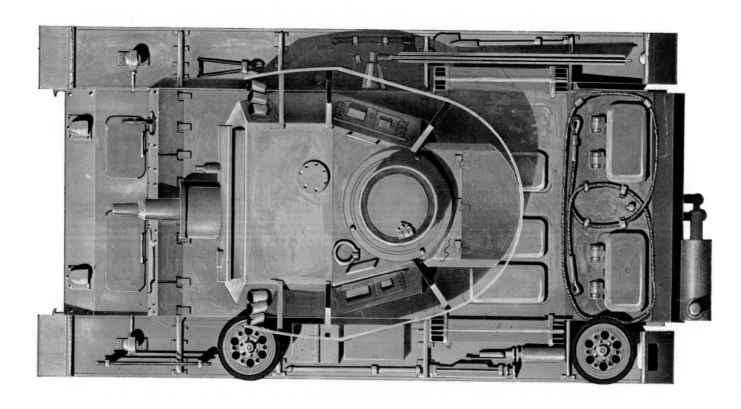

Danilo Renzulli

114

Panzerkampfwagen III Ausf N

Here is a close view of the divisional insignia of 1st Armoured Division 'Camicie Nere', as marked on the vehicle in 1943. After the Italian armistice this regiment was reformed on the Allied side, first as the Armoured Legion Division, then as 134th Armoured Division 'Centauro II' in September 1943.

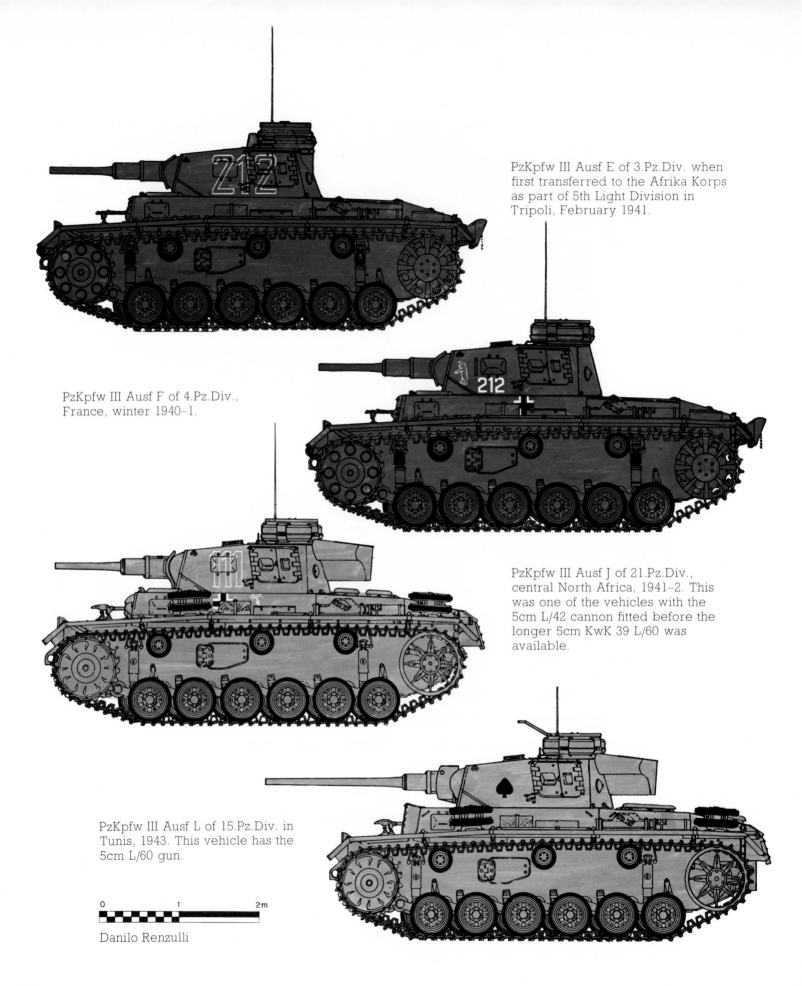

PzKpfw III Ausf E of 3.Pz.Div. when first transferred to the Afrika Korps as part of 5th Light Division in Tripoli, February 1941.

PzKpfw III Ausf F of 4.Pz.Div., France, winter 1940–1.

PzKpfw III Ausf J of 21.Pz.Div., central North Africa, 1941–2. This was one of the vehicles with the 5cm L/42 cannon fitted before the longer 5cm KwK 39 L/60 was available.

PzKpfw III Ausf L of 15.Pz.Div. in Tunis, 1943. This vehicle has the 5cm L/60 gun.

0   1   2m

Danilo Renzulli

Panzerkampfwagen III

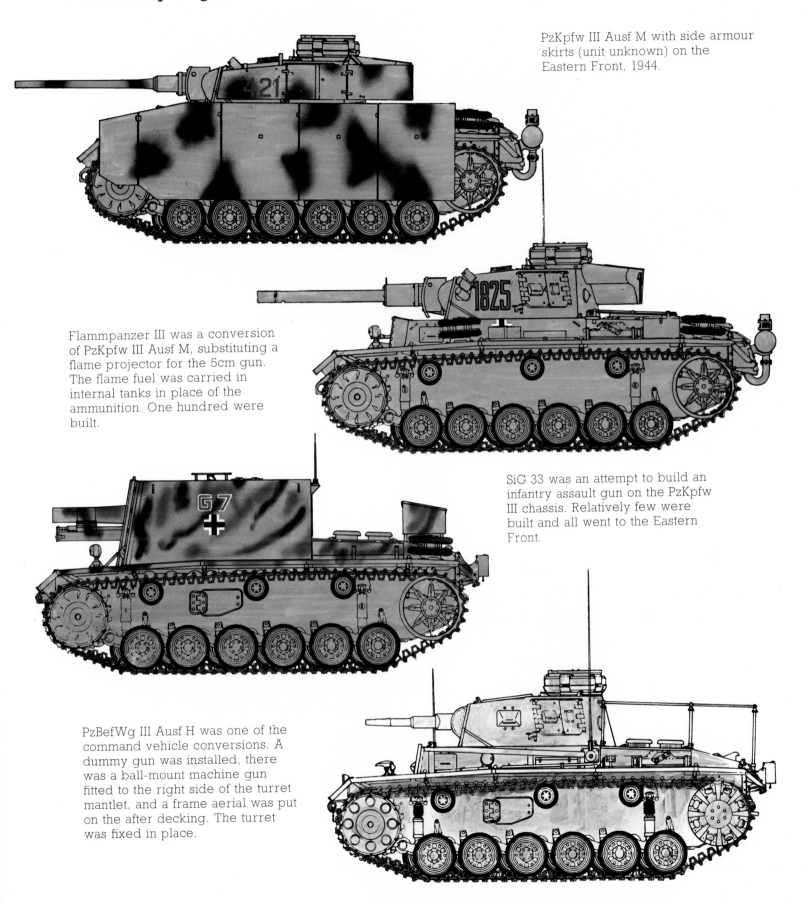

PzKpfw III Ausf M with side armour skirts (unit unknown) on the Eastern Front, 1944.

Flammpanzer III was a conversion of PzKpfw III Ausf M, substituting a flame projector for the 5cm gun. The flame fuel was carried in internal tanks in place of the ammunition. One hundred were built.

SiG 33 was an attempt to build an infantry assault gun on the PzKpfw III chassis. Relatively few were built and all went to the Eastern Front.

PzBefWg III Ausf H was one of the command vehicle conversions. A dummy gun was installed, there was a ball-mount machine gun fitted to the right side of the turret mantlet, and a frame aerial was put on the after decking. The turret was fixed in place.

This is the formidable PzKpfw IV Ausf G, known to the British when it first appeared as the 'Panzer IV Special'. It was fitted with the 7·5cm KwK L/43, then with the longer 7·5cm KwK L/48 gun. A formidable opponent, it gave the Germans the upper hand when it first appeared in North Africa, and was a useful and timely arrival on the Eastern Front. More than 8,000 of this model were built.

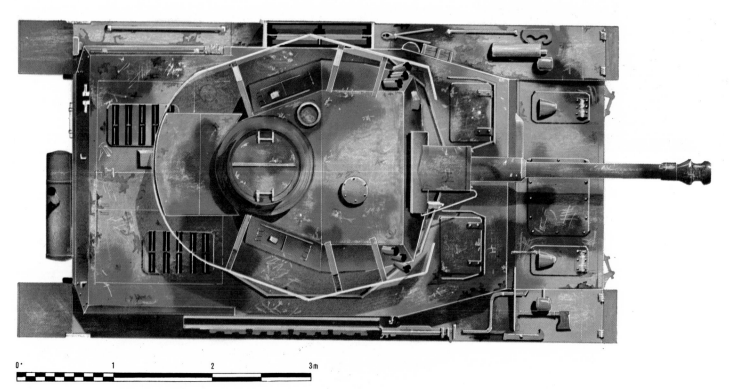

0·   1   2   3m

Danilo Renzulli – Nicola Pignato

118

Panzerkampfwagen IV Ausf G

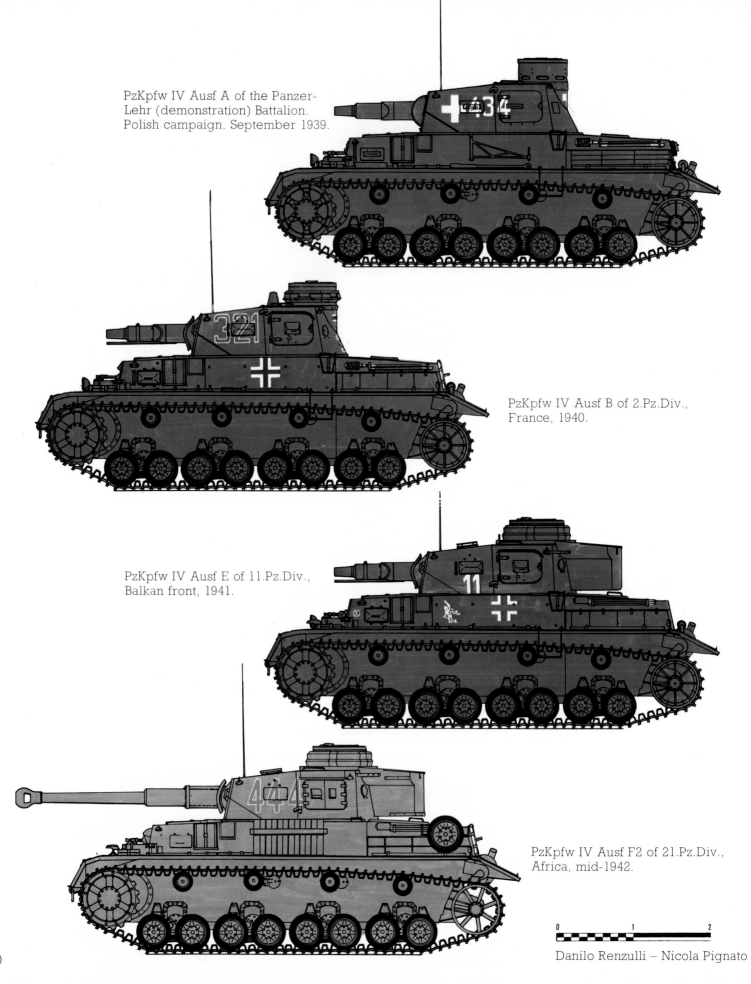

PzKpfw IV Ausf A of the Panzer-Lehr (demonstration) Battalion, Polish campaign, September 1939.

PzKpfw IV Ausf B of 2.Pz.Div., France, 1940.

PzKpfw IV Ausf E of 11.Pz.Div., Balkan front, 1941.

PzKpfw IV Ausf F2 of 21.Pz.Div., Africa, mid-1942.

0　　　1　　　2

Danilo Renzulli – Nicola Pignato

Panzerkampfwagen IV

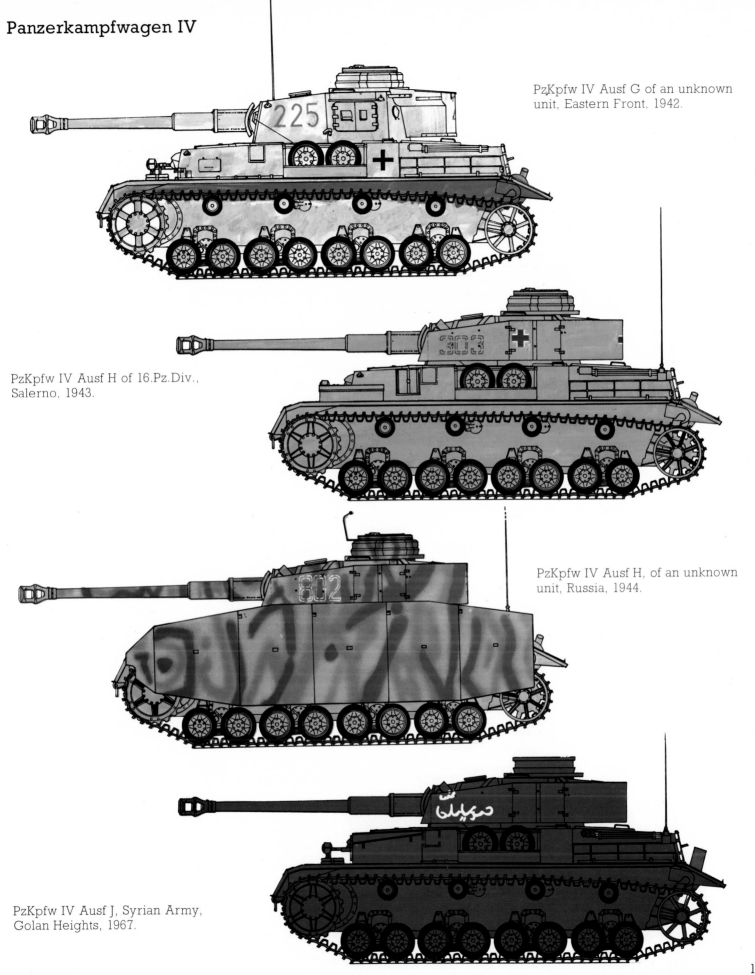

PzKpfw IV Ausf G of an unknown
unit, Eastern Front, 1942.

PzKpfw IV Ausf H of 16.Pz.Div.,
Salerno, 1943.

PzKpfw IV Ausf H, of an unknown
unit, Russia, 1944.

PzKpfw IV Ausf J, Syrian Army,
Golan Heights, 1967.

Panzerkampfwagen IV

In 1935 the contract for this 'medium' or 'close support' tank was given to Krupp, although a prototype VK 2001 (Rh-b) had already been completed in mild steel by Rheinmetall-Borsig at the end of 1934, and tested during 1935–6. Krupp's MKA prototype incorporated the hull shape and form, and the simple suspension which was to become a hallmark of the Panzerkampfwagen IV.

This basic design proved sound and reliable, though it underwent considerable improvements to the guns and armour, in order to keep pace with the changing requirements of combat and technology. The design provided for mass-production, and, like the Panzerkampfwagen III, was divided into four major sub-assemblies: the turret, hull, front superstructure and rear superstructure. These were complete structural units and were bolted together at the final assembly stage. The hull was divided into three by two bulkheads, and the engine was mounted at the rear, with the drive shaft brought forward under the fighting compartment floor to the driving compartment. The turret's power-traverse was operated by a generator driven by a 500cc two-stroke petrol engine situated to the left of the main engine. This was deleted in later production vehicles, in order to allow more space for fuel storage. There were three fuel tanks under the floor beneath the turret turntable, and the rear superstructure could be moved for the purpose of changing the engine. The superstructure overhung the hull sides, and allowed good internal stowage and a 168cm (66in) diameter turret ring.

The gearbox was in the middle of the front compartment, with the driver on the left and the radio operator on the right. The driver had a vision flap and a binocular episcope, and both the driver and radio operator had a roof hatch. There were hinged flaps on the glacis plate giving access to the steering mechanism in the nose, and the hull machine gun was ball-mounted in the right of the superstructure. The turret traverse gear and gun elevating gear were on the left side of the gun in the fighting compartment, and these were operated by the gunner. The gunner had either a sighting telescope or an open sight bar in the left front port of the turret.

The commander was provided with an armoured cupola towards the rear centre of the turret, and sat immediately behind the deflector plate of the gun on a tip-up seat. He could also stand on the turret floor, sit in the cupola, or stand on a footrest looking out of the cupola top. The loader normally stood to load the 7.5cm gun and the co-axial machine gun, to ensure an adequate supply of ammunition, but there was a tip-up seat provided for him to the right of the gun. On each side of the turret there were vision ports in the front, and access doors on the side, also with armoured vision ports and (depending on the model) pistol ports.

Each side had two bogies, carrying two rubber-tyred wheels, and under the leading axle of each bogie there were quarter-elliptic leaf springs, with the tail of the spring resting under a trailing axle on a roller. Each side had four return rollers, a rear idler and a front drive sprocket and, on the rear of the hull (in early models), there were rear smoke emitters. In later models electrically fired smoke-discharger cups, fitted on the turret sides, replaced the smoke emitters. The spring-loaded radio aerial could be deflected into its trough by a special rail on the gun assembly (in later models on the gun barrel itself), or alternatively could be retracted inside the tank by the crew. Although the Panzerkampfwagen IV/BW were slow to come into production (at first they were only built in small pre-production batches), they preceded the Panzerkampfwagen III into service, and outlived them by a considerable margin.

Production models ran from the Ausf D of 1940 with short 7.5cm gun to the Ausf J of 1944 with long KwK L/48 gun and added side skirt armour. The PzKpfw IV was numerically the most important German tank.

MODELS Panzerkampfwagen IV Ausf A-J.

COUNTRY OF ORIGIN Germany.

WEIGHT **A-D:** 17·5 tonnes (17·3 tons); **E-H:** 21–23·6 tonnes (20·6–23·2 tons); **J:** 25 tonnes (24·6 tons).

LENGTH 5·6m (18ft 8½in).

WIDTH 2·8m (9ft 4in).

HEIGHT 2·6m (8ft 7in).

GROUND CLEARANCE 0·4m (1ft 3½in).

ARMOUR 8–50mm.

ENGINES **A-D:** HL 108 TR 250hp, gasoline; **E-J:** Maybach HL 120 TRM 300hp, gasoline.

MAXIMUM SPEED **A-D:** 30km/h (18·5mph); **E-J:** 38km/h (23·6mph).

RANGE 150km (93 miles).

CREW 5.

ARMAMENT 2 × 7·92mm MG plus **A-E:** 1 × 7·5cm KwK L/24 gun, **F-G:** 1 × 7·5cm KwK L/43 gun, **H, J:** 1 × 7·5cm KwK L/48 gun.

AMMUNITION MG: 2,700 rds; L/24 (**A-E**): 80 rds, L/43 (**F, G**): 87 rds, L/48 (**H, J**): 87 rds.

TRENCH CROSSING 2·3m (7ft 6½in).

TRACK WIDTH 0·38m (1ft 3in).

MAXIMUM ELEVATION 20°.

FORDING DEPTH 0·8cm (2ft 9in).

Panzerkampfwagen V Panther

It was decided to develop the Panther when the existence of the Russian T-34 and KV-1 tanks was discovered in July 1941. The superiority of the T-34 became evident in October 1941 when the 4 Pz.Div. with PzKpfw IIIs and IVs suffered severe defeat against this powerful Russian vehicle. General Guderian appointed a Panzer Commission to study the situation, and by January 1942 this commission supplied detailed specifications to MAN and Daimler-Benz.

The new vehicle was to weigh 35 tons, have an armour maximum of 100mm (turret) and 35mm (rear), with a top speed of 60km/h (37mph), and a 7·5cm gun. The engine was to be a Maybach HL 210, and the vehicle was to have a fording depth of 4m (13ft). The major features of the T-34 were the large road wheels and wide tracks, giving a steadier ride, the sloped all-round armour which allowed optimum deflection of shot, and an overhanging gun and turret, which the Germans had previously avoided. The Daimler-Benz prototype was a close copy of the T-34 in both looks and layout. Work was started on building a running prototype, but because the Panther committee set up to evaluate the designs decided in favour of more conventional engineering this was never completed.

The MAN design was selected 'off the drawing board'. Production of a pilot model and the establishment of production for the Panther was the most intensive effort of all German wartime tank programmes. A syndicate of engineering firms was made responsible for various key components such as track, wheels and torsion bars. The assumption that the weight of the tank would not exceed 35 tons proved optimistic, and a big increase in estimated weight led to several mechanical problems which were to beset the development. Limitations in the design became apparent when the two pilot models (VK 3002 MAN) were being tested. On Hitler's orders the glacis plate armour was increased from 60mm to 80mm, and the total effect of the increased weight put a great strain on the engine and transmission system originally planned for the 35-ton vehicle. The Maybach HL 230 engine replaced the previous Maybach HL 210, giving a maximum speed of 45km/h (28mph).

The urgent need prompted the original production target of 250 Panthers by May 1943 to be increased to 600, and Henschel, Daimler-Benz and MNH were brought in to build them. The first 20 vehicles completed were similar to the VK 3002 MAN prototype, with the new engine and gearbox fitted, but still with 60mm glacis plates, a single baffle muzzle brake on the L/70 gun, and the cupola on the far left of the turret, bulging into the turret side. The main production Ausf D had the 80mm glacis plates and the commander's cupola shifted to the right. This allowed a smooth turret side, which simplified production, with a double baffle muzzle brake on the gun. This model also included a drum-shaped cupola with vision slits and pistol and shell case disposal ports in the turret sides. There was a 'letterbox' vertical flap for the radio-operator's hull machine gun, a vision flap for the driver, both of which were in the glacis, and a binocular gun sight on the left side of the mantlet.

The five crew-members were: driver, radio-operator, gunner, loader and commander. The driver and radio-operator were provided with two periscopes each. There was a full turret cage, and the turret could be traversed either by hydraulic power, or by an optional hand traverse.

Despite the teething troubles (including engine over-heating and mechanical breakdowns), the production of Panthers continued until the end of the war in May 1945, although the phasing out of these vehicles started in July 1943. First used in service at the Kursk Offensive in July 1943, over 600 Ausf Ds were built in all. Subsequent models were the Panther Ausf A, with improved cupola and ball-mounted hull machine gun, and the Ausf G with new hull front and sides and many small improvements.

MODELS Panzerkampfwagen V Panther Ausf D, A and G.

COUNTRY OF ORIGIN Germany.

WEIGHT 46·2 tonnes (45·5 tons).

LENGTH 6·88m (22ft 5in).

WIDTH 3·43m (11ft 2½in).

HEIGHT 3·1m (10ft 2in).

GROUND CLEARANCE 0·56m (1ft 10in).

ARMOUR **A, G:** 15–110mm; **D:** 15–100mm.

ENGINE 12-cylinder Maybach HL 230, 700hp, gasoline.

MAXIMUM SPEED 45km/h (28mph).

RANGE 177km (110 miles).

CREW 5.

ARMAMENT 1 × 7·5cm KwK L/70 gun, 3 × 7·92mm MG.

AMMUNITION **A, D:** 7·5cm: 79 rds, MG: 4,200 rds; **G:** 7·5cm: 81 rds, MG: 4,800 rds.

TRENCH CROSSING 1·91m (6ft 3in).

TRACK WIDTH 0·65m (2ft 1½in).

MAXIMUM ELEVATION 25°.

FORDING DEPTH 1·7m (5ft 7in).

The Panther was considered to be technically the finest German tank of World War 2, and in terms of engineering perfection and sophistication it was one of the best AFVs produced. The sloped superstructure and over-hanging gun were a direct result of the appearance of the T-34 which outclassed all previous German tanks. The need to counter the T-34 led to the design of the Panther, copying many of the T-34's features. Inset, above, is the MG 34 used for AA defence on the cupola ring. The soldier gives an indication of size of the vehicle.

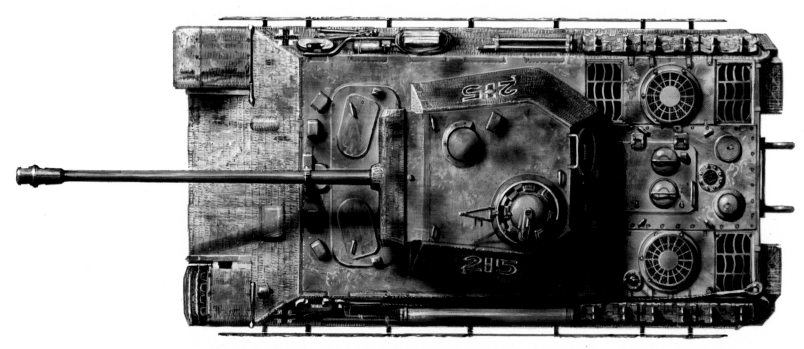

Pino dell'Orco – Nicola Pignato

Panzerkampfwagen V Ausf D Panther

The vehicle illustrated is a PzKpfw V Panther Ausf D, the original production model. The later Ausf A had a ball-mounted machine gun in the glacis plate instead of the machine gun flap, while the Ausf G had the driver's visor eliminated with episcopes provided instead. The side skirts were intended to protect the suspension from hollow charge rounds (such as are fired by bazookas). This vehicle was in action at the Anzio beachhead on 23 March 1944.

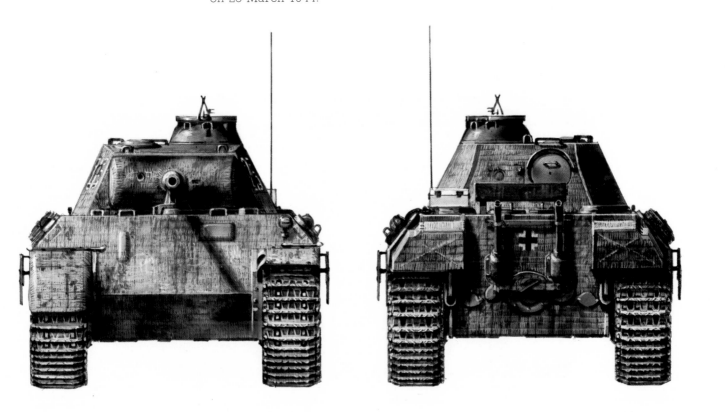

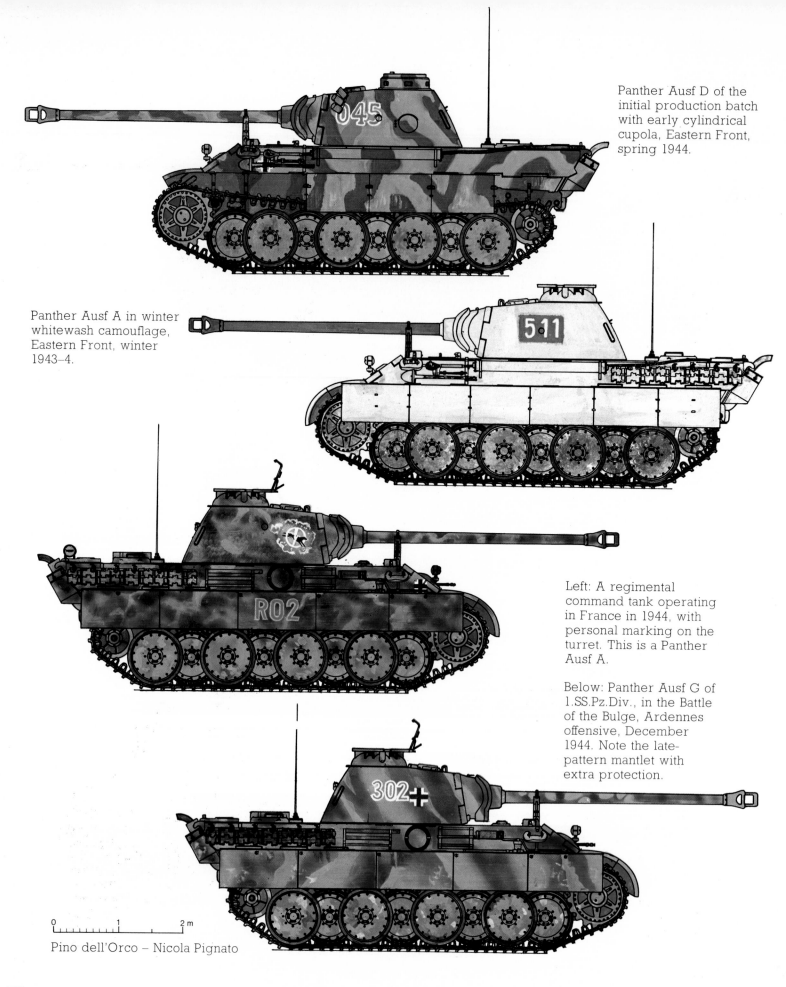

Panther Ausf D of the initial production batch with early cylindrical cupola, Eastern Front, spring 1944.

Panther Ausf A in winter whitewash camouflage, Eastern Front, winter 1943–4.

Left: A regimental command tank operating in France in 1944, with personal marking on the turret. This is a Panther Ausf A.

Below: Panther Ausf G of 1.SS.Pz.Div., in the Battle of the Bulge, Ardennes offensive, December 1944. Note the late-pattern mantlet with extra protection.

0   1   2 m

Pino dell'Orco – Nicola Pignato

Panzerkampfwagen V Panther

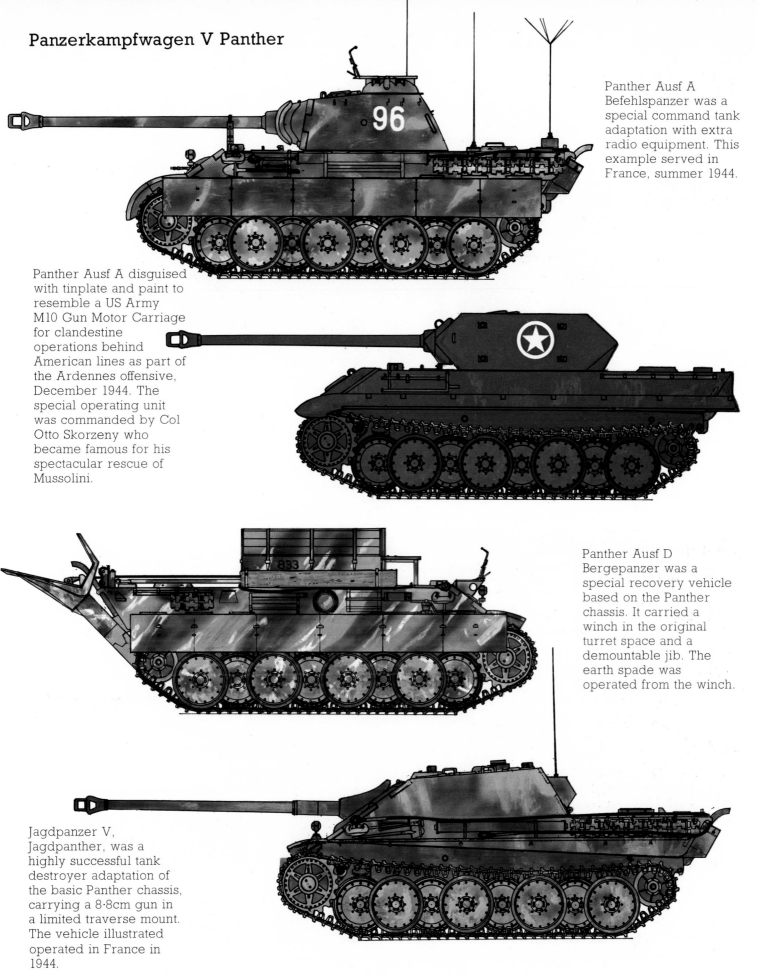

Panther Ausf A Befehlspanzer was a special command tank adaptation with extra radio equipment. This example served in France, summer 1944.

Panther Ausf A disguised with tinplate and paint to resemble a US Army M10 Gun Motor Carriage for clandestine operations behind American lines as part of the Ardennes offensive, December 1944. The special operating unit was commanded by Col Otto Skorzeny who became famous for his spectacular rescue of Mussolini.

Panther Ausf D Bergepanzer was a special recovery vehicle based on the Panther chassis. It carried a winch in the original turret space and a demountable jib. The earth spade was operated from the winch.

Jagdpanzer V, Jagdpanther, was a highly successful tank destroyer adaptation of the basic Panther chassis, carrying a 8·8cm gun in a limited traverse mount. The vehicle illustrated operated in France in 1944.

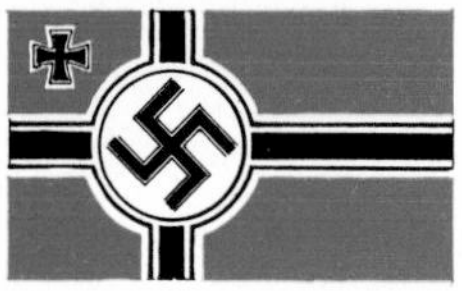

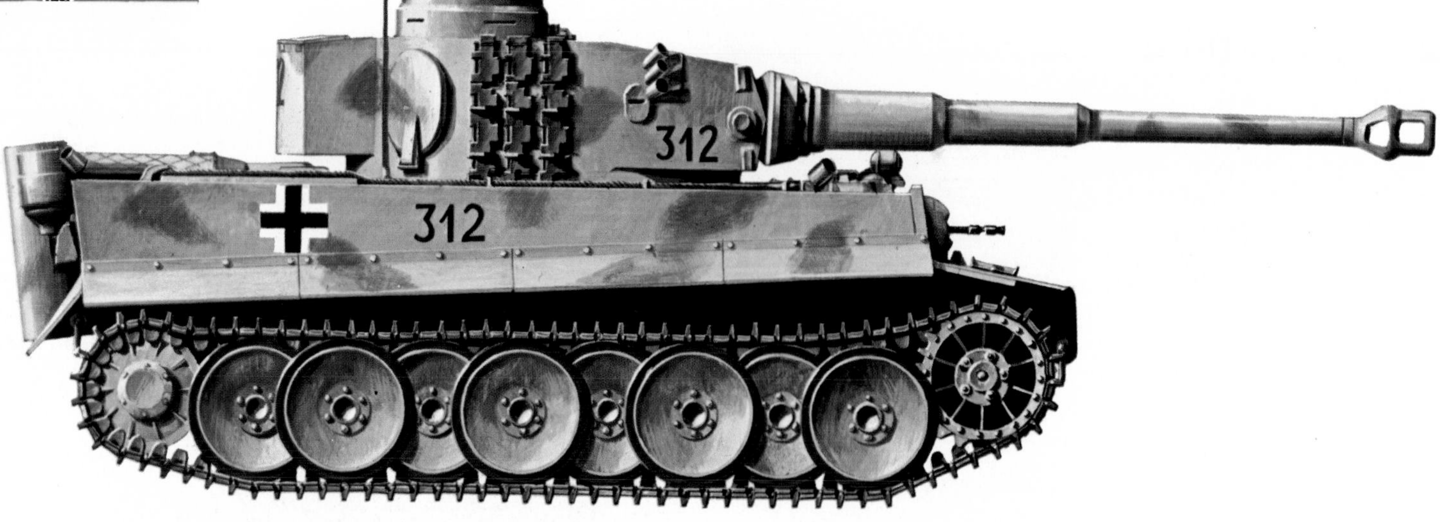
312
312

At the time of its introduction the Tiger tank was the most heavily armed and armoured tank in the world. It was first encountered by the British at Pont du Fahs in Tunis in early 1943, when two vehicles were knocked out by 6pdr anti-tank guns firing into the sides of the German tanks at close-range. However, the Tiger's very first taste of action in late 1942 was also unsuccessful. because of its deployment on the Eastern Front on swampy ground which restricted movement. The drawing shows an early-production PzKpfw VI Tiger Ausf H with full tropical filter (Feifel) system fitted above the engine compartment. Provision was also made for deep wading with a 'schnorkel' tube and rubber sealing. Later production vehicles had all this equipment omitted. From February 1944 the tank was redesignated PzKpfw VI Ausf E.

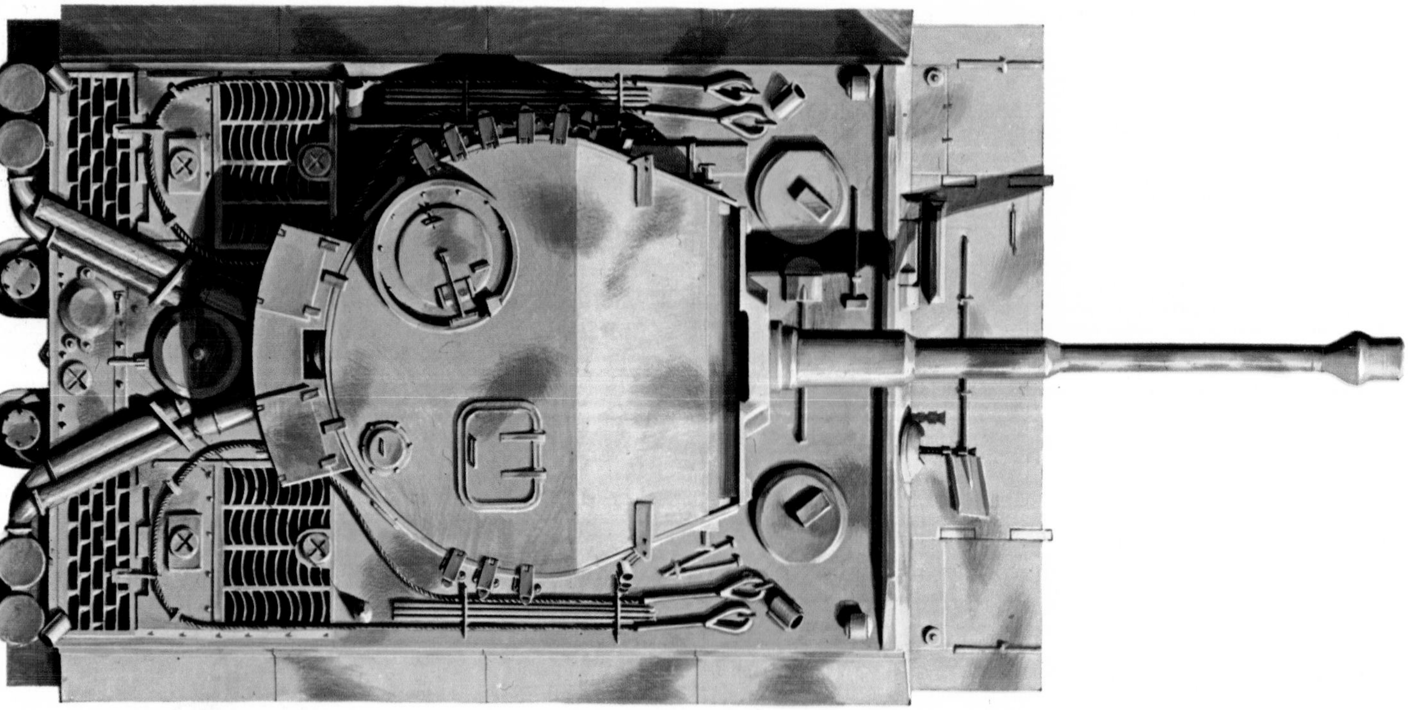

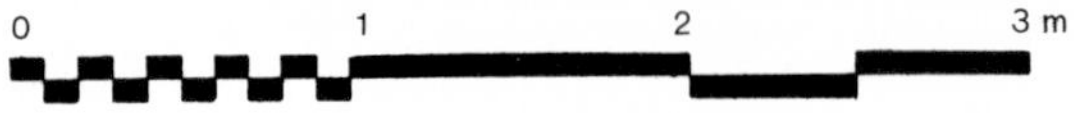
0
1
2
3 m

Gistudio – Tatangelo

Panzerkampfwagen VI Tiger Ausf H

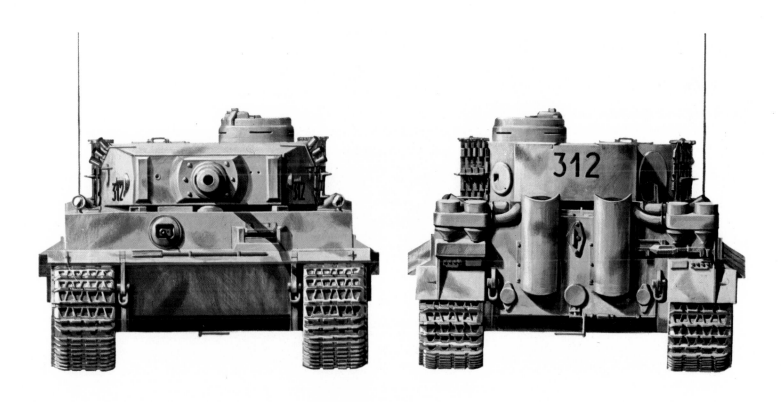

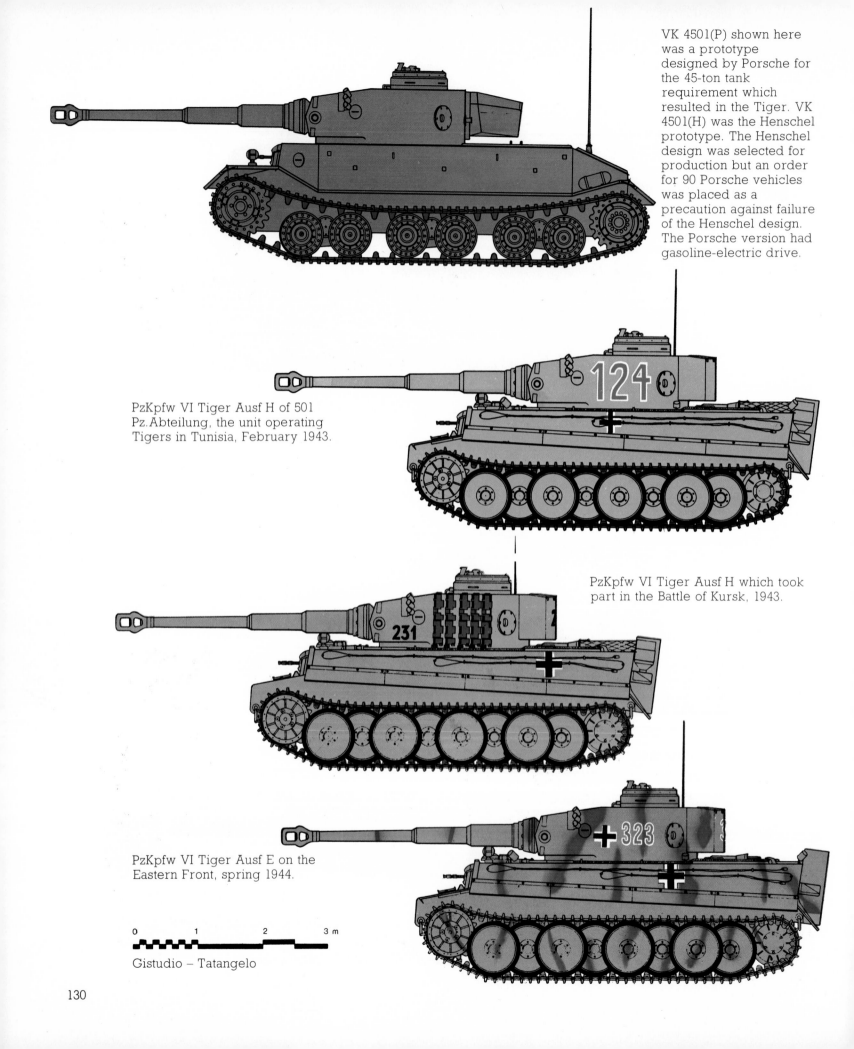

VK 4501(P) shown here was a prototype designed by Porsche for the 45-ton tank requirement which resulted in the Tiger. VK 4501(H) was the Henschel prototype. The Henschel design was selected for production but an order for 90 Porsche vehicles was placed as a precaution against failure of the Henschel design. The Porsche version had gasoline-electric drive.

PzKpfw VI Tiger Ausf H of 501 Pz.Abteilung, the unit operating Tigers in Tunisia, February 1943.

PzKpfw VI Tiger Ausf H which took part in the Battle of Kursk, 1943.

PzKpfw VI Tiger Ausf E on the Eastern Front, spring 1944.

Gistudio – Tatangelo

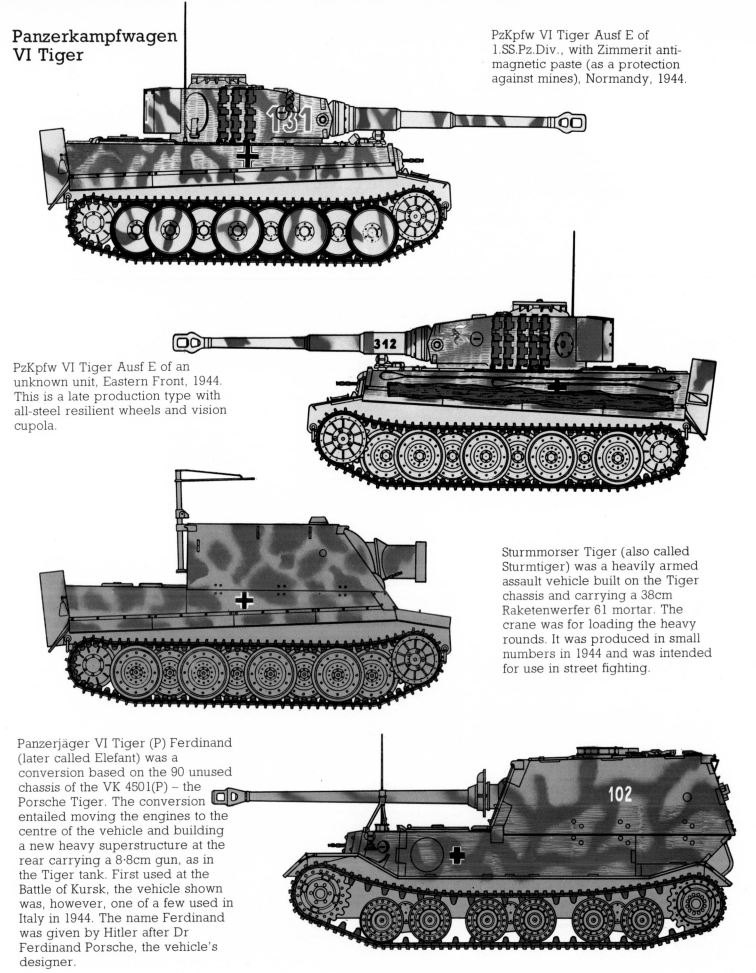

Panzerkampfwagen VI Tiger

PzKpfw VI Tiger Ausf E of 1.SS.Pz.Div., with Zimmerit anti-magnetic paste (as a protection against mines), Normandy, 1944.

PzKpfw VI Tiger Ausf E of an unknown unit, Eastern Front, 1944. This is a late production type with all-steel resilient wheels and vision cupola.

Sturmmorser Tiger (also called Sturmtiger) was a heavily armed assault vehicle built on the Tiger chassis and carrying a 38cm Raketenwerfer 61 mortar. The crane was for loading the heavy rounds. It was produced in small numbers in 1944 and was intended for use in street fighting.

Panzerjäger VI Tiger (P) Ferdinand (later called Elefant) was a conversion based on the 90 unused chassis of the VK 4501(P) – the Porsche Tiger. The conversion entailed moving the engines to the centre of the vehicle and building a new heavy superstructure at the rear carrying a 8·8cm gun, as in the Tiger tank. First used at the Battle of Kursk, the vehicle shown was, however, one of a few used in Italy in 1944. The name Ferdinand was given by Hitler after Dr Ferdinand Porsche, the vehicle's designer.

Panzerkampfwagen VI Tiger

In May 1941, Hitler, impressed by the heavy armour of the British Matilda and the French Char B tanks, pointed out the need for a tank heavier than the Panzerkampfwagen IV, to become the main weapon of the panzer divisions. Since 1937, work had been done on developing heavier tanks than the PzKpfw IIIs and IVs, but these designs were not adopted as the existing PzKpfws seemed satisfactory.

However, the need became urgent in June 1941, when the invasion of Russia started and the Russian T-34 and the KV-1 proved far superior, both in firepower and in armour. The Germans were prompted to develop new vehicles which would restore the superiority of their AFVs. Initially, the requirement was for a tank with a gun capable of penetrating armour 100mm thick at 1,500m (1 mile), and able to withstand a hit from a comparable gun. Henschel was asked to produce a vehicle of 36–40 tons, with a tapered bore gun (Waffen 0725), while another requirement was issued to Porsche to develop a 45-ton vehicle, designation VK 4501, to take a tank adaptation of the 8·8cm gun.

Krupp was to build the turrets for each vehicle, but the original Henschel Project (VK 3601) was shortlived; the tapered bore guns required tungsten steel, and, as this was in short supply, Hitler cancelled the Waffen 0725. It was therefore decided to use the turret designed for the VK 4501 on the VK 3601, but this turret had a diameter of 185cm as against 165cm, which meant that the hull superstructure needed to be widened to accommodate this, and overhung the top run of the track. The vehicle weight was greatly increased, as the superstructure and tracks were widened, and it now had an extra run of road wheels to decrease the ground pressure. The project was redesignated VK 4501 (H).

The Porsche design, now redesignated VK 4501 (P), used most of the design features from the earlier VK 3001 (P), which had been cancelled. It had air-cooled engines, which proved so troublesome that Porsche considered changing from electric to hydraulic transmission, and petrol-electric drive. The prototypes were demonstrated in front of Hitler on 20 April 1942, his birthday, and the Henschel design was accepted for production.

Apart from its conventional engineering, the VK 4501 (H) seemed more suitable for mass-production. After the trials Henschel prepared to build 1,300 vehicles, and production commenced in August 1942 at the rate of 12 vehicles per month. By November the output had been increased to 25 per month. In August 1944, when production finished, the total output was 1,335 tanks. The name Tiger was adopted for this vehicle, although this was the name originally given to the Porsche design, and the vehicles were given the full designation of PzKpfw VI Tiger Ausf E, subsequently changed on Hitler's orders to PzKpfw Tiger Ausf E.

At the time of its introduction the Tiger was the most powerful tank in the world, weighing over 55 tons, yet light to control, due to the fully automatic gearbox and fully regenerative steering. It was equipped to wade up to 4m (13ft) deep and had a cumbersome system of two separate tracks, a 72·5cm (28·5in) 'battle' track and a 'transportation' track of 52cm (21in) width.

In its later years, the Tiger underwent various changes, mainly to cut the construction time and costs. The wading facility was deleted, as it was rarely used and proved very expensive. The first 250 tanks had the Maybach HL 210, 21·3-litre, petrol engine (642hp), but this was later replaced by the Maybach HL 230 engine, giving 694hp.

The Tiger was never used, as originally intended, to spearhead the panzer divisions, because of its great weight and relatively low speed. It was mainly operated in a defensive role, where, owing to the effectiveness of its armour, it presented many problems to the Allied forces. Provided they were well maintained, Tigers proved to be effective but, with badly trained crews, problems often developed.

MODEL Panzerkampfwagen VI Tiger Ausf E.

COUNTRY OF ORIGIN Germany.

WEIGHT 55·8 tonnes (55 tons).

LENGTH 6·29m (20ft 8½in).

WIDTH 3·78m (12ft 5½in).

HEIGHT 2·89m (9ft 6in).

GROUND CLEARANCE 0·43m (1ft 5in).

ARMOUR 26–100mm.

ENGINE Maybach HL 230 694hp, gasoline.

MAXIMUM SPEED 37·9km/h (23·5mph).

RANGE 100km (62 miles).

CREW 5.

ARMAMENT 1 × 8·8cm gun, 2 × 7·92mm MG.

AMMUNITION 8·8cm: 92 rds, MG: 3,920 rds.

TRENCH CROSSING 1·8m (5ft 11in).

TRACK WIDTH 0·72m (2ft 4in).

MAXIMUM ELEVATION 25°.

FORDING DEPTH First 495 vehicles: 3·96m (13ft); remainder: 1·2m (3ft 11in).

Panzerkampfwagen VIB Königstiger

In August 1942, Hitler ordered that the Tiger should be equipped with the long-barrelled 8·8cm gun, and by January 1942 he demanded that it should have 150mm frontal armour. Within a month, the German Army Weapons Office had ordered Henschel to revise the design to incorporate fully sloped armour. In addition, both Henschel, who built the Tiger, and MAN, who built the Panther, were asked to produce 'second generation' versions to replace the existing vehicles, ensuring that most of the components were interchangeable.

Dr Porsche was also requested to submit a design, VK 4502, to fit this requirement. Porsche's design (the VK 4502 (P)/Porsche Typ 180) offered two different layouts, with the turret mounted either at the front or back of the hull, and the latter was provisionally accepted. The hull itself was compact and had sloped faces like the Panther. Petrol-electric drive was offered, as in earlier Porsche designs, but this was rejected, not only because of the preference for conventional drive, but also because the electric motors required a considerable amount of copper, which was in short supply. As with previous Porsche designs, the suspension included paired bogies with longitudinal torsion bars. Wegmann undertook the turret design, according to which the main gun was to be 8·8cm KwK 43 L/71. Some 50 of these turrets were put into production, but the VK 4502 (P) was abandoned.

The MAN project (VK 4502 MAN) was accepted and production plans went ahead, but the war ended before the vehicle, which was to be the PzKpfw Panther II, could enter production.

Henschel's initial design, the VK 4502 (H), was rejected, and a revised version was then designed. The second design, the VK 4503 (H) was a logical development of the Tiger Ausf E. It was powered and driven conventionally, had sloped armour, and its turret was large enough to carry the 8·8cm KwK 43 L/71. The design was accepted and ordered into production as a top priority, but the detail design was not completed until 1943, three months behind schedule, on account of the extensive redesigning and the extra work which was needed to standardize components with the Panther II. By November 1943, however, the pilot model was ready and, with production beginning at the Henschel factory in Kassell in December, the first models had been completed by February 1944. The first 50 tanks were fitted with the Wegmann turrets originally intended for the abandoned VK 4502 (P). All the others were given a new Krupp-designed turret that was simpler to build and free from the shot-trap under the mantlet which was a fault in the Porsche design.

The new tank was variously known as the Tiger Ausf B, Tiger II, Königstiger (King Tiger), or – to the Western Allies – Royal Tiger. Externally it looked like the Panther, but it had many of the features of the last Tiger Ausf Es. The engine, cupola and engine covers were common to the late Tiger E and later Panther, and the all-steel resilient wheels were common to the late production Tiger E and the very late production Panther Ausf G. The Tiger Ausf B had hull armour up to 150mm thick and was larger and heavier than previous vehicles. It also had a small conical saukopf (pig's head) mantlet, the 8·8cm KwK 43 L/71 gun, ball-mounted hull machine gun and overlapped wheels.

The rationalization programme of Autumn 1944 provided for the production of only two tank models with traversing turrets in 1945, the Panther Ausf G and the Tiger Ausf B, but, as the latter was more difficult to build, production was concentrated on the Panther, of which two could be built for every one Tiger. Production was scheduled at 20 a month, increasing to 145, but the highest output reached was 84 in August 1944, and in March 1945 the the figure fell to only 25. The Tiger Ausf B was the heaviest tank in active service in World War 2, first seeing action on the Eastern Front in May 1944 and on the Western Front in August 1944.

MODEL Panzerkampfwagen VI Ausf B Königstiger.

COUNTRY OF ORIGIN Germany.

WEIGHT 70·8 tonnes (69·7 tons).

LENGTH 7·39m (24ft 3in).

WIDTH 3·8m (12ft 6in).

HEIGHT 3·1m (10ft 3in).

GROUND CLEARANCE 0·5m (1ft 7½in).

ARMOUR 25–150mm.

ENGINE Maybach HL 230 700hp, gasoline.

MAXIMUM SPEED 37·8km/h (23·5mph).

RANGE 110km (68 miles).

CREW 5.

ARMAMENT 1 × 8·8cm KwK L/71 gun, 2 × 7·92mm MG.

AMMUNITION 8·8cm: 84 rds, MG: 5,850 rds.

TRENCH CROSSING 2·5m (8ft 2in).

TRACK WIDTH 0·8m (2ft 7in).

MAXIMUM ELEVATION 35°.

FORDING DEPTH 1·6m (5ft 3in).

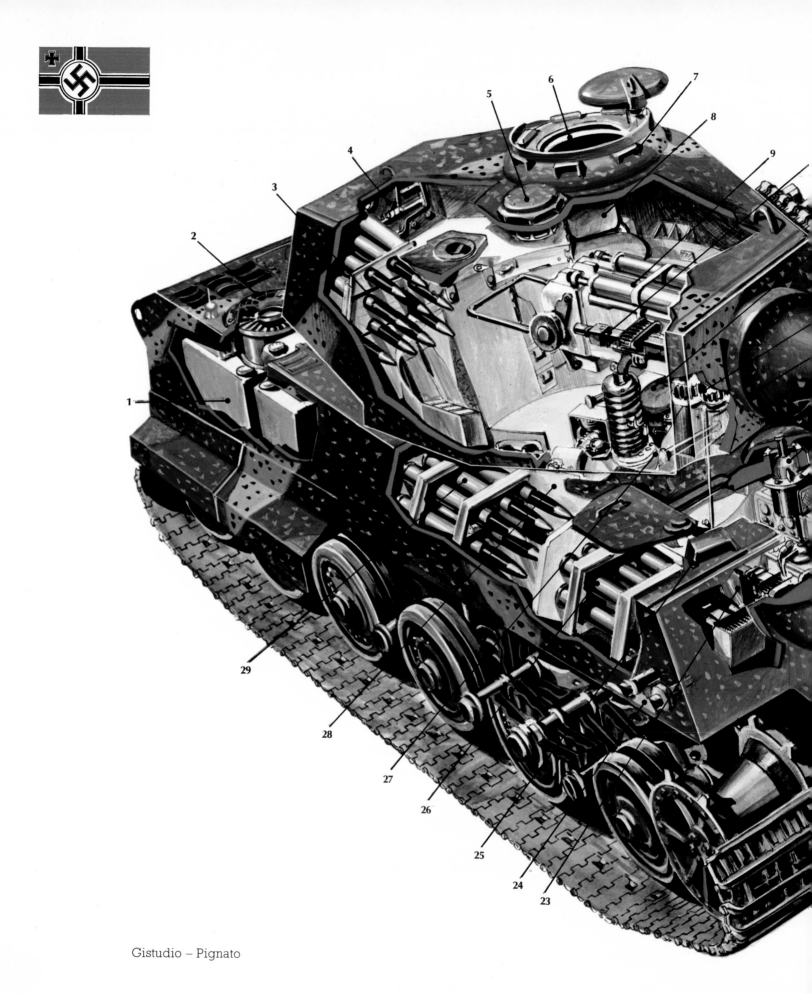

Gistudio – Pignato

Panzerkampfwagen VI Ausf B Tiger II

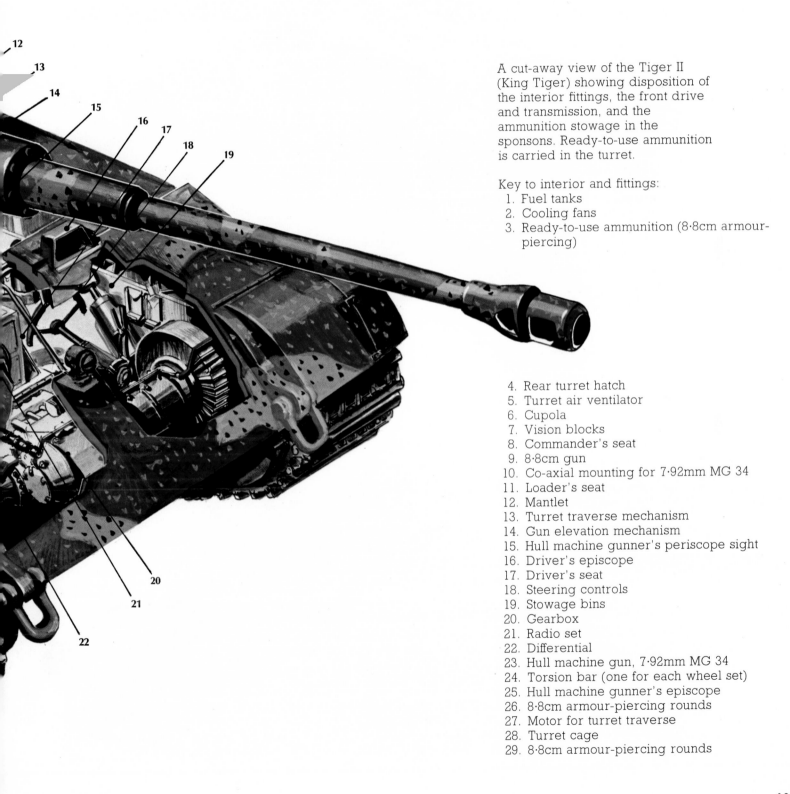

A cut-away view of the Tiger II (King Tiger) showing disposition of the interior fittings, the front drive and transmission, and the ammunition stowage in the sponsons. Ready-to-use ammunition is carried in the turret.

Key to interior and fittings:
1. Fuel tanks
2. Cooling fans
3. Ready-to-use ammunition (8·8cm armour-piercing)
4. Rear turret hatch
5. Turret air ventilator
6. Cupola
7. Vision blocks
8. Commander's seat
9. 8·8cm gun
10. Co-axial mounting for 7·92mm MG 34
11. Loader's seat
12. Mantlet
13. Turret traverse mechanism
14. Gun elevation mechanism
15. Hull machine gunner's periscope sight
16. Driver's episcope
17. Driver's seat
18. Steering controls
19. Stowage bins
20. Gearbox
21. Radio set
22. Differential
23. Hull machine gun, 7·92mm MG 34
24. Torsion bar (one for each wheel set)
25. Hull machine gunner's episcope
26. 8·8cm armour-piercing rounds
27. Motor for turret traverse
28. Turret cage
29. 8·8cm armour-piercing rounds

Panzerkampfwagen VI Ausf B Tiger
II of 501 Panzerabteilung (battalion)
during initial training with the type
at Münsterlager in 1944. This was
the first Tiger II production type
with the Porsche turret.

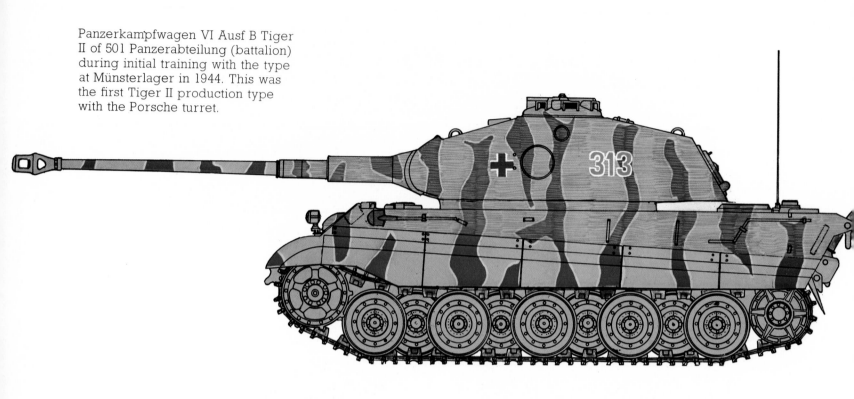

Panzerjäger Tiger Ausf B Jagdtiger
(Sd Kfz 186). This was an
experimental version fitted with
Porsche suspension, as running in
April 1945. It was contemplated
producing later vehicles with this
new suspension, but the war ended
before anything else was done.

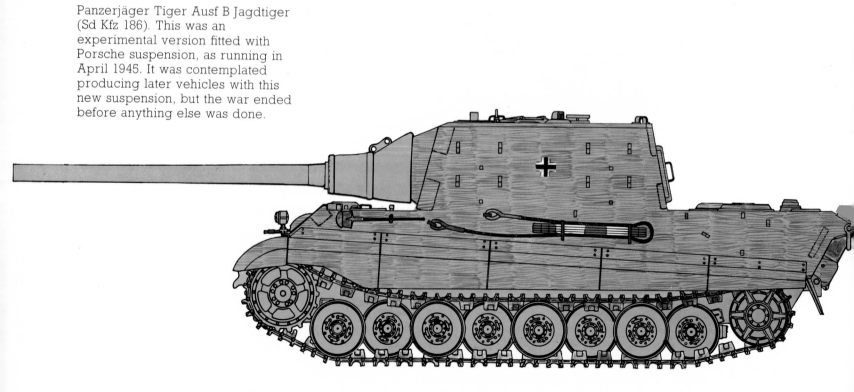

Panzerkampfwagen VIB Königstiger

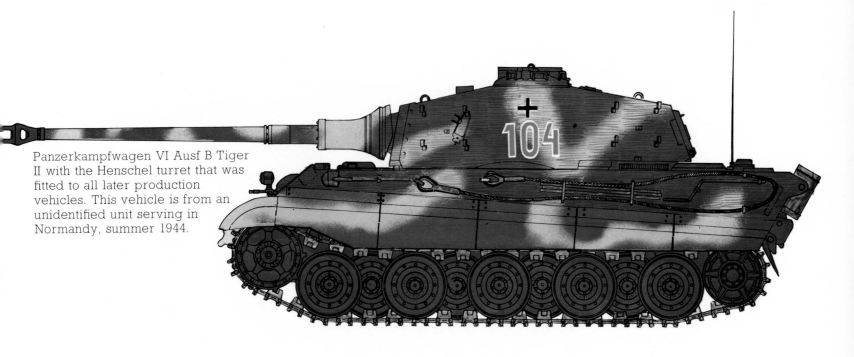

Panzerkampfwagen VI Ausf B Tiger II with the Henschel turret that was fitted to all later production vehicles. This vehicle is from an unidentified unit serving in Normandy, summer 1944.

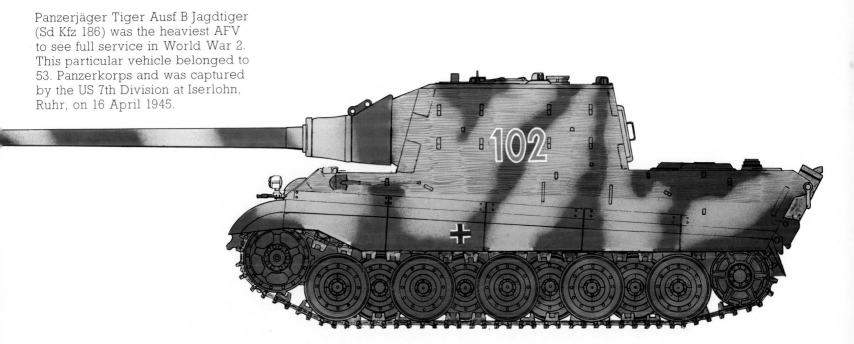

Panzerjäger Tiger Ausf B Jagdtiger (Sd Kfz 186) was the heaviest AFV to see full service in World War 2. This particular vehicle belonged to 53. Panzerkorps and was captured by the US 7th Division at Iserlohn, Ruhr, on 16 April 1945.

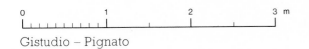

Gistudio – Pignato

The illustration here shows a standard-production Sexton as it appeared in service in Normandy, France, in the summer of 1944. This example is from 147th Field Regiment, Royal Artillery (The Essex Yeomanry) and the vehicle is marked for 'B' battery. All self-propelled batteries of field regiments of 21 Army Group were equipped with Sextons shortly after the Normandy landings in June 1944 so that 21 Army Group standardized on 25pdr ammunition. Many regiments had previously been equipped with M7 Priests which were all handed over to the US Army at this time so that US units could standardize on 105mm ammunition.

Shown in the illustration are most of the modifications introduced during production including M4-type bogies with trailing return rollers, a towing hook at the rear for the ammunition trailer, provision of an auxiliary generator, stowage for extra equipment, and mounts for Bren AA machine guns. Sextons remained in British and Canadian service for many years postwar, and they were also supplied to other armies, including those of Spain and Italy.

A further variant was the Sexton GPO produced in late 1943. This was a Sexton with the gun removed and extra equipment added for gun position officers (GPO) of Sexton batteries. It was fitted with extra radio, map tables, additional telephone cables, and an extra Tannoy unit. A Sexton GPO is shown in the illustration bottom right.

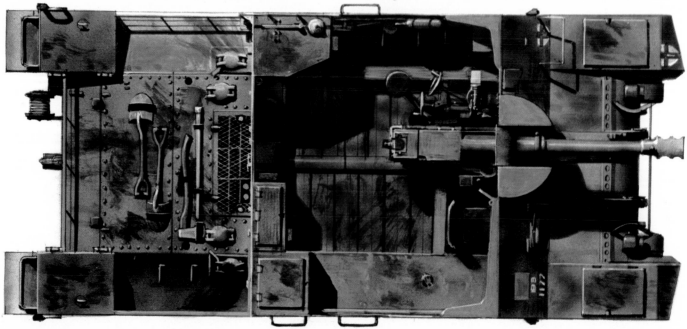

Pino dell'Orco – Nicola Pignato

25pdr Self-propelled Gun Sexton

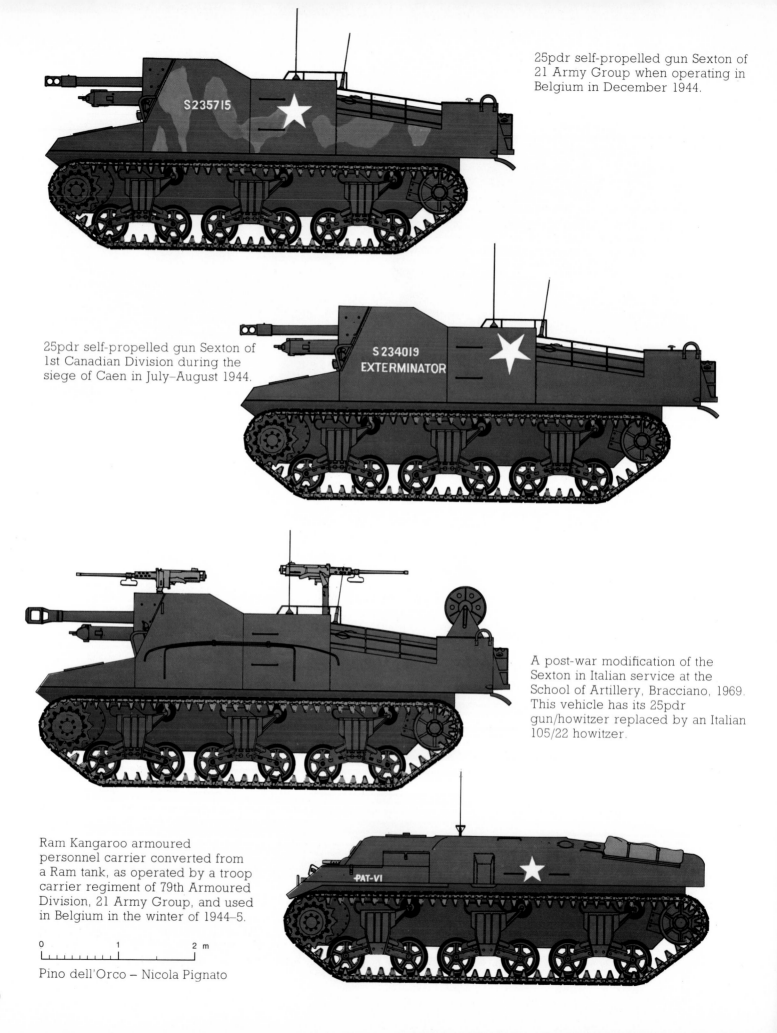

25pdr self-propelled gun Sexton of 21 Army Group when operating in Belgium in December 1944.

25pdr self-propelled gun Sexton of 1st Canadian Division during the siege of Caen in July–August 1944.

A post-war modification of the Sexton in Italian service at the School of Artillery, Bracciano, 1969. This vehicle has its 25pdr gun/howitzer replaced by an Italian 105/22 howitzer.

Ram Kangaroo armoured personnel carrier converted from a Ram tank, as operated by a troop carrier regiment of 79th Armoured Division, 21 Army Group, and used in Belgium in the winter of 1944–5.

0   1   2 m

Pino dell'Orco – Nicola Pignato

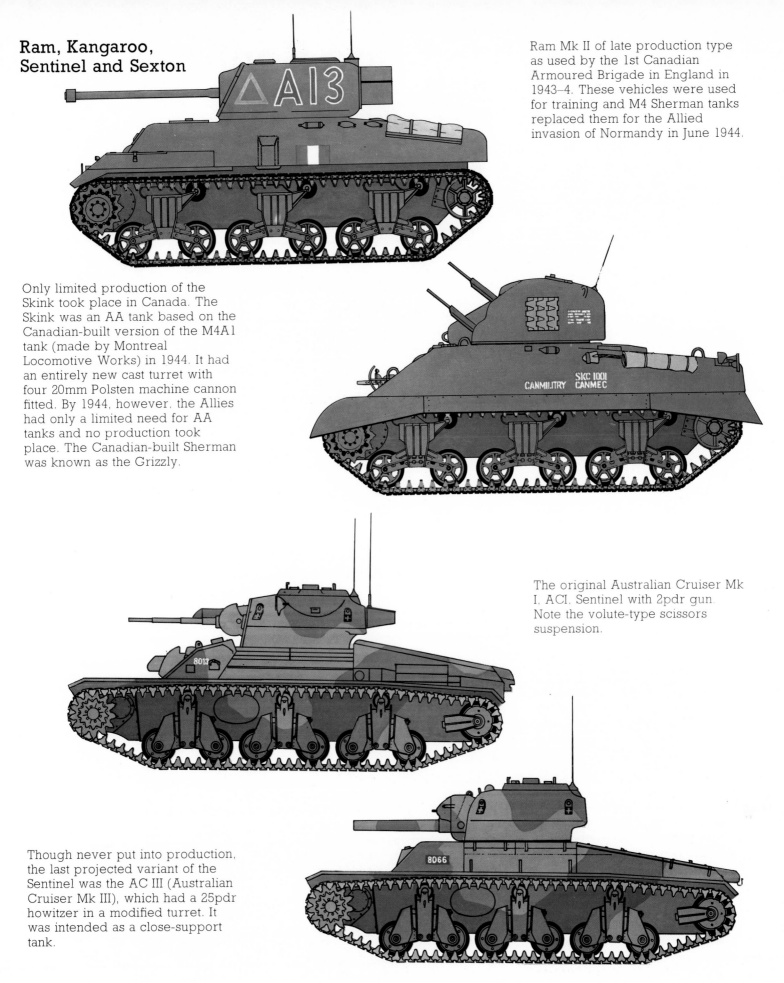

Ram, Kangaroo, Sentinel and Sexton

Ram Mk II of late production type as used by the 1st Canadian Armoured Brigade in England in 1943–4. These vehicles were used for training and M4 Sherman tanks replaced them for the Allied invasion of Normandy in June 1944.

Only limited production of the Skink took place in Canada. The Skink was an AA tank based on the Canadian-built version of the M4A1 tank (made by Montreal Locomotive Works) in 1944. It had an entirely new cast turret with four 20mm Polsten machine cannon fitted. By 1944, however, the Allies had only a limited need for AA tanks and no production took place. The Canadian-built Sherman was known as the Grizzly.

The original Australian Cruiser Mk I, AC1, Sentinel with 2pdr gun. Note the volute-type scissors suspension.

Though never put into production, the last projected variant of the Sentinel was the AC III (Australian Cruiser Mk III), which had a 25pdr howitzer in a modified turret. It was intended as a close-support tank.

Ram, Kangaroo, Sentinel and Sexton

In spring 1940 a decision was taken to build a Tank Arsenal in Canada under the administration of Montreal Locomotive Works, with the assistance of its parent organization, American Locomotive. It was further decided that a Canadian-built cruiser tank design would be produced. This was to be based on that of the US M3 medium tank, then at the pilot model stage, both to save time and to utilize mechanical and chassis components already in production for the M3. By late 1940, it became clear that many of the design features being finalized on the M3 medium tank would be far from satisfactory for British and Canadian users.

In January 1941, it was decided to continue the Canadian design using the mechanical components of the M3 medium, but incorporating hull and turret to suit Canadian requirements, with a British main armament. This vehicle was to be known as the Ram.

It was planned to provide 6pdr gun mount drawings from Britain but these did not materialize in time and the mantlet, cradle and elevating gear were designed in Canada. Pending the final development and production of the 6pdr mountings, the first 50 vehicles were fitted with 2pdrs and were designated Ram Mk I. Production vehicles with 6pdrs then became Ram Mk II, the latter coming into full production in January 1942.

Rams did not see action as gun tanks, but were largely used for training in Canada or Britain. Most were converted for special purposes, mainly as Kangaroos. The Kangaroo was an armoured personnel carrier (APC) made by removing the turret and cage and installing seats for infantry in the fighting compartment. Ram Kangaroos equipped the armoured troop carrier battalions of 79th Armoured Division in the NW Europe campaign and were the first tracked APCs used in quantity by the British.

The Australian Ministry of Munitions first considered the idea of building tanks in early July 1940. In November, the Australian General Staff drew up precise requirements for the sort of tank they thought necessary. They estimated that 2,000 would be needed, with first deliveries in July 1941 and output of 70 a week from then on. A tank design expert was sent out from Great Britain to set up plans. For the proposed vehicle AC I (AC=Australian Cruiser), it was planned to use a copy of the M3 final drive and gearbox. For a power plant, Cadillac engines were finally adopted, arranged in 'clover leaf' formation. In early 1941, a wooden mock-up of AC I was built. The vehicle was to have cast or rolled armour throughout, using only alloys available in Australia. The first cast hull was successfully manufactured in October, and the prototype AC I was completed in January 1942. In August the first production vehicle was finished at Chullona Tank Assembly Shops, NSW, and a total of 66 AC I 'Sentinels' were built when production ceased and all orders were cancelled in July 1943.

The Sexton was developed in the latter half of 1942 to meet British General Staff requirements for a self-propelled gun with all the mobility and characteristics of the M7 HMC Priest, but with the standard British 25pdr field howitzer in place of the American 105mm weapon. As a basis, the Ram chassis was used. Layout was similar to that of the M7, but the driving position was on the right and the gun was offset to the left, since the Ram chassis had the driver's position shifted to the right-hand side. A small ammunitioning hatch was provided in the left-hand side. The standard 25pdr howitzer was mounted, but, in order to give sufficient elevation, it was necessary to limit the recoil throw.

Built by Montreal Locomotive, the pilot model was shipped to Britain for tests and approval, and production commenced at Montreal Locomotive Works in early 1943. Some 424 vehicles were completed by the end of 1943. Successive orders from Britain kept the vehicle in production until the end of 1945, by which time 2,150 had been completed.

MODELS Cruiser Tank Ram Mk I; Cruiser Tank Sentinel AC1; Sexton.

COUNTRY OF ORIGIN **Ram:** Canada; **Sentinel:** Australia; **Sexton:** Canada.

WEIGHT **Ram:** 29 tonnes (28·5 tons); **Sentinel:** 28·4 tonnes (28 tons); **Sexton:** 25·8 tonnes (25·3 tons).

LENGTH **Ram:** 5·7m (18ft 8in); **Sentinel:** 6·3m (20ft 9in); **Sexton:** 6·1m (20ft 1in).

WIDTH **Ram:** 2·87m (9ft 5in); **Sentinel:** 2·5m (8ft 2in); **Sexton:** 2·7m (8ft 11in).

HEIGHT **Ram:** 2·6m (8ft 9in); **Sentinel:** 2·8m (9ft 1in); **Sexton:** 2·43m (8ft).

GROUND CLEARANCE **Ram:** 0·43m (1ft 5in); **Sentinel:** 0·39m (1ft 3in); **Sexton:** 0·43m (1ft 5in).

ARMOUR **Ram:** 25–87mm; **Sentinel:** 25–65mm; **Sexton:** 10–38mm.

ENGINES **Ram:** Wright Continental R-975, 400hp, gasoline; **Sentinel:** 3 × Cadillac, 117hp, gasoline; **Sexton:** Wright Continental R-975, 400hp, gasoline.

MAXIMUM SPEED **Ram:** 40km/h (25mph); **Sentinel:** 32km/h (20mph); **Sexton:** 40km/h (25mph).

RANGE **Ram:** 232km (144 miles); **Sentinel:** 321km (200 miles); **Sexton:** 290km (180 miles).

CREW **Ram:** 5; **Sentinel:** 5; **Sexton:** 6.

ARMAMENT **Ram:** 1 × 2pdr gun, 3 × ·30 cal. MG; **Sentinel:** 1 × 2pdr, 2 × ·303in MG; **Sexton:** 1 × 25pdr, 2 × ·303in MG.

AMMUNITION **Ram:** 2pdr: 92 rds, MG: 880 rds; **Sentinel:** 2pdr: 130 rds, MG: 4,250 rds; **Sexton:** 25pdr: 112 rds, MG: 1,500 rds.

TRENCH CROSSING **Ram:** 2·26m (7ft 5in); **Sentinel:** 2·43m (8ft); **Sexton:** 2·5m (8ft 3in).

TRACK WIDTH **Ram:** 0·41m (1ft 4½in); **Sentinel:** 0·41m (1ft 4½in); **Sexton:** 0·39m (1ft 3½in).

MAXIMUM ELEVATION **Ram:** 20°; **Sentinel:** 40°; **Sexton:** 40°.

FORDING DEPTH **Ram:** 1m (3ft 4in); **Sentinel:** 1·22m (3ft 11½in); **Sexton:** 1·16m (3ft 10in).

Renault R-35

The French infantry called for a new light tank in 1934 which would eventually succeed the old Renault FT in service. Four firms were asked to submit designs; Renault, FCM, Delaunay-Belleville, and CGL. Renault were the first to produce a design late in 1934 with a prototype designated ZM. This was based quite closely on a fast light reconnaissance vehicle, *Automitrailleuse de Reconnaissance 1935, Type ZT*, which Renault had already designed for the cavalry. The only common feature was the suspension and running gear – the rest of the vehicle was lightly built – but the utilization of an existing design feature enabled Renault to produce the ZM very quickly.

The Renault ZM prototype had 30mm armour, increased to 40mm in production vehicles. This took the weight from the 8 tons originally specified to 10 tons. The infantry had asked for a speed of 15–20km/h (9–12mph) and an armament of a 37mm gun or two 7·5mm machine guns. A two-man crew was envisaged – driver and commander, who was also the gunner. While the prototypes were under test, the Germans reoccupied the Rhineland in March 1935, provoking an urgent demand for rearmament. So the Renault ZM was ordered into production at once with an initial batch of 300. By 1940 over 1,600 had been built and it was the most widely produced of the infantry light tanks, the other type being the FCM 36. The ZM in military service was designated Renault R-35.

To give the required armour protection, the hull was made in three sections bolted together, all with rolled plates. The side plates carried the track bogies and front driving sprocket. The differentials and final drive were housed under the cast nose plate, and the superstructure was also all cast. The driver sat slightly to the left, with two cast visor doors. The armament was carried in a cast APX-R turret which was also used on other tanks like the R-40, H-35 and H-39. This turret had a heavy cast cradle for the gun and a prominent domed cupola with vision slits. Inside the vehicle the commander had a seat attached to the turret but normally he stood to work it. A hatch flap dropped down at the back of the turret and formed a seat when required. The armament was the Model 1918 37mm gun with a co-axial machine gun. Suspension consisted of bell-crank bogies and a trailing idler, and a skid tail could be fitted to assist in trench crossing.

By 1939 Renault R-35s were in wide service, and export sales had been made to Poland, Turkey, Romania and Yugoslavia. A couple of experimental models had been made with the FCM turret fitted, but there was no development in this direction. A few tanks were equipped as fascine carriers with a girder framework arranged so that fascines could be carried above the turret and launched over the nose.

With the fall of France many R-35s fell into German hands. Though the design did not accord with German concepts, the perpetual shortage of equipment meant that R-35s were pressed into service in any case. About 200 were used to equip German reconnaissance companies for Operation Barbarossa, the invasion of Russia, and these were designated PzKpfw R-35 (4·7cm), the 37mm French gun having been replaced by a Czech 47mm in the meantime. With turrets removed, other R-35s were used as ammunition carriers on the Russian front. In this guise they were named Munitionspanzer 35 R (f).

The R-35 was also used as the basis for at least two types of SP gun. The original turret was removed and replaced by an open-topped armoured superstructure. One such conversion featured the standard Czech 4·7cm anti-tank gun and was designated 4·7cm Pak (t) auf Gw R-35 (f) – a combination of captured equipment from two different sources. Later in the war (1943–4) a 10·5cm field howitzer was fitted in a similar mount to give a conversion designated 10·5cm Le FH 18 auf Gw 35R(f). Finally there was another turretless conversion which could carry an 8cm howitzer and crew, made only in small numbers.

MODEL Renault R-35.

COUNTRY OF ORIGIN France.

WEIGHT 10·1 tonnes (10 tons).

LENGTH 4m (13ft 2in).

WIDTH 1·85m (6ft 1in).

HEIGHT 2·08m (6ft 10in).

GROUND CLEARANCE 0·32m (1ft ½in).

ARMOUR Max. 40mm.

ENGINE 4-cylinder Renault, gasoline, 82hp.

MAXIMUM SPEED 20km/h (12·5mph).

RANGE 140km (87 miles).

CREW 2.

ARMAMENT 1 × 37mm gun, 1 × co-axial 7·5mm MG.

AMMUNITION 37mm: 100 rds, MG: 2,400 rds.

TRENCH CROSSING 1·6m (5ft 3in).

TRACK WIDTH 0·30m (11in).

MAXIMUM ELEVATION 10°.

FORDING DEPTH 0·8m (2ft 7in).

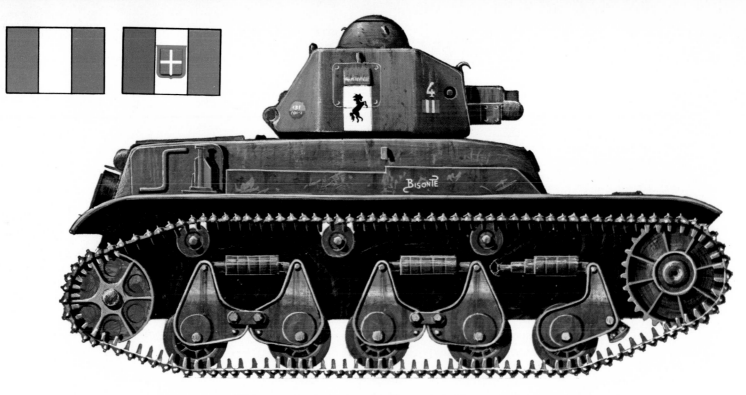

This standard production Renault R-35 was in service in 1940 with the 101st Battalion, 2nd Company, of the Italian 131st Infantry Regiment (brigade). The inset close-up shows details of the unit marking. The Ram's head was the insignia of the 2nd Company, but the side elevation immediately above shows a vehicle of the 1st Company whose emblem was a prancing horse carried in place of the Ram's head on each side of the turret.

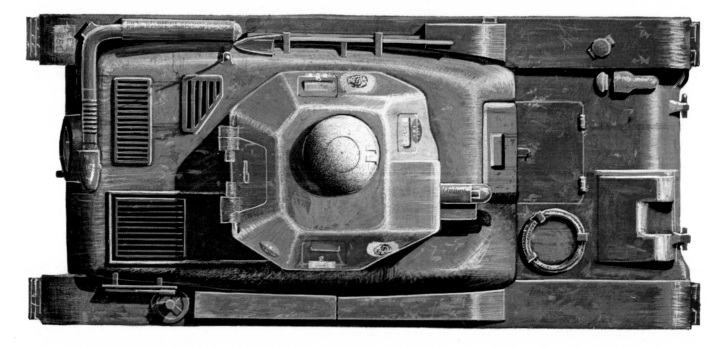

0   1 m

Danilo Renzulli – Nicola Pignato

Renault R-35

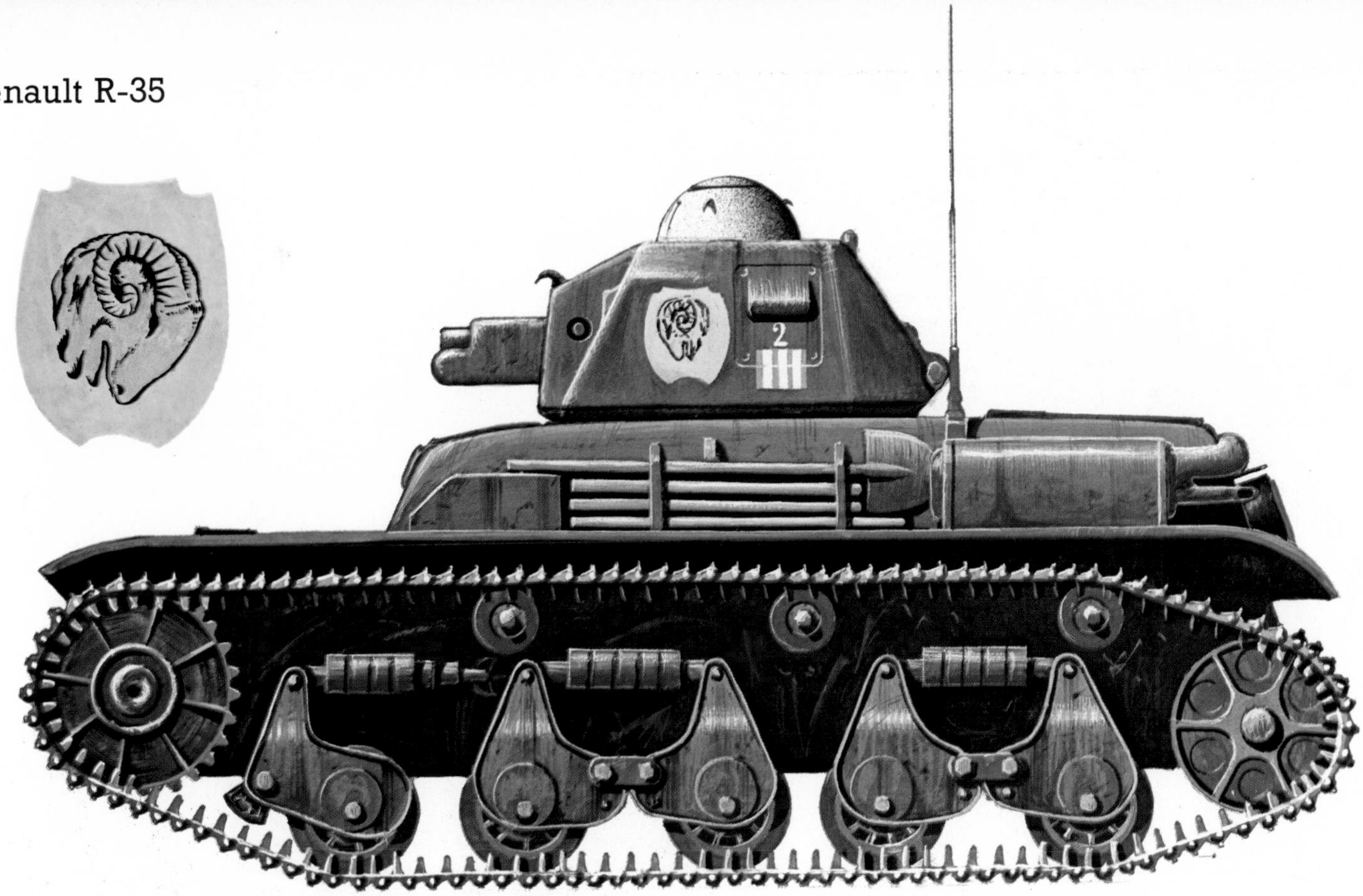
2

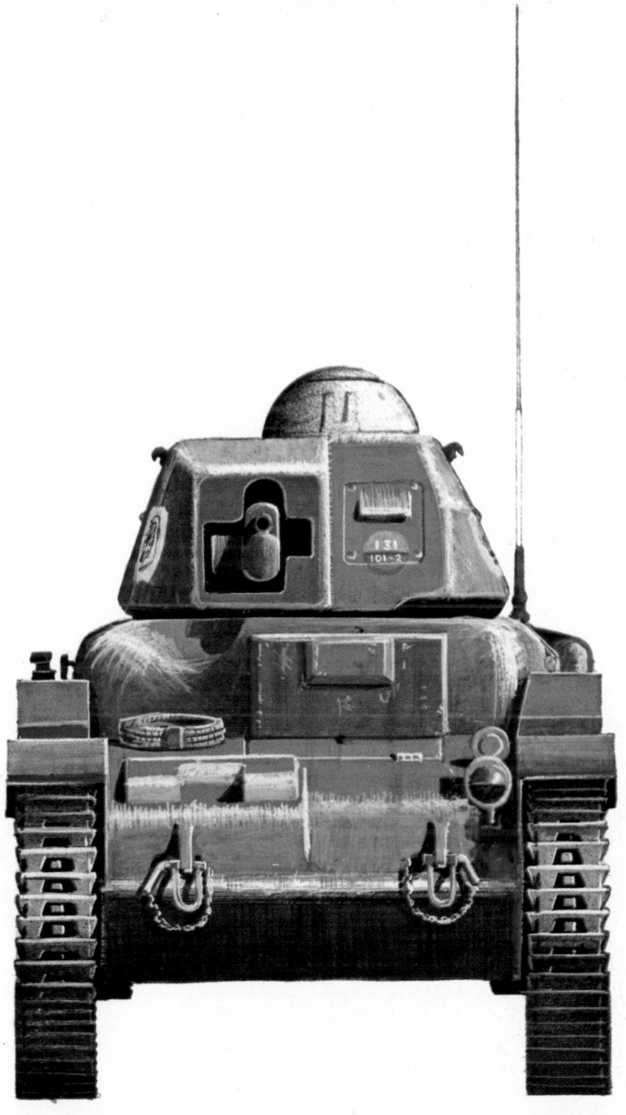

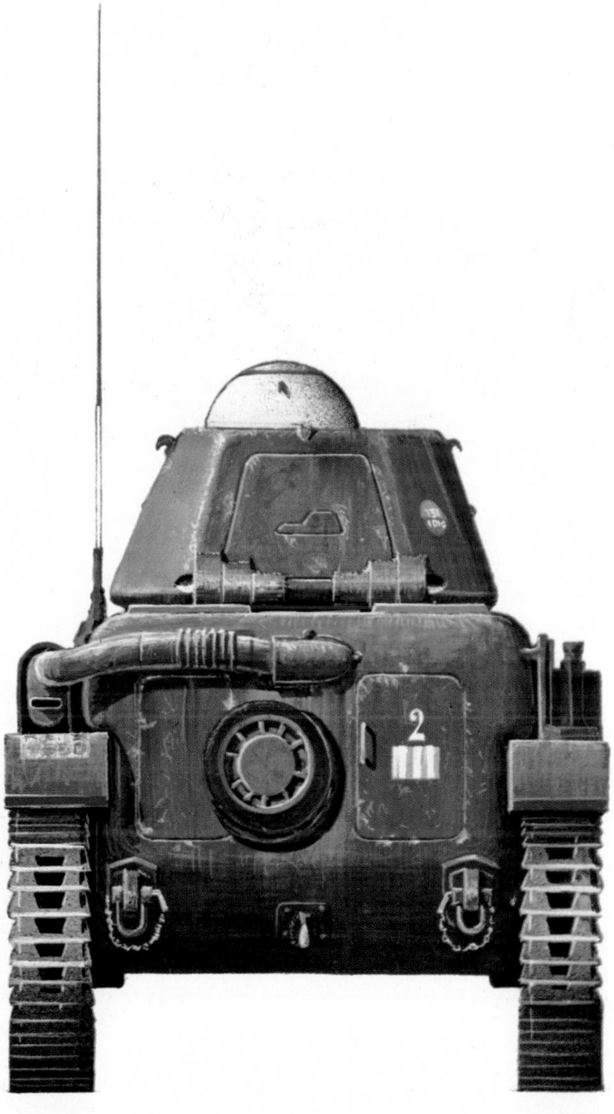
2

French Renault R-35, taking part in summer exercises in 1938.

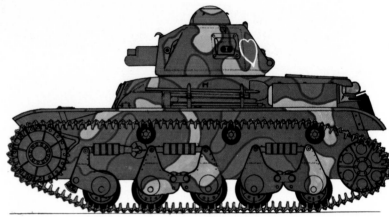

Renault R-35 in French markings during the Battle of France, May 1940.

Renault R-35 of the Vichy French forces in Libya, 1941.

Renault R-40 (AMX 40) armed with 47mm gun at the test establishment, Issy-les-Moulineaux, February 1940. The R-40 was essentially the standard R-35, with its suspension replaced by a new vertical springing type developed by AMX. The small wheels and coil springs were covered by side skirts, and the gun was the new long-barrel 47mm type.

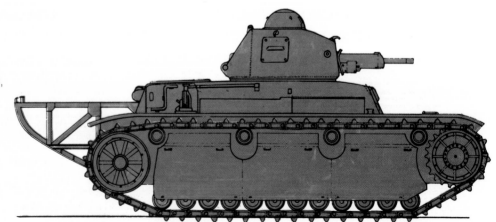

0   1   2 m

Danilo Renzulli – Nicola Pignato

Renault R-35

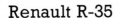

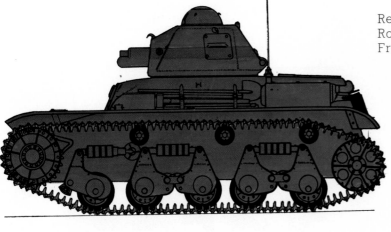

Renault R-35 (ex-French service) in Romanian Army Service, Eastern Front, 1942.

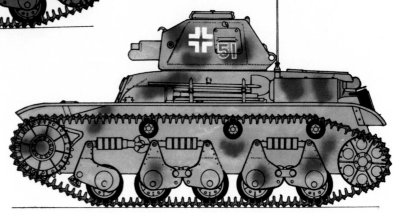

Renault R-35 in German service, with modified turret cupola, used by German occupation forces in Greece, 1943.

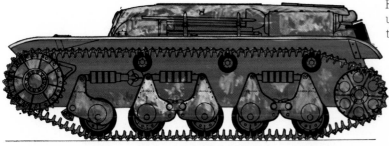

Renault R-35 Schlepper (tractor), used as a munitions carrier and tractor, Eastern Front, 1944.

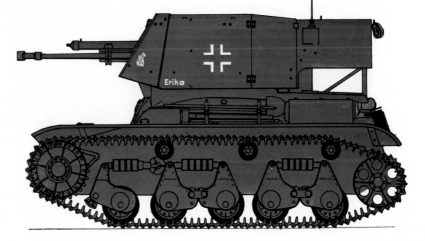

Panzerjäger 4·7cm Pak (t) auf Gw R-35 (f), Normandy, early 1944.

This Sd Kfz 234/2 Puma armed with the 5cm KwK 39 gun was one of the most elegant fighting vehicles to appear in World War 2. This example equipped the elite Panzer Lehr division in the defence of the Falaise Gap, Normandy, in 1944 The Puma is the best-known of a series of German eight-wheel armoured cars and was a 'second generation' type within the series development.

The hull of the Sd Kfz 234/2 (and all other models) was all-welded. The chassis frame was relatively light (the rigidity of the hull permitted this), and was essentially two longitudinal girders joined by two tubular cross-members. Four suspension springs were attached to the cross-members. A Tatra diesel engine was mounted at the front of the frame. All four axles were driven via reduction boxes and there was a six-speed gearbox. Because there were different turning circles made by the various wheels on full lock, there was an inter-axle differential to compensate for this.

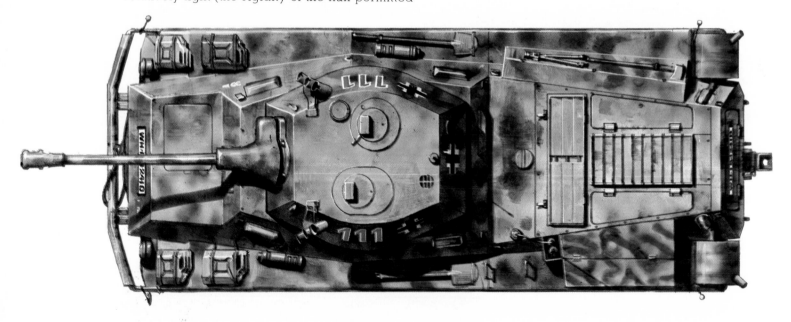

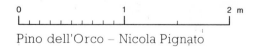

Pino dell'Orco – Nicola Pignato

Panzerspähwagen Sd Kfz 234/2 Puma

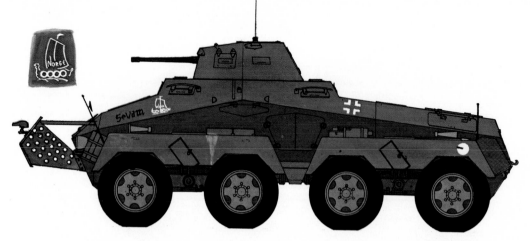

Sd Kfz 231 (8 rad) of the Luftwaffe
Division 'Hermann Goering', a
fighting division composed of
Luftwaffe personnel. Inset is a
close-up of the individual vehicle
marking.

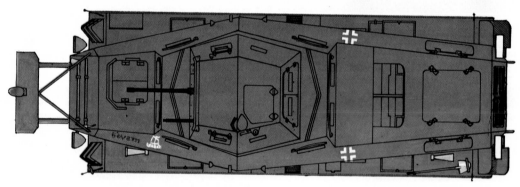

Sd Kfz 232 of Waffen-SS division
'Viking', on the Eastern Front in
1942.

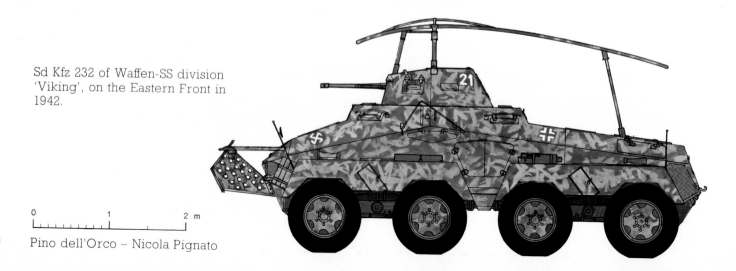

Sd Kfz 231 and 234 Puma

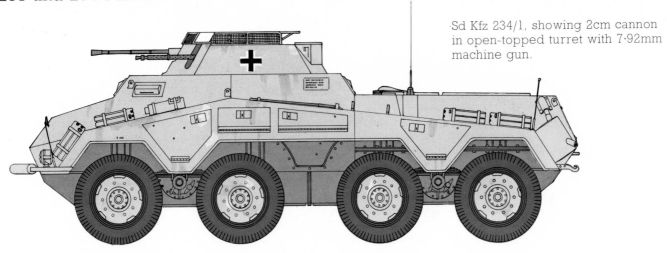

Sd Kfz 234/1, showing 2cm cannon in open-topped turret with 7·92mm machine gun.

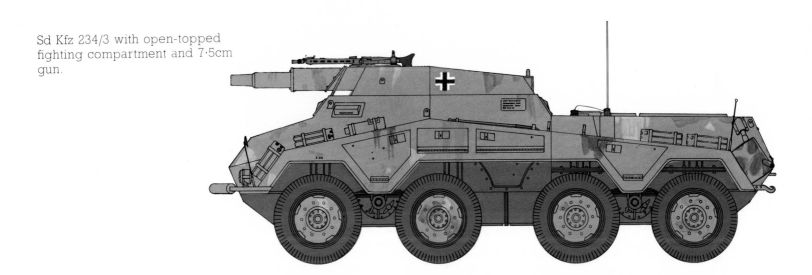

Sd Kfz 234/3 with open-topped fighting compartment and 7·5cm gun.

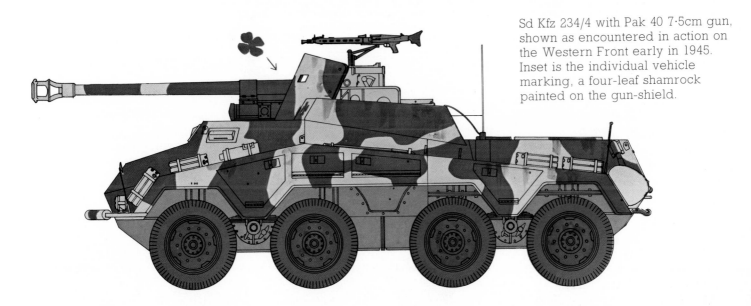

Sd Kfz 234/4 with Pak 40 7·5cm gun, shown as encountered in action on the Western Front early in 1945. Inset is the individual vehicle marking, a four-leaf shamrock painted on the gun-shield.

Sd Kfz 231 and 234 Puma

In the German eight-wheel armoured cars, steering wheels and controls were provided for each direction of travel and the body was placed on the chassis so that the engine was at the rear. As the car would drive equally well in either direction there was strictly speaking no front or back – the engine end of the chassis was considered to be the front even though it was the rear in the normal mode of travel! In purely technical terms the eight-wheeler was an extremely advanced and sophisticated design.

The Sd Kfz 231 (8 rad) had a simple turret armed with a 2cm KwK 30 or 38 gun and a co-axial MG 34 machine gun. There was a four-man crew; gunner, commander and two drivers. The seats for the two turret men were attached to the turret which was hand traversed with sophisticated gearing. The hull was well faceted, with a prominent stowage box at the front. Some vehicles had a 10mm armour plate fixed to the stowage box front for extra protection.

The second model was the Sd Kfz 232 (Fu) (8 rad), Fu standing for Funkwagen, or radio car. It was identical in construction to the Sd Kfz 231, except that a large 'bedstead' frame aerial was carried above the vehicle, with pivots on the supports above the turret so that it could still traverse despite the considerable top hamper. The car was intended to act as a rear link in the reconnaissance role and carried extensive radio equipment. Later vehicles had the big bedstead replaced by a much simpler pole aerial and a star aerial which could be erected as required. The Sd Kfz 232 (Fu) (8 rad) was in service from 1939.

By 1942 there was a need for armoured car units to play their part in offensive operations. The Sd Kfz 233 (7·5cm), in effect a wheeled assault gun (which entered service in October 1942), was an adaptation of the basic design to fit the short 7·5cm KwK 37 L/24 gun into a modified hull. The top of the superstructure was cut away, with the gun mount offset to the right front. There was a three-man crew: front

driver, loader/rear driver, and commander/gunner.

The Sd Kfz 633 (Fu) (8 rad) was another signals vehicle developed, with modifications, from the Sd Kfz 232. The turret was dropped in favour of a large body with small fixed turret on top, but the bedstead aerial (or later pole and star) was the same as on the Sd Kfz 232. The Sd Kfz 633 could be used as a long-range command vehicle and carried medium-wave radio equipment, and was mainly employed by signals platoons of armoured reconnaissance regiments.

As a replacement for this original series of eight-wheelers, Büssing-NAG was asked in August 1940 to come up with a new design with fully monocoque hull and no chassis. A diesel engine was called for, suitable for operation in all climes, and a Tatra V12 engine was eventually chosen. The armour on the new vehicle was thicker than on the previous types, 30mm at the front and 8mm on the sides. A long one-piece mudguard each side replaced the twin mudguard arrangement of the earlier vehicles. It was intended that these new types would be used in North Africa, but the fighting there had ceased when the first vehicles appeared in early 1943. Various models, numbering over 2,000 in all, were built and all were used in Europe. The Sd Kfz 234/1 was the equivalent of the Sd Kfz 231 with similar turret and armament.

The Sd Kfz 234/2 Puma was an elegant armoured car with a 5cm KwK 39 gun in a fully enclosed streamlined turret, as befitted its offensive reconnaissance role. Because of its handsome looks it has always been the best-known of German armoured cars.

The Sd Kfz 234/3 was the equivalent of the Sd Kfz 233 with similar armament, while Sd Kfz 234/4 was a late war expedient to mount a complete 7·5cm Pak 40 gun and reduced field mount into the open topped hull of the Sd Kfz 233. Few of these were built, but they were used in action and proved successful as tank destroyers in the later stages of World War 2.

MODELS Sd Kfz 231 and 234/2 Puma.

COUNTRY OF ORIGIN Germany.

WEIGHT **231:** 7·8 tonnes (7·7 tons); **234/2:** 11·74 tonnes (11·6 tons).

LENGTH **231:** 5·85m (19ft 2in); **234/2:** 6·8m (22ft 4in).

WIDTH **231:** 2·2m (7ft 4in); **234/2:** 2·4m (7ft 10in).

HEIGHT **231:** 2·35m (7ft 10in); **234/2:** 2·28m (7ft 8in).

GROUND CLEARANCE **231:** 0·27m (8⅝in); **234/2:** 0·35m (1ft 1¾in).

ARMOUR **231:** 5–18mm; **234/2:** 8–30mm.

ENGINES **231:** Büssing NAG L8V, 155hp, gasoline; **234/2:** Tatra 103, 220hp, diesel.

MAXIMUM SPEED **231:** 85km/h (52mph); **234/2:** 80km/h (50mph).

RANGE **231:** 300km (186 miles); **234/2:** 900km (559 miles).

CREW 4.

ARMAMENT **231:** 1 × 2cm KwK 30, 1 × 7·92mm MG; **234/2:** 1 × 5cm KwK 39/1, 1 × 7·92mm MG.

AMMUNITION **231:** 2 cm: 180 rds, MG: 2,100 rds; **234/2:** 5cm: 55 rds, MG: 1,050 rds.

TRENCH CROSSING 1·24m (4ft ½in).

TRACK WIDTH 0·5m (1ft 7¼in).

MAXIMUM ELEVATION **231:** 26°; **234/2:** 30°

FORDING DEPTH **231:** 1m (3ft 3in); **234/2:** 1·2m (3ft 11in).

Sd Kfz 251

Germany led the world in half-track design during the 1930s; the unsophisticated types developed in France, Britain and America were little more than trucks with the rear wheels replaced by tracked suspension units. The tracks on these vehicles were usually rubber or steel links, and steering was by the front wheels. By contrast the German half-tracks were engineered to the same high quality as tanks, with manganese webbed steel track shoes, interleaved torsion-bar suspension, and a Cletrac-type brake system so that the tracks also helped in steering the vehicle as the front wheels were turned.

All the infantry and artillery units for supporting the proposed panzer divisions were to be motorized and mechanized, and a whole family of half-track vehicles (from 1 ton to 18 tons) was designed for the purpose.

The Sd Kfz 11 was the 3-ton class vehicle, built and developed by Hanomag, and intended, in its basic form, to tow medium field artillery. With a top speed of 53km/h (33mph) and a maximum road range of 250km (155 miles), it was 5·5m (18ft) long, weighed 7 tons, and carried a crew of nine. Variants on this chassis included munitions carriers, smoke layers, and decontamination vehicles.

Armoured versions of the 1-ton and 3-ton class half-tracks were developed in 1939 specifically to equip the infantry of the Panzer-Grenadiers. One of the three infantry batallions in each panzer division was equipped with these armoured half-tracks, the other battalions having trucks or unarmoured half-tracks. These vehicles had the same chassis as the normal models, but were fitted with a well-shaped and angled armoured body. The most famous of all these was the Sd Kfz 251, built by Hanomag on the 3-ton chassis, with an armour basis of 12mm. In order to speed production, models which appeared in 1942 were simplified in shape at front and rear. Each vehicle carried a squad of ten infantrymen with their machine gun team. Another machine gun was fitted in a front shield on the vehicle – and the second gun could be pintle-mounted at the rear for AA use, though it was normally dismounted and carried by the troops.

The flak-gun version of the Sd Kfz 10 1-ton half-track had a 2cm AA gun mounted and the sides folded outwards to form a platform for the crew. Flak units were integral to every armoured formation and provided anti-aircraft defence in the field. The gun on this vehicle, which had a crew of seven, could also be used against ground targets.

Extensively used on the Russian front was the Sd Kfz 251/1, an armoured model with attachments for firing 28cm rockets. These were an inexpensive way of putting down a heavy, though inaccurate, barrage of fire during street fighting. The rockets, three a side, were dropped into the frames in their carrying cases, which then also became the launchers. The Sd Kfz 251/6 command vehicle (Kommandopanzerwagen) was used by the headquarters staff of armoured formations. It was virtually a mobile signal office with radio receiver and transmitter, associated bedstead aerial, cipher equipment and map tables.

The Sd Kfz 251/10, which was a platoon commander's vehicle, mounted an old 3·7cm Pak (anti-tank gun), added to the vehicle by utilizing an obsolescent field gun mount, less wheels and trail. This was a good way of making use of a redundant and otherwise obsolete weapon to give a degree of extra firepower to the Panzer-Grenadier's half-track platoon.

The Sd Kfz 251/7 was an engineer equipment vehicle. It carried a small assault bridge in sections for erecting over ditches, as well as a full range of demolition equipment and inflatable rubber assault boats. The bridge sections were carried in racks on the superstructure top. Other versions of the Hanomag vehicle included an armoured ambulance and a flame-throwing vehicle, while an SP with 75mm gun was also produced.

MODEL Sd Kfz 251.

COUNTRY OF ORIGIN Germany.

WEIGHT 8·9 tonnes (8·76 tons).

LENGTH 5·79m (19ft).

WIDTH 2·11m (6ft 11in).

HEIGHT 1·75m (5ft 9in).

GROUND CLEARANCE 0·30m (1ft).

ARMOUR 6–14·5mm.

ENGINES Maybach HL42 TRKM, 100hp, gasoline.

MAXIMUM SPEED 53km/h (33mph).

RANGE 200km (124 miles).

CREW 12.

ARMAMENT 2 × 7·92mm MG.

AMMUNITION 2,010 rds.

TRENCH CROSSING 1·98m (6ft 6in).

TRACK WIDTH 0·234m (9¼in).

FORDING DEPTH 0.6m (2ft).

The Sd Kfz 251 half-track was the most important
of German troop carrier vehicles and equipped
the leading Panzer-Grenadier battalions. One of 22
variants, the Sd Kfz 251/5 shown here was used as
a squad or section transport. The vehicle is from
9.Pz.Div., Russian Front, August 1941.

0   1   2 m

Gistudio – Tatangelo

Mitteler Schützenpanzerwagen Sd Kfz 251/5 Ausf B

The Sd Kfz 251 carried the elite Panzer-Grenadier armoured infantry. Their best-known weapon was the MP 38 machine pistol, carried by the men shown here.

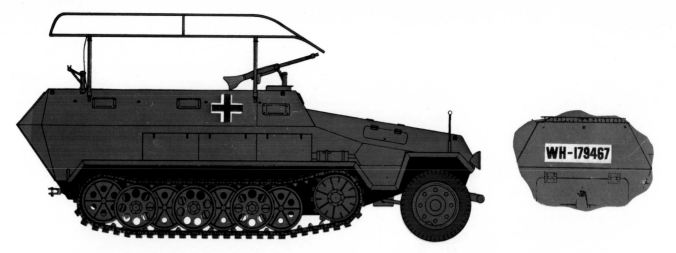

Above: Sd Kfz 251/3 Ausf A was a special signal vehicle version (Funkwagen). This vehicle was the personal command car of General Guderian in the French campaign of 1940.

Right: Sd Kfz 251/8 Ausf D armoured ambulance. This vehicle was used in the Ardennes offensive, winter 1944–5.

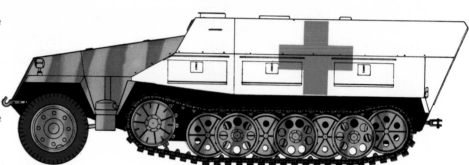

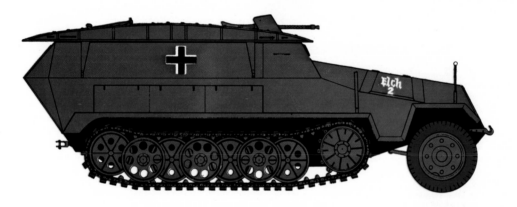

Sd Kfz 251/7 Ausf C assault engineer vehicle, Eastern Front, 1943.

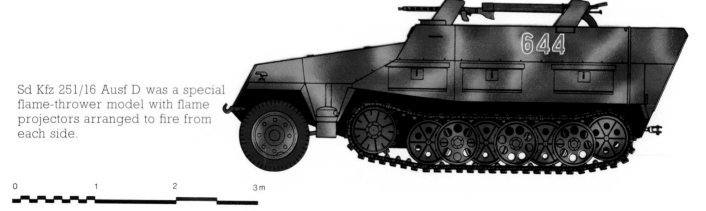

Sd Kfz 251/16 Ausf D was a special flame-thrower model with flame projectors arranged to fire from each side.

0   1   2   3 m

Gistudio – Tatangelo

156

Sd Kfz 251

Sd Kfz 251/9 Ausf D was a self-propelled gun model with 7·5cm short gun in a limited traverse mount.

Sd Kfz 251/1 Ausf D was the basic troop carrier version and the Ausf D type had simplified front and rear.

This Sd Kfz 251/10 Ausf B was the platoon commander's vehicle fitted with a 3·7cm anti-tank gun. The Ausf B was the early production model with faceted front and rear armour plates. This vehicle carries the palm and swastika marking of the Afrika Korps.

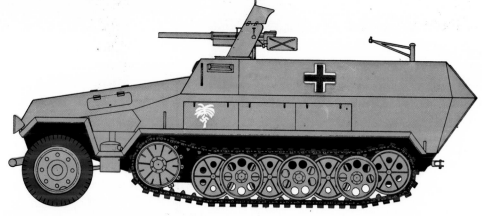

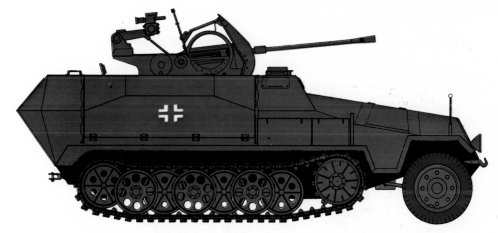

Sd Kfz 251/17 Ausf C was a special AA version with modified sides which folded outwards when the gun was in action. This one belonged to Luftwaffe Division 'Hermann Goering', a ground unit composed of Luftwaffe personnel.

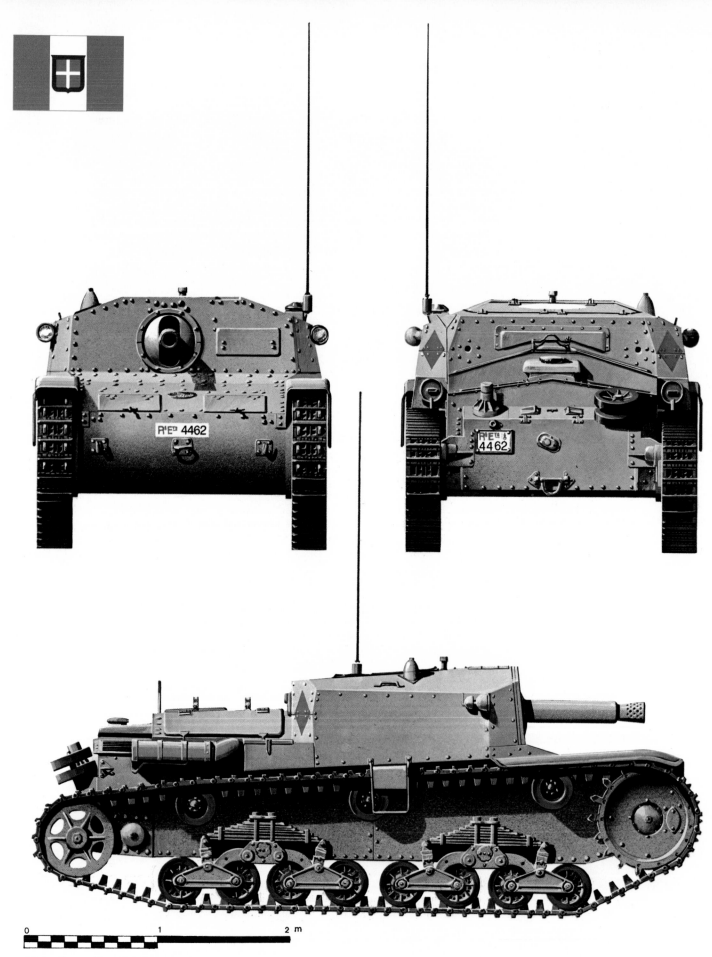

Gistudio – Claudio Tatangelo

Semovente da 75/18 M40

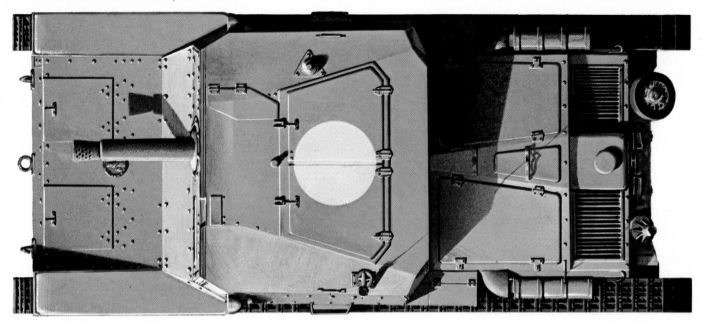

This Semovente da 75/18 was operated by DLIV Gruppo of the 'Littorio' Division. It was commanded by Capt Davide Beretta and was knocked out in the fighting at El-Alamein in October 1942. Though the M13/40 was not particularly successful as a tank, it gave rise to the development of this Semovente which was one of the best AFVs of its type to appear during World War 2. The Italian Inspectorate of Technical Services saw that an assault gun version of the M13/40 was a fairly straightforward adaptation, and a chassis was taken in hand for conversion as a prototype. A simple box-like shape replaced the original tank superstructure, and the Model 75/18 gun howitzer was fitted in a limited traverse housing slightly offset to the right. The overall height of the vehicle was substantially reduced as a result (to 1·8 metres), emphasizing one of the great tactical advantages of the assault gun, a low silhouette.

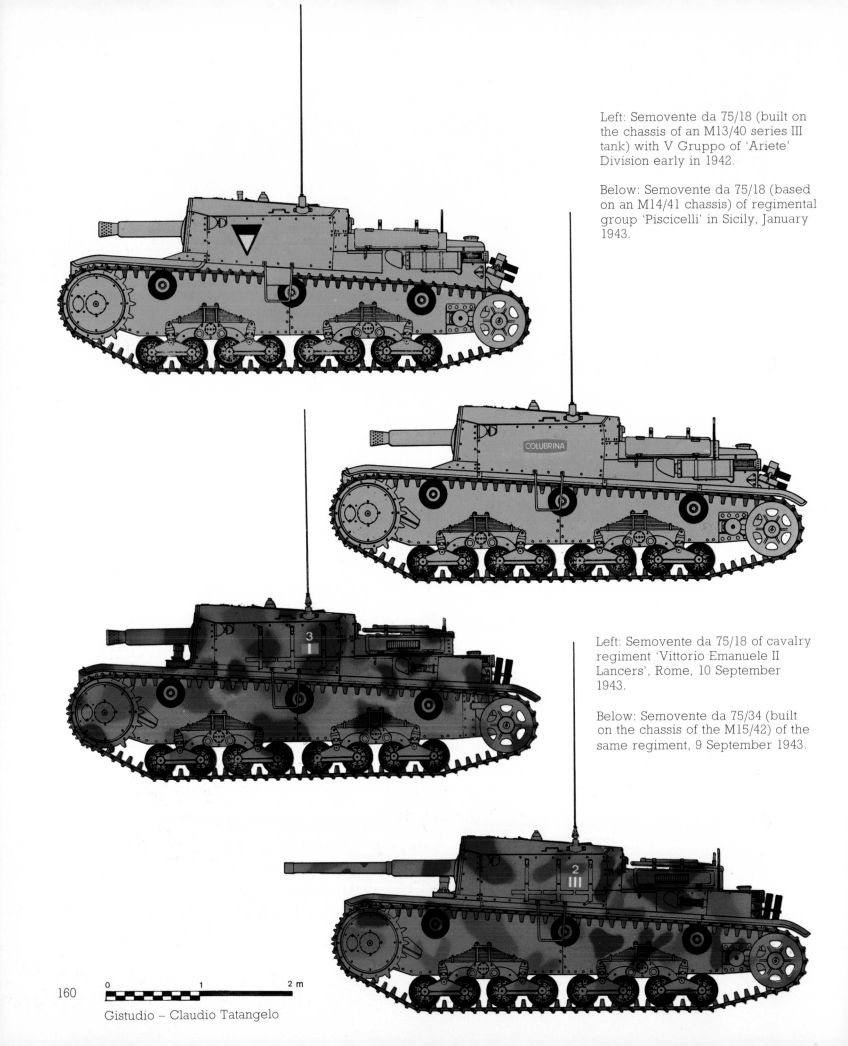

Left: Semovente da 75/18 (built on the chassis of an M13/40 series III tank) with V Gruppo of 'Ariete' Division early in 1942.

Below: Semovente da 75/18 (based on an M14/41 chassis) of regimental group 'Piscicelli' in Sicily, January 1943.

Left: Semovente da 75/18 of cavalry regiment 'Vittorio Emanuele II Lancers', Rome, 10 September 1943.

Below: Semovente da 75/34 (built on the chassis of the M15/42) of the same regiment, 9 September 1943.

Gistudio – Claudio Tatangelo

Semovente da 75/18

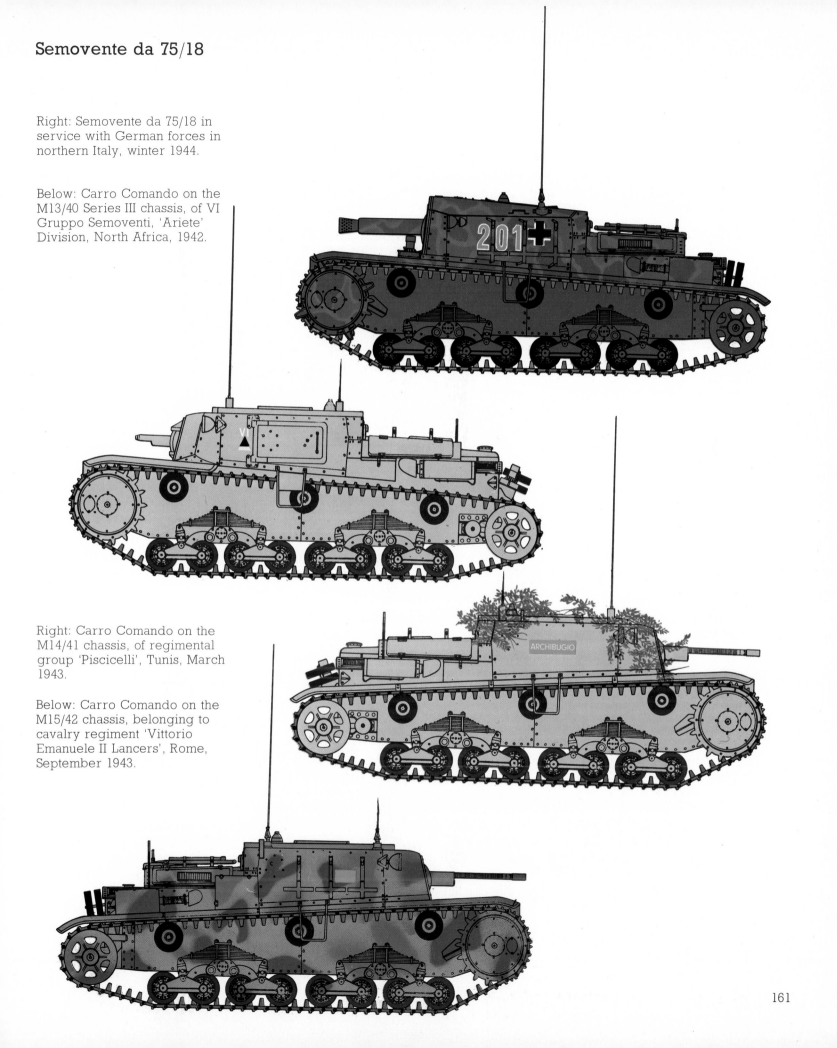

Right: Semovente da 75/18 in service with German forces in northern Italy, winter 1944.

Below: Carro Comando on the M13/40 Series III chassis, of VI Gruppo Semoventi, 'Ariete' Division, North Africa, 1942.

Right: Carro Comando on the M14/41 chassis, of regimental group 'Piscicelli', Tunis, March 1943.

Below: Carro Comando on the M15/42 chassis, belonging to cavalry regiment 'Vittorio Emanuele II Lancers', Rome, September 1943.

Semovente da 75/18

The Semovente was an assault gun development of the M13/40 tank. The prototype of the new vehicle, designated Semovente M40 da 75/18, was tested early in 1941 and production vehicles were ready later that year.

All the early vehicles were on the M13/40 chassis which had abbreviated track covers. As production proceeded, later vehicles were built on the M14/41 chassis with the improved engine. These were designated Semovente M41 da 75/18. In 1943 came a third production series based on the chassis of a lengthened improvement of the M14/41 – the M15/42. These later vehicles were now designated Semovente M42 da 75/18 and had full track covers and other detail refinements. In September 1943 production ceased.

As the Italian tanks were proving to be unsatisfactory, and in the absence of German replacement vehicles, the Semovente became the dominant type produced by the Italians (they had asked to produce German PzKpfw IIIs under licence but never went into production). A new variant was developed as a command vehicle for the Semovente groups. This was the Carro comando per reparto semovente da 75/18 (command vehicle for assault guns), which was essentially a basic vehicle lacking the 75mm gun. This was replaced by an 8mm Breda machine gun on the M13/40 chassis and a 13·2mm machine gun on the later M14/41s. The vehicle carried extra map tables and radio sets for the group commander.

In the closing stages of hostilities there were further and even better Semovente developments. The first, the M41 da 75/32 in which the 75/18 gun/howitzer was replaced by a 75/32 field gun with a much longer barrel, was a stop-gap of which about 25 only were built. The first few delivered went to an armoured cavalry division which fought against the Germans at the time of the armistice in September 1943. All were captured and used by the Germans in the confusion of the time. The next model was the Semovente M42M da 75/34, which carried the 75/34 gun –

the same long 75mm weapon which had been developed for a planned new tank, the P.40. The M42M prototype was ready in March 1943, when production was put in hand, but the armistice was signed before any could be used. Of the 90 built, some were seized by the Germans while others were used by the reformed Italian units which fought on the Allied side after the armistice.

All Italian tank production was dropped in favour of the Semovente in early 1943 and the production lines were kept busy bringing out the gradually improved models. For true infantry support a lengthened M15/42 chassis was developed, and this was used as a basis for a big new Semovente, the M42L (later M43) da 105/25. Dubbed the Dachshund, this had a greatly lengthened hull and chassis with extra suspension units, and the same 50mm frontal armour which had been successful on the earlier models. Only one group had the vehicle in service by the time of the armistice but a number were seized by the Germans then and others were built for the Germans later.

At the time of the armistice, a number of Semoventes of all sorts were seized in North Italy by the Germans who were forewarned that Italian troops were to surrender. A few of the 75/18 models had already been used and appreciated by German units in Libya. Captured Semoventes were handed over to Panzer-Grenadier units and they were used both in Italy and the South of France. The Germans made some modifications and re-works of their own. The German designations were, for example, StuG M40 (or M41) mit 75/18, depending on the model. The Carro comando vehicle was designated PzBefWg M42.

One further Semovente was the M41M da 90/53 which was a true SP gun with a 90mm AA weapon mounted at the rear of the vehicle in an open mount with shield. Finally there was a wholly German version, the M42L da 75/46, essentially the M42L da 105/25 with a German 75mm gun replacing the 105mm howitzer.

MODEL Semovente da 75/18.

COUNTRY OF ORIGIN Italy.

WEIGHT 13·1 tonnes (12·89 tons).

LENGTH 4·92m (16ft 2in).

WIDTH 2·2m (7ft 3in).

HEIGHT 1·85m (6ft).

GROUND CLEARANCE 0·38m (1ft 4in).

ARMOUR 10–30mm.

ENGINE SPA 8 TM 40, 125hp, diesel.

MAXIMUM SPEED 32km/h (20mph).

RANGE 200km (124 miles).

CREW 3.

ARMAMENT 1 × 75mm gun, 1 × 8mm MG.

AMMUNITION 75mm: 44 rds, MG: 1,104 rds.

TRENCH CROSSING 2m (6ft 6¾in).

TRACK WIDTH 0·3m (1ft).

MAXIMUM ELEVATION 22°.

FORDING DEPTH 1m (3ft 3½in).

M4 Sherman

While design work was carried out on the M3 in 1941, the American Armored Force Board drew up requirements for its successor with a 75mm gun in a fully traversing turret. Final M3 working drawings were completed in March 1941, and Rock Island Arsenal offered the Armored Force Board five suggested schemes for the M4 at a meeting the following month. The most straightforward scheme was to use the M3 medium chassis, and provide a completely new hull top, either cast or welded, with a central turret mounting the 75mm gun. Doors were provided in each side of the hull as in the M3.

On President Roosevelt's personal orders tank production schedules for 1942, provisionally set at 1,000 medium tanks a month, were doubled. To achieve this, additional production facilities were required and Pacific Car and Foundry, Fisher, Ford, and Federal Machine and Welder were added to the list of plants earmarked to build the new medium tank. In October 1941, the design was standardized as the Medium Tank M4 and plans were made to introduce the M4 on to the production line, in those plants building M3s, at some convenient point early in 1942. This would mean that M4 medium tanks would be built at a total of 11 plants in 1942. A major proposal was that a further purpose-built tank production plant be built on the lines of Detroit Arsenal. In September 1941 Fisher was asked to erect and operate this at Grand Blanc, Michigan.

The M4 pilot model was built by Lima Locomotive works in February 1941, differing from the T6 prototype principally in the elimination of the hull side doors. Full production in three plants, Lima, Pressed Steel, and Pacific Car and Foundry started the following month, all these initial production types being cast hull vehicles, designated M4A1. By the autumn of 1942 all other plants in the programme were in full production, and in October 1942, at the Battle of Alamein, the first M4 mediums went into action with British forces.

The M4 series was the most widely produced, most widely used, and most important of all tanks in service with American, British, and Allied forces in World War 2. While not the best Allied tank in qualitative terms, and certainly inferior in armour and hitting power to the best German and Soviet tanks, the M4 medium tank (popularly known by its British name of Sherman) had the virtues of simplicity of maintenance, reliability, speed, ruggedness, and an uncomplicated design. In terms of cost-effectiveness, the M4 Sherman was supremely suited to the needs of the hour, a fact reflected in the total output of more than 40,000 tanks (and associated AFVs) based on the M4 chassis in the years 1942–6. Shermans were used by every Allied nation in every armour role on every fighting front.

The Medium Tank M4 had the same basic chassis as the M3 medium, with vertical volute suspension, rear engine and front drive. Apart from very early models, the bogies were altered, however, so that the return rollers were set behind, instead of on top of, the spring units. Hull was either welded, cast, or welded with cast/rolled nose, while the 75mm gun was set in a simple cast turret and provided with a gyro-stabilizer as in the M3. Initially the engine was a Continental R-975 air-cooled radial type, but an ever-persistent shortage of this Wright-built power unit (which was essentially an aircraft engine and needed as such by the aero industry) forced the adoption of alternative engines, giving rise to the main production variants.

Main production types were M4 (Wright engine, welded hull), M4A1 (as M4 but with cast hull), M4A2 (as M4 but with GM diesel motor), M4A3 (as M4 but with Ford GAA engine), M4A4 (Chrysler engines, longer hull) and M4A6 (part cast hull). Late production tanks had the 76mm gun in M23 type turret, horizontal volute spring suspension, 58cm (23in) wide tracks, and ammunition 'wet' stowage. The British fitted a 17pdr gun to make the powerful Sherman Firefly of 1944, and there was a close support version with 105mm gun.

MODEL M4 Sherman.

COUNTRY OF ORIGIN USA.

WEIGHT 30·1 tonnes (29·6 tons).

LENGTH 5·9m (19ft 4in); **M4A4, M4A6:** 6·1m (19ft 10in).

WIDTH 2·6m (8ft 7in).

HEIGHT 2·74m (9ft).

GROUND CLEARANCE 0·43m (1ft 5in).

ARMOUR 25–50mm.

ENGINES **M4, M4A1:** 9-cylinder Continental R-975 CI, 400hp, gasoline; **M4A2:** 2 × GM 6-71, diesel; **M4A3:** Ford GAA V8, gasoline; **M4A4:** Chrysler WC Multibank, gasoline; **M4A6:** Caterpillar RD-1820 radial, diesel.

MAXIMUM SPEED 38km/h (24mph).

RANGE 160km (100 miles).

CREW 5.

ARMAMENT 1 × 75mm gun, 3 × ·30 cal. MG.

AMMUNITION 75mm: 97 rds; ·30 cal.: 4,750 rds.

TRENCH CROSSING 2·28m (7ft 6in).

TRACK WIDTH 0·58m (1ft 11in).

MAXIMUM ELEVATION 25°.

FORDING DEPTH 0·91m (3ft).

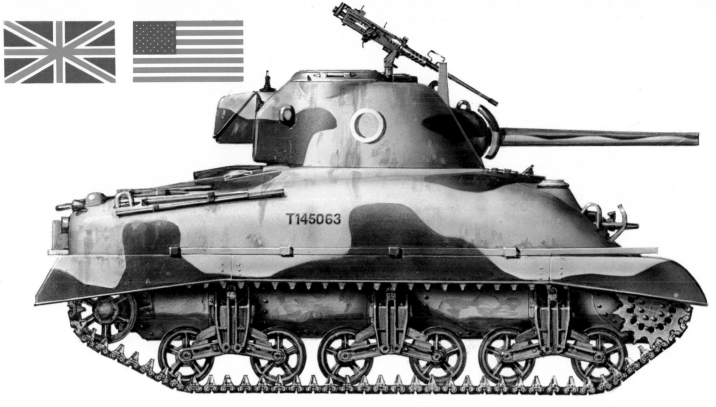

The Sherman was the classic American tank of World War 2, used by all Allied nations under Lend-Lease arrangements. Total production of all variants ran to 48,071 units, making it by far the most important of Allied AFVs. Numerous production models and special-purpose derivatives were built, and the basic tank was continually updated in armour and armament as World War 2 progressed. The example shown here is an early production Medium Tank M4A1, as issued to 'C' Squadron of the 9th Lancers ('The Bays'), of 2nd Armoured Brigade, 1st Armoured Division, of the 8th Army at the Battle of El-

Alamein in October 1942. The 'rhino' is the formation sign of 1st Armoured Division, '86' is the unit serial number, and '2' on the turret is the individual tank number in its squadron. The M4A1 was the first model of the series in service, being designated Sherman II by the British. It had a cast hull (most other models had a welded hull) and the early type had the return rollers of the suspension system mounted on top of the bogie brackets. Later vehicles had trailing return rollers. Medium Tanks M4 and M4A1 replaced the Medium Tank M3 series in production.

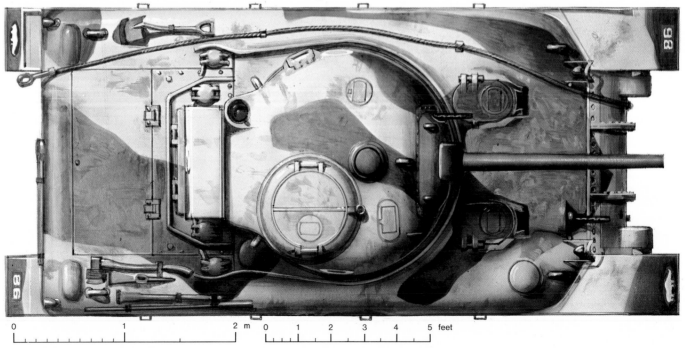

0   1   2 m   0 1 2 3 4 5 feet

Pino dell'Orco – Nicola Pignato

Medium Tank M4A1 Sherman

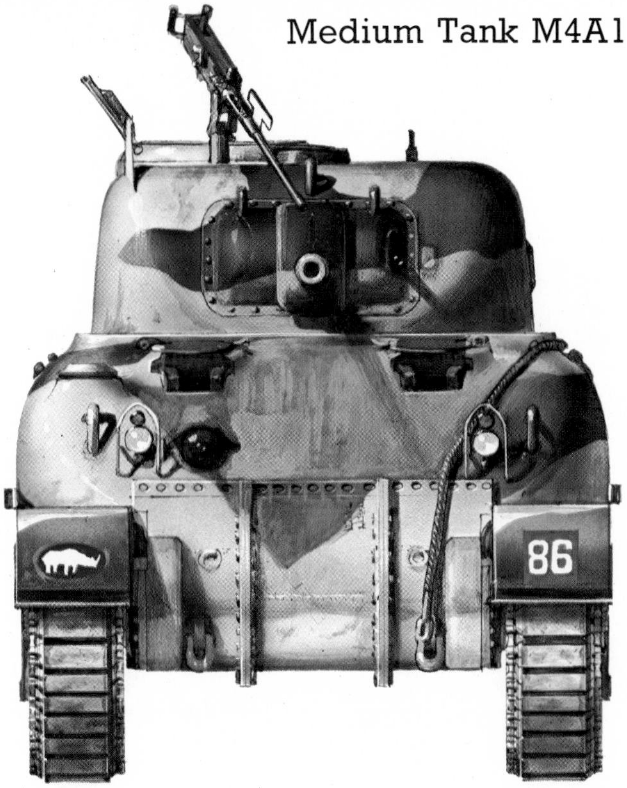
86

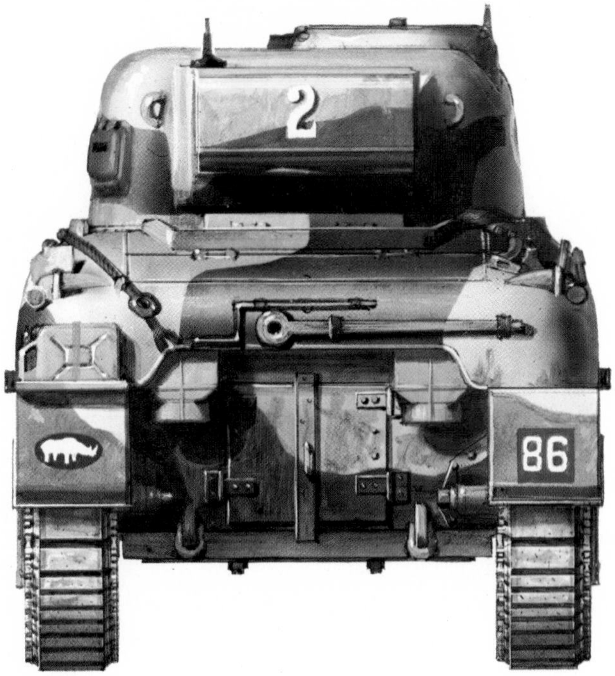
2
86

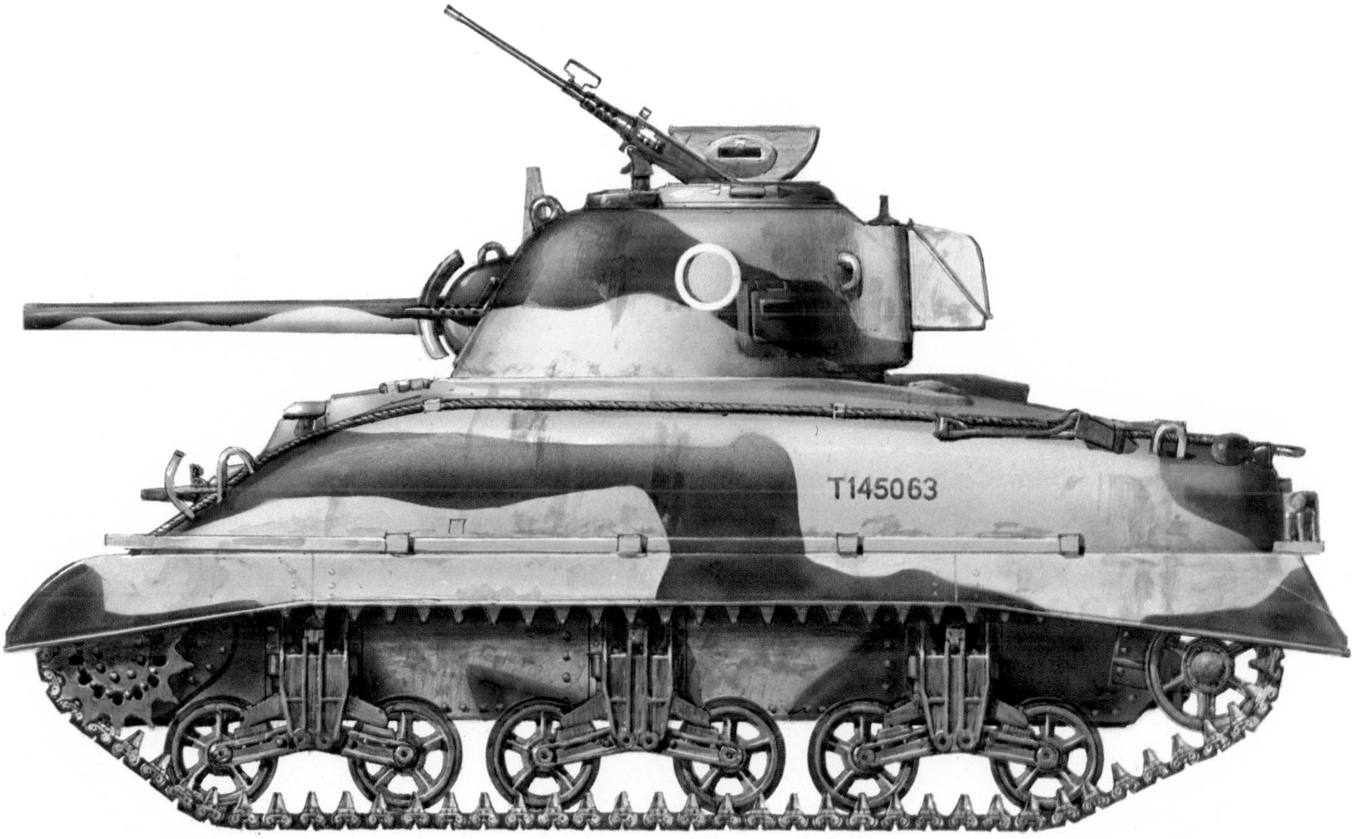
T145063

Medium Tank M4A2 was designated Sherman III by the British. This example took part in the Anzio landings in 1943 and belonged to a Canadian unit.

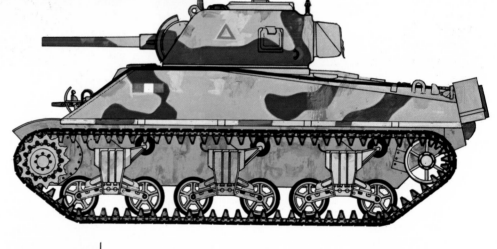

Right: Medium Tank M4A2, Sherman III, of the British 22nd Armoured Brigade, during the occupation of Naples.

Below: Medium Tank M4A3 with 105mm howitzer was produced as a close-support tank late in the war. It was designated Sherman IVB by the British. This example served in the immediate post-war period with the Italian Ariete armoured division.

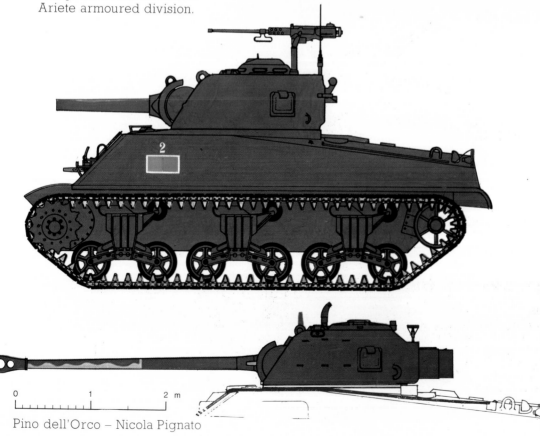

Below: The most powerfully armed of all Sherman variants was the British Sherman Firefly, a British conversion in which the 75mm gun was replaced by a British 17pdr. In order to do this the gun had to be mounted on its side, with an armoured extension to the turret rear to hold the radio which was displaced by the length of the breech. This conversion was first carried out late in 1943 and Sherman Firefly tanks were available for the Normandy landings in June 1944. As they were in short supply they were allocated in small numbers to each British armoured battalion in the assault divisions. Since they offered the biggest threat to German armour they were picked off first by German tanks. The artist Rex Whistler, then with Guards Armoured Division, devised the painting pattern shown to disguise the length of the barrel and make it look at a distance like a 75mm gun.

0   1   2 m

Pino dell'Orco – Nicola Pignato

M4 Sherman

Right: Medium Tank M4 of French 2nd Armoured Division (12th Armoured Regiment) in Alsace early in 1945. The M4 was designated Sherman I by the British.

Below: Designated Medium Tank M4A3 (76mm), this was the later production M4A3 which was made from late 1943. It was up-gunned by fitting the high-velocity long barrel M1 (later M1A1) 76mm gun in place of the original 75mm weapon, and a larger turret, originally developed for the T23 Medium Tank. was used to hold the bigger gun. The hull front was given a 47° slope both to increase frontal protection and simplify production.

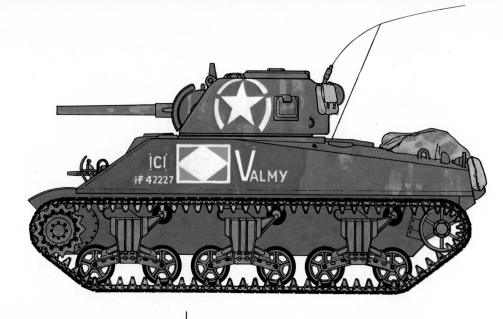

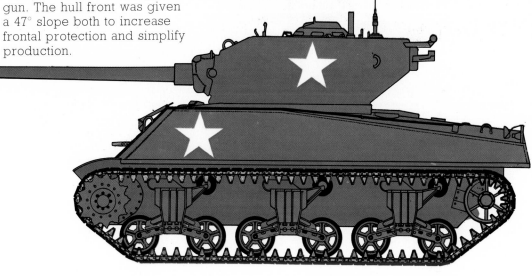

Below: The Sherman DD was a British development worked out by Nicholas Straussler. He started with a Tetrarch tank in 1941, then developed a Valentine version, before producing a design for the Sherman. The DD (Duplex Drive) system provided rear propellers which could be geared to a power take-off, for propulsion in water. In the drawing they are shown folded up and disconnected. Flotation was provided by a folding canvas screen, held up by air tubes and iron hoops to the height shown. This gave sufficient buoyancy for the vehicle to 'swim' ashore under its own power. With the screens lowered and propellers disconnected, the vehicle could fight as a gun tank. Several battalions of 79th Armoured Division were equipped with Sherman DDs for the Normandy landings in 1944, and some vehicles were supplied to the US Army at this time.

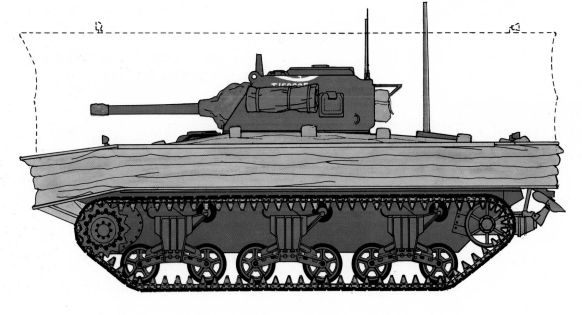

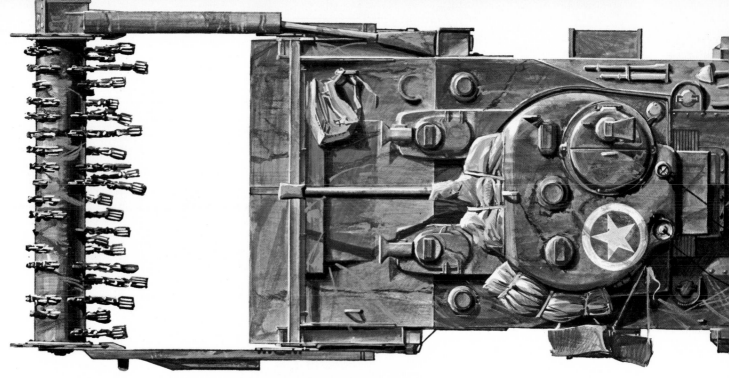

The Sherman Crab Mk I of 1943 was a British conversion of the M4A4, Sherman Mk V, the type most widely used by the British Army. The heavy rotor arms were driven by a power take-off from the main engine, and the arms could be lifted hydraulically to clear the ground. Tanks swept a cleared line by moving in echelon in twos or sometimes threes, with the remaining vehicle of each troop standing to give covering fire. Marker lights were carried on the back of each vehicle so that the driver of the following vehicle could keep station. Lane markers, releasing either chalk dust or flagged metal spigots, were carried at the rear side of each tank to indicate the lane which the tank was just clearing. The Crab Mk II differed in having a contouring device to give superior mine sweeping ability on undulating ground. The example illustrated belonged to the Westminster Dragoons, one of the special flail units attached to 79th Armoured Division whose bull's head formation sign is shown. A few Crabs were supplied by Britain to the US Army in 1944–5.

City of Gloucester

0   1   2 m

Gistudio-Tatangelo

Sherman Crab Mk I

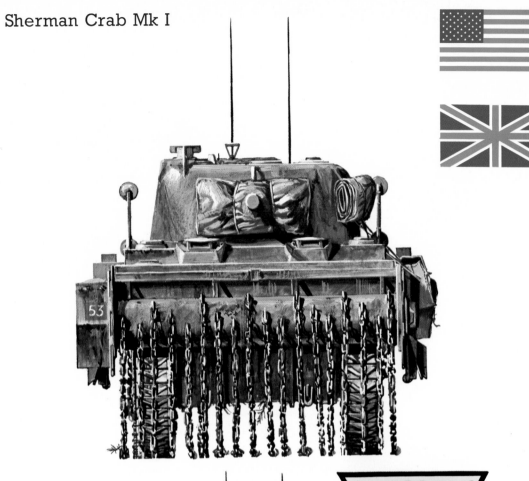

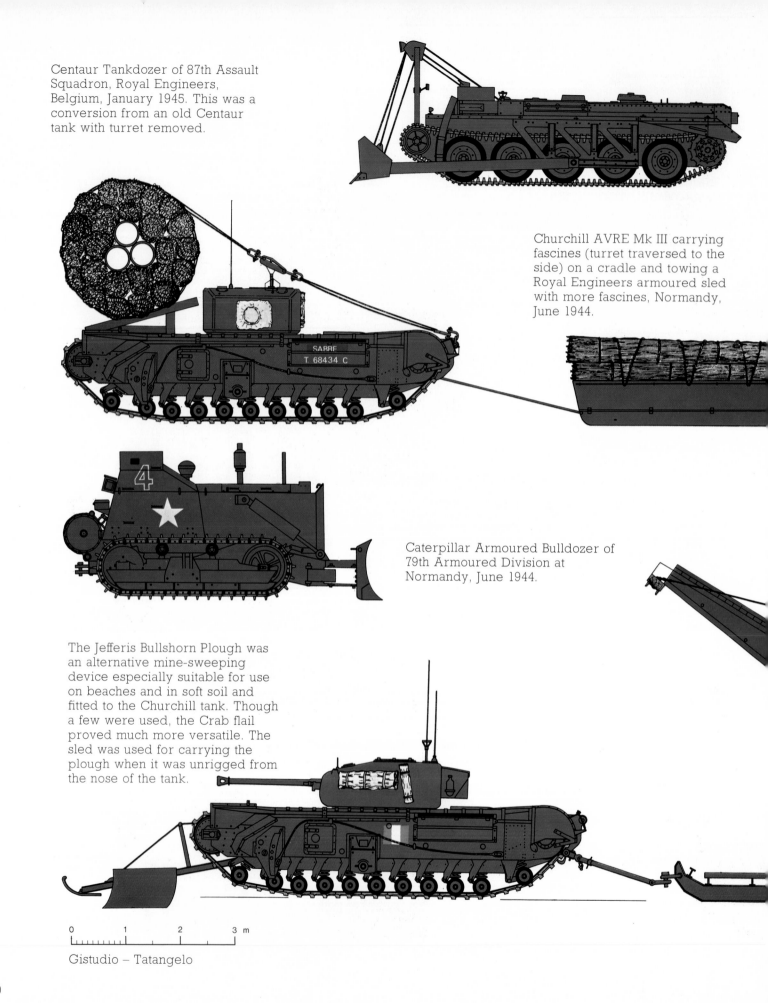

Centaur Tankdozer of 87th Assault Squadron, Royal Engineers, Belgium, January 1945. This was a conversion from an old Centaur tank with turret removed.

Churchill AVRE Mk III carrying fascines (turret traversed to the side) on a cradle and towing a Royal Engineers armoured sled with more fascines, Normandy, June 1944.

SABRE
T. 68434 C

Caterpillar Armoured Bulldozer of 79th Armoured Division at Normandy, June 1944.

The Jefferis Bullshorn Plough was an alternative mine-sweeping device especially suitable for use on beaches and in soft soil and fitted to the Churchill tank. Though a few were used, the Crab flail proved much more versatile. The sled was used for carrying the plough when it was unrigged from the nose of the tank.

0   1   2   3 m

Gistudio – Tatangelo

Allied special purpose vehicles

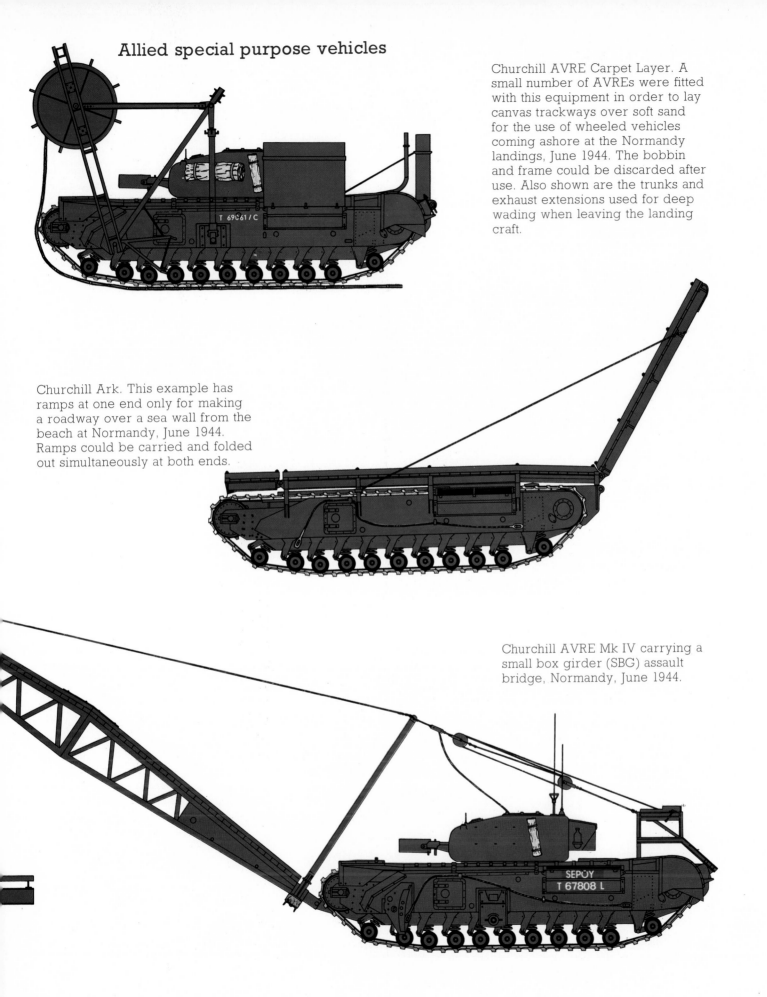

Churchill AVRE Carpet Layer. A small number of AVREs were fitted with this equipment in order to lay canvas trackways over soft sand for the use of wheeled vehicles coming ashore at the Normandy landings, June 1944. The bobbin and frame could be discarded after use. Also shown are the trunks and exhaust extensions used for deep wading when leaving the landing craft.

Churchill Ark. This example has ramps at one end only for making a roadway over a sea wall from the beach at Normandy, June 1944. Ramps could be carried and folded out simultaneously at both ends.

Churchill AVRE Mk IV carrying a small box girder (SBG) assault bridge, Normandy, June 1944.

Allied special purpose vehicles

A major contribution to tank development made by the British during the war years was in the production of special purpose vehicles – tanks adapted to perform specific battlefield roles and popularly known as 'Funnies'. British ingenuity was seen in a whole succession of strange designs intended to facilitate the advance of armoured divisions in the amphibious invasion of the Continent and the subsequent advance into Germany.

The paramount reason for these developments was the need to breach the notorious 'West Wall', the formidable beach defence system built along the Channel coast of France by the Germans in 1940–42. One particular type of equipment shown to be lacking was a protected vehicle for the engineers engaged in clearing obstacles; the Canadian engineers had sustained heavy casualties while trying to breach the sea wall and clear other obstructions on the Dieppe beaches.

The Churchill tank was considered the most suitable vehicle for conversion. Its side (or pannier) escape doors were also at a more convenient height for access and the vehicle offered armour protection superior to that of the Ram or Sherman. By December 1942 the first prototype had been converted from a Churchill II, in which all ammunition bins were removed as well as the co-driver's seat, the turret basket and main armament. A mock-up of a spigot mortar was mounted in the turret front. Work on the actual mortar which was to arm this vehicle was commenced in September 1942. To be known as the Petard, it was to be capable of fitment in the 2pdr mounting of the Churchill tank. The Petard's projectile was given the name of 'Flying Dustbin'.

In December 1943 the prototype Churchill AVRE (Armoured Vehicle Royal Engineers) production vehicle was made ready by Cockbridge and Co. of Ipswich who had been appointed to prepare the necessary production drawings and to manufacture 475 AVRE conversion kits.

Early in 1944 it was decided to form and equip three RE regiments as armoured assault regiments for participation in Operation Overlord, the Normandy landings. These regiments, each with an establishment of approximately 60 AVREs, formed the 1st Assault Brigade, RE, of the 79th Armoured Division which had been formed to train and administrate all special purpose armour taking part in the invasion. At the same time, it was decided that these tanks should be capable of being fitted with various devices such as fascines, bridges and mine ploughs.

The Matilda Baron was an early type of mine-clearing tank developed in Britain with Bedford truck engines driving the rotor arms. A further improved type was the Scorpion fitted to both the Crusader and Sherman. This type entered service in 1943 but was not widely used in action, being superseded by the Sherman Crab which had power take-off to drive the flails.

Even though there was no official demand for the tank flame-thrower, work was carried out by the Petroleum Warfare Department (PWD) to develop trailer-type equipment. This PWD model fulfilled the requirements of the War Office and the Crocodile, as it was to be called, was subsequently officially adopted. Prompted by the need for this equipment in Operation Overlord, scheduled for the following spring, an order was placed for 250 Crocodiles in August 1943 despite the fact that normal troop trials had not taken place with the prototype vehicles. By October the production of six prototypes was going ahead, but it was then decided to modify the design to enable the flame-thrower to be fitted to the improved Churchill Mk VII which was just in production. It was now necessary that the flame-throwing equipment could be fitted to any Mk IV or VII Churchill by unit personnel in the field. These tanks were built ready to 'accept' complete Crocodile sets of parts. Only the Mk VII saw service in the role.

The DD (Duplex Drive) equipment was a flotation device invented by engineer Nicholas Straussler as a means of converting a standard tank into a temporary amphibious vehicle for sea or river crossing. The equipment was first tested in June 1941 on a Tetrarch light tank, and production was started during 1942 on DD equipment for its adaptation to the Valentine tank. These vehicles were later relegated to a training role, a few being used operationally in Italy during 1945. By April 1943 the DD equipment had been developed for fitment to the Sherman tank, the vehicles used in the DD role undergoing various modifications that included the fitting of a sprocket rear idler wheel and assemblies to drive the propulsion unit.

The other important type was the bridging vehicle. While some experiments were carried out before the war, it was not until after Dieppe that serious efforts were made to produce bridging vehicles in quantity. The following principal types were produced:

Ark Mk I: Ark stood for 'armoured ramp carrier' and the original Ark was a turretless Churchill with trackways along the top and ramps front and rear which could be lowered to complete a bridge. Considered to be expendable, the tank drove into the gap to be spanned and stayed there if necessary.

Ark Mk II: This had wider trackways on one side to allow smaller vehicles (eg Jeeps) to cross. The 'Italian Pattern' version had ramps made from US-type bridge sections and were built by and for units serving in Italy in 1943–4.

Sherman Ark II: This was a Sherman conversion in Italy in similar style to the Churchill, though few were made.

Churchill Bridgelayer: This was a conversion with a bridge capable of carrying up to 60 tons, and hydraulic launching equipment in the original fighting compartment. The 9·1m (30ft) bridge was launched horizontally by a pivoted arm. These vehicles were used for many years post-war, being very successful. Other variants were the Churchill Mobile Bailey and Skid Bailey, essentially Bailey bridge sections adapted for pushing or pulling by Churchill AVRE towing vehicles.

M3/M5 Stuart

The Light Tank M3 Stuart was an improved version of the M2A4 designed at Rock Island Arsenal in the spring of 1940. It incorporated lessons learned from the tank fighting in Europe in the 1939–40 campaigns. The main requirement was for increased armour thickness, but this in turn called for stronger suspension. Front armour was increased to 38mm (51mm on the nose), the vision ports in the turret sides were removed, and a large trailing idler was fitted to increase ground contact. Other changes included a lengthened rear superstructure and thicker armour on the engine covers as a precaution against strafing from the air. The M3 was approved and standardized in July 1940. It entered production in March 1941 at American Car and Foundry, and was introduced immediately after completion of the M2A4 contract.

Several other improvements were made during production, first of them being a welded turret, replacing the riveted type, which was developed in late 1940 and introduced almost immediately in March 1941. This change was mainly to reduce weight, though it also stopped the danger of 'popping' rivets in event of a hit. Further change was introduced in early 1941 with a welded/cast homogeneous rounded turret replacing the multi-faced turret used until then. From mid-1941 a gyro-stabilizer was fitted for the gun and in the autumn of 1941, following British experience with M3 light tanks in the North African desert fighting, two external fuel tanks – capacity 114 litres (25 gallons) each – were introduced to increase the range. From early 1942 an all-welded hull was adopted, and to ease engine supply problems, 500 M3 light tanks were completed with Guiberson T1020 diesel engines replacing the standard Continental gasoline engine. These vehicles were designated M3 (Diesel), and were identical externally to the standard M3.

A further improved model was designed, tested, approved and standardized in August 1941. This had the cupola removed to reduce overall height, a gyro-stabilizer for the gun, power traverse for the turret, and a turret basket. Designated M3A1, it was introduced to the American Car and Foundry production line in June 1942 to follow on the M3 which finally went out of production in August 1942. Another change in the M3A1 was the removal of the two sponson machine guns carried in the M3. These were fired remotely by the driver but proved to be of limited value, being finally sacrificed to reduce weight and increase interior stowage. The British had already removed these guns from many of the M3s delivered to them.

The final production type, the M3A3, represented a radical change, with a new all-welded hull enlarged by extending the side sponsons and the driver's compartment forward and upward. This gave room for extra fuel tanks and increased ammunition stowage. Sandshields (a lesson from the desert fighting) were added and many other small changes were made. Standardized in August 1942, the M3A3 entered production in early 1943.

Meanwhile, a further related model had appeared – Light Tank M5. This stemmed from a suggestion by the Cadillac car firm to the Ordnance Department that they should try the M3 light tank with twin Cadillac engines installed and the commercial Cadillac Hydramatic transmission which was produced for automobiles. In late 1941, a standard M3 was converted as a trials vehicle (the M3E2) to test the idea and proved most successful. It made a faultless trial run of 800km (500 miles), and proved easy to drive and smooth to operate. Because of the continual shortage of Continental radial engines, the Cadillac-modified vehicle was approved for production and standardized as the Light Tank M5 in 1942.

In order to fit the twin Cadillac engines, the rear engine covers were stepped up. But the hull was otherwise similar in shape to that of the welded M3A1 apart from a sloping nose. The M5A1 was an improved model to the standard of the M3A3.

MODELS M3/M5 Stuart.

COUNTRY OF ORIGIN USA.

WEIGHT **M3:** 12·5 tonnes (12·3 tons); **M5:** 15·2 tonnes (15 tons).

LENGTH **M3:** 4·5m (14ft 10in); **M5:** 4·33m (14ft 2½in).

WIDTH **M3:** 2·23m (7ft 4in); **M5:** 2·24m (7ft 4½in).

HEIGHT **M3:** 2·51m (8ft 3in); **M5:** 2·29m (7ft 6½in).

GROUND CLEARANCE 0·40m (1ft 4in).

ARMOUR **M3:** 21–55mm; **M5:** 12–67mm.

ENGINES **M3:** 7-cylinder Continental Radial, 250hp, gasoline; **M5:** Twin Cadillac, 121hp, gasoline.

MAXIMUM SPEED **M3:** 56km/h (35mph); **M5:** 64km/h (40mph).

RANGE **M3:** 112km (70 miles); **M5:** 160km (100 miles).

CREW 4.

ARMAMENT **M3:** 1 × 37mm gun, 5 × ·30 cal. MG; **M5:** 1 × 37mm gun, 2 × ·30 cal. MG.

AMMUNITION **M3:** 37mm: 103 rds, MG: 8,720 rds; **M5:** 37mm: 123 rds, MG: 6,250 rds.

TRENCH CROSSING **M3:** 1·82m (6ft); **M5:** 1·62m (5ft 4in).

TRACK WIDTH 0·29m (11½in).

MAXIMUM ELEVATION 20°.

FORDING DEPTH 0·91m (3ft).

Light Tank M3A1 of the US 1st Armored Division in North Africa in January 1943. At this time the divisional commander was General Patton. The 1st and 13th Armored Battalions were included in this division from which 'El Diablo' came. The British designation for the M3A1 was Stuart III and it was also popularly called the 'Honey'.

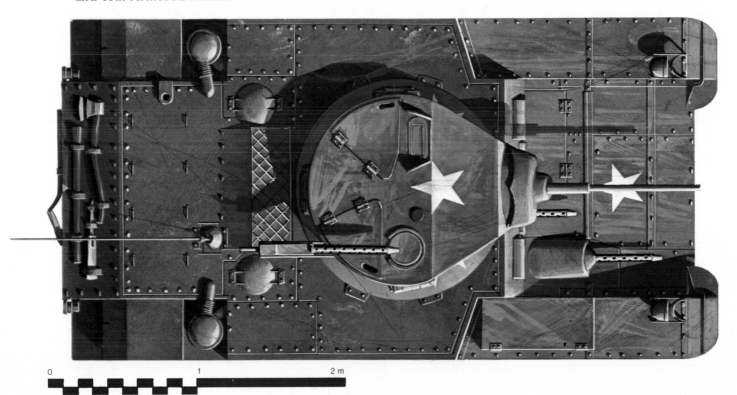

Light Tank M3A1 (Stuart III)

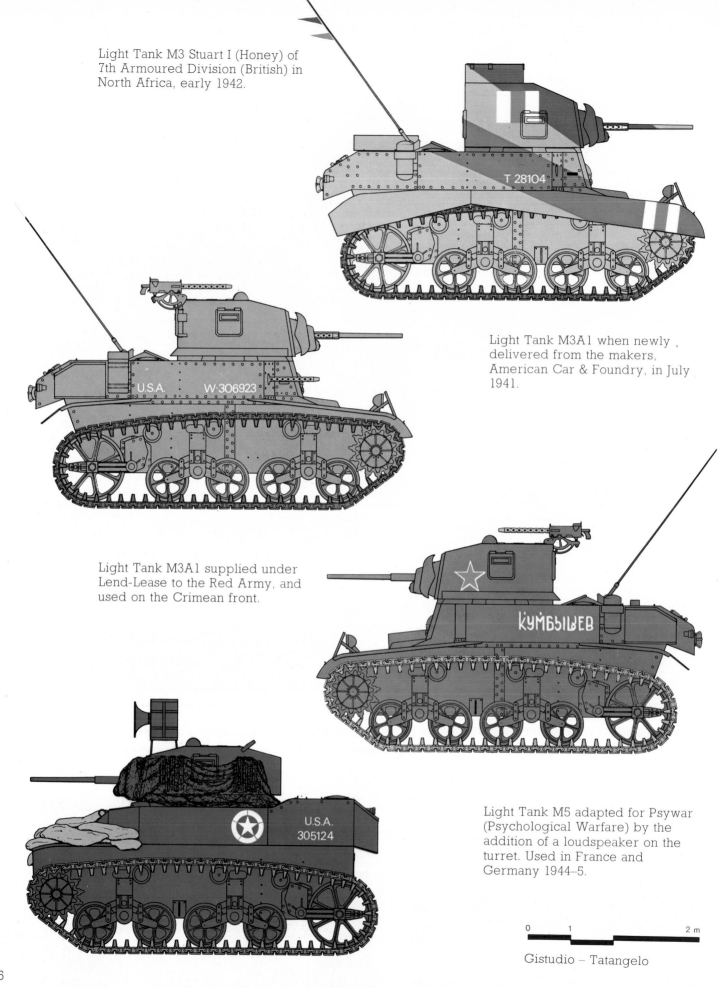

Light Tank M3 Stuart I (Honey) of 7th Armoured Division (British) in North Africa, early 1942.

Light Tank M3A1 when newly delivered from the makers, American Car & Foundry, in July 1941.

Light Tank M3A1 supplied under Lend-Lease to the Red Army, and used on the Crimean front.

Light Tank M5 adapted for Psywar (Psychological Warfare) by the addition of a loudspeaker on the turret. Used in France and Germany 1944–5.

0   1   2 m

Gistudio – Tatangelo

M3/M5 Stuart

Reconnaissance Car T8E1, one of a
limited number of turretless M5s
produced in 1944. Others of this
sort were converted by removing
turrets from existing tanks.

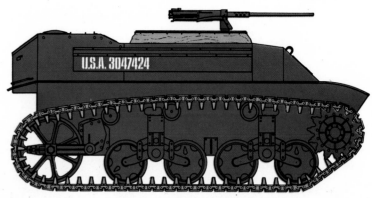

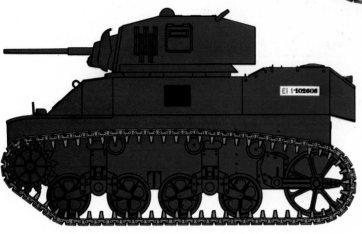

Light Tank M5 of the Italian
'Montebello Lancers' regiment,
post-war.

75mm Howitzer Motor Carriage
M8, France 1944. These vehicles
equipped the HQ companies of
American armoured battalions.

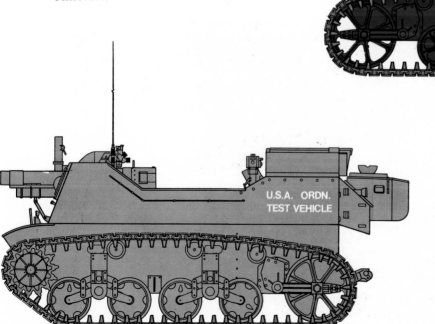

Howitzer Motor Carriage T82 was
an experimental conversion of an
M5 with a 105mm howitzer.

The German Sturmgeschütz III was one of the most successful German AFVs of World War 2. It arose from an original concept of the pre-war panzer divisions, whereby a special vehicle for infantry support work was planned. In the war years the StuG III was rapidly developed and up-gunned, and was used both in its original role as an assault gun and also as a tank destroyer. The vehicle illustrated in four-view is a StuG 40 which was operated in France in 1943. The last drawing (opposite) shows a StuG III Ausf G which operated on the Eastern Front in 1944.

0   1   2 m

Sturmgeschütz III Ausf G

This StuG III Ausf G shows many characteristics of the later model assault guns. The gun is held in a 'saukopf' (pig's head) cast mantlet; the skirt armour plates are fitted (these were to protect the suspension from hollow charge projectiles such as bazooka rounds); there is a shield to the machine gun on the superstructure roof; and foliage is used extensively for concealment in an ambush position. This vehicle is from a Panzer-Grenadier unit in Normandy, summer 1944.

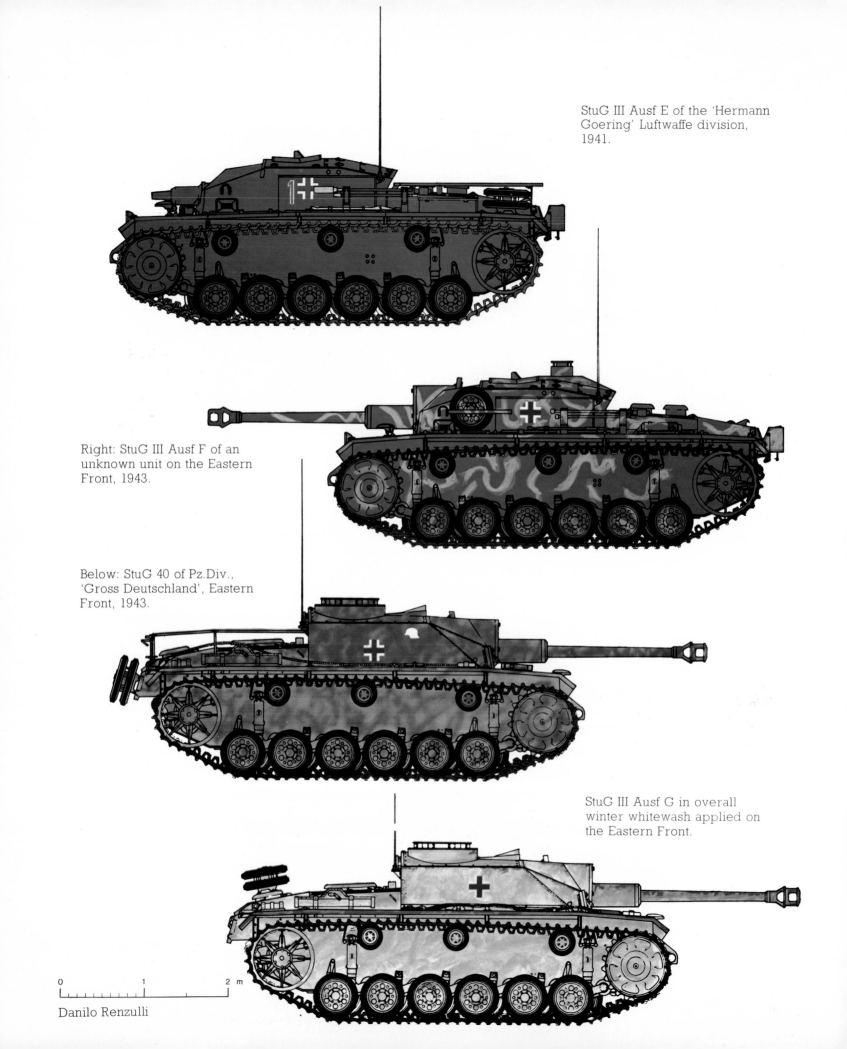

StuG III Ausf E of the 'Hermann Goering' Luftwaffe division, 1941.

Right: StuG III Ausf F of an unknown unit on the Eastern Front, 1943.

Below: StuG 40 of Pz.Div., 'Gross Deutschland', Eastern Front, 1943.

StuG III Ausf G in overall winter whitewash applied on the Eastern Front.

0   1   2 m

Danilo Renzulli

Sturmgeschütz III

StuG III Ausf G of the Finnish
Army, 1944.

StuG III Ausf G with 105mm
howitzer, Kursk, 1943.

StuG III Ausf G of 1.SS-Pz.
Div., Belgium 1944. This is a
late vehicle with 'saukopf'
mantlet.

StuG III Ausf G of 287
Abteilung, Caucasus Front,
1943.

Sturmgeschütz III

Part of the original concept of the German panzer divisions in 1936 was the provision of an infantry support vehicle. This would be based on a standard tank chassis, but with its gun mounted low in the superstructure on a limited traverse and without a turret. Other factors apart, such a vehicle would be simpler to produce than a tank and would have a lower overall height. A prototype series was built based on the chassis and mechanical gear of the new PzKpfw III tank. The gun was the low velocity short 7·5cm StuK infantry weapon. The superstructure was turtle-like in appearance and the overall height of the vehicle was lower than that of a soldier. The armour on the front and the superstructure was thicker than that of the PzKpfw III.

After successful trials an initial production order was placed, and the first 30 had been built by early 1940 when they took part with great success in the French campaign. This first model was designated StuG III Ausf A. The Ausf B model, which had mechanical improvements but was structurally similar to the Ausf A, ran to 320 examples built in the June 1940–May 1941 period.

Changes came with the StuG III Ausf C and Ausf D, which had altered front armour on the superstructure and better gun sights. Some vehicles were fitted as command vehicles with added armoured boxes on the superstructure sides for radio installation. Only 200 Ausf D vehicles were built and most were used on the Russian Front although three Ausf D vehicles were sent to North Africa. The StuG III Ausf E was in production from late 1941 to March 1942; it had increased stowage in armoured panniers and further revisions to armour layout and superstructure.

StuG III Ausf F was more correctly designated 7·5cm StuG 40, and it was the model which introduced the long 7·5cm StuK 40 gun in place of the short 7·5cm weapon. Hitler suggested this re-arming, and the adoption of thicker armour. As a result the new vehicle began to roll off the production lines in March 1942 and over 350 were built in the next six months, later ones being fitted with the longer L/48 gun. The mantlet was redesigned in this model and roof fans were installed to clear the firing fumes. The next model, the StuG 40 Ausf F/8, of which 334 were built, had alterations to the hull bringing it mechanically to the standards of the PzKpfw III Ausf J. Hull armour thickness was increased to 50mm and extra armour was bolted to the nose. The 7·5cm StuG 40 Ausf G (or StuG III Ausf G) was the major production type with no less than 7,720 being built in the December 1942–March 1943 period. New superstructure, extra front armour, a cupola, machine gun shield and sometimes side skirts (anti-bazooka shields) were fitted. Later vehicles had the fabricated mantlet replaced by a cast saukopf (sow's head) design. Some late vehicles of this type were used to control Goliath remote-control explosive tanks, and had extra radio equipment for this task. The StuG 40 Ausf G was a major German type very widely used.

Concurrent with the StuG 40 Ausf G was the 10·5cm StuH 42, of which more than 1,200 were built from October 1942 until the end of the war. This was an excellent close support gun and a true assault gun where the other models were now more strictly speaking tank destroyers. Further variants on the basic design were mainly to supplement it. There was the StuG III (F1) flame-thrower with a flame projector replacing the gun. Later some old vehicles had the gun removed and the embrasure plated over for use as munitions carriers.

One further and unsuccessful variant – only 24 were built – was the Sturm-Infantrie Geschütz 33 B, which mounted the 15cm SiG 33 in a large high superstructure. However, a company of these vehicles was used at the battle of Stalingrad.

The Russians also made a type of assault gun based on captured PzKpfw IIIs. They removed the turret, added a big superstructure, and mounted their 7·62cm gun, which was the same as that on the T-34.

MODEL Sturmgeschütz III.

COUNTRY OF ORIGIN Germany.

WEIGHT 22·3 tonnes (22 tons).

LENGTH 5·49m (18ft).

WIDTH 2·95m (9ft 8in).

HEIGHT 1·94m (6ft 4in).

GROUND CLEARANCE 0·36m (1ft 2in).

ARMOUR 11–50mm.

ENGINE Maybach HL 120 TRM, 300hp, gasoline.

MAXIMUM SPEED 40km/h (25mph).

RANGE 164km (102 miles).

CREW 4.

ARMAMENT 1 × 7·5cm StuK gun.

AMMUNITION 44 rds.

TRENCH CROSSING 2·3m (7ft 6in).

TRACK WIDTH 0·4m (1ft 4in).

MAXIMUM ELEVATION 20°.

FORDING DEPTH 0·8m (2ft 8in); later models 1m (3ft 3in).

Sturmgeschütz IV, Jagdpanzer IV and Sturmpanzer IV

After the general acceptance of the original assault gun, the firm of Alkett suggested a heavy assault version of the PzKpfw IV, essentially a vehicle with a heavily armoured box-like structure on the chassis and the running gear of the existing PzKpfw IV. A 10·5cm StuH 42 was fitted in a limited traverse mount and the superstructure had no less than 100mm of armour (at 40°) at the front, with 50mm at the sides. The frontal hull armour was 80mm thick (though the earliest vehicles had 100mm), this being achieved by bolting further armour to the original tank nose plates. The driver had an extended armoured housing with the same sort of sliding shutter vision slit as the Tiger tank. On later vehicles this was dispensed with, and the driver had a periscope instead. Also on the later production vehicles there was the addition of a ball-mounted machine gun on the right side of the front superstructure, as well as a cupola on the roof for the commander – early vehicles merely had a hatch.

Hitler ordered its immediate production because he considered that the vehicle was ideal for the close fighting being experienced in streets and towns on the Eastern front, where the Soviet Army was showing stiff and determined resistance. The very heavy armour protection of the vehicle would be useful in these conditions. By February 1943 production was ordered, with 40 vehicles to be ready for May when the summer offensives would begin. The first unit equipped with the new vehicle was in action in the great Kursk battle. The type was named Sturmpanzer IV Brummbär (Grizzly Bear), and production continued until the war's end. Most were built on the chassis of the PzKpfw IV Ausf G though some were built on earlier chassis.

Following the success of the original StuG III assault gun/tank destroyer, a test was made to see if the low superstructure being mass-produced for the StuG III (which was based on the PzKpfw III chassis), could be fitted to the PzKpfw IV chassis. This proved feasible and, as StuG III production had been badly disrupted by the bombing of the Alkett factory, Krupp was asked in December 1943 to produce this type, as the StuG IV, using the PzKpfw IV chassis already in production. As the PzKpfw IV was longer than the PzKpfw III, it was necessary to modify the body by making an extended armoured cover for the driver's position, and plating in other areas of the hull to fit the new superstructure. The driver's cover section was given an access hatch and two periscopes. In some later vehicles a remote-control machine gun was mounted on the roof instead of the manually operated version, and 15cm (6in) concrete was sometimes added to the superstructure front as additional armour. This vehicle, with its 7·5cm StuK 40 L/48 gun, was a very successful type, albeit an extemporization, and more than 1,000 were built.

As a complete replacement for the StuG III, an entirely new design was produced on the PzKpfw IV chassis. This was the Jagdpanzer IV (Sd Kfz 162) which had a new low superstructure of well-sloped shape with the original PzKpfw IV nose altered to allow for the slope of the low front plate. A prototype was approved in December 1943 and immediate production was undertaken by Vomag. The original armoured front was 60mm thick, and was later increased to 80mm. The long 7·5cm Pak L/48 gun was fitted, having a heavy cast saukopf (pig's head) mantlet. So important was this fine vehicle considered that, from May 1944, Vomag ceased to make PzKpfw IVs and concentrated only on Jagdpanzer IVs. Over 750 were built, the first being in service in March 1944. A variation of this vehicle was the Panzer IV/70, made by Niebelungenwerke, which was essentially the Jagdpanzer IV superstructure placed on the chassis and lower hull of a PzKpfw IV. As the original nose was retained, it was necessary to set the superstructure higher, with vertical front and side plates to complete the vehicle. It was very much a last minute stop-gap, easier to build than any tank, and 278 were made in 1944 and 1945.

MODELS Sturmgeschütz IV and Jagdpanzer IV.

COUNTRY OF ORIGIN Germany.

WEIGHT **StuG:** 24·2 tonnes (23·9 tons); **Jagdpz:** 24 tonnes (23·6 tons).

LENGTH **StuG:** 5·59m (18ft 4in); **Jagdpz:** 7·29m (23ft 11in).

WIDTH **StuG:** 2·95m (9ft 8in); **Jagdpz:** 3·21m (10ft 6½in).

HEIGHT **StuG:** 2·15m (7ft ½in); **Jagdpz:** 1·96m (6ft 5in).

GROUND CLEARANCE **StuG:** 0·39m (1ft 3in); **Jagdpz:** 0·4m (1ft 3¾in).

ARMOUR **StuG:** 20–100mm; **Jagdpz:** 40–80mm.

ENGINE 12-cylinder Maybach HL 120 TRM, 300hp, gasoline.

MAXIMUM SPEED 40km/h (25mph).

RANGE 169km (105 miles).

CREW 4.

ARMAMENT **StuG:** 1 × 7·5cm StuK 40, 1 × 7·92mm MG; **Jagdpz:** 1 × 7·5cm Pak 39 L/48, 2 × 7·92mm MG.

AMMUNITION **StuG:** 7·5cm: 36 rds, MG: 600 rds; **Jagdpz:** 7·5cm: 79 rds, MG: 600 rds.

TRENCH CROSSING 2·59m (8ft 6in).

TRACK WIDTH 0·4m (1ft 4in).

MAXIMUM ELEVATION **StuG:** 20°; **Jagdpz:** 15°.

FORDING DEPTH 0·8m (2ft 7in).

The Jagdpanzer IV was the final development of the tank destroyer on the chassis of a standard tank, though in this model the nose shape was altered in order to fair-in the well-sloped superstructure front. Development of this vehicle was championed by Heinz Guderian when Inspector-General of Armoured Forces in 1942–3. It was intended to replace the various models of StuG III and StuG IV as a standard production type, and was produced in the last year or so of the war. This vehicle is from 116.Pz.Div. operating in the Ardennes offensive (the Battle of the Bulge) in December 1944. The divisional insignia can be seen with the tank unit tactical sign on the nose. The last view (opposite) is a Jagdpanzer IV Ausf F on the Italian Front late in 1944, and shows the added skirt armour carried by many vehicles.

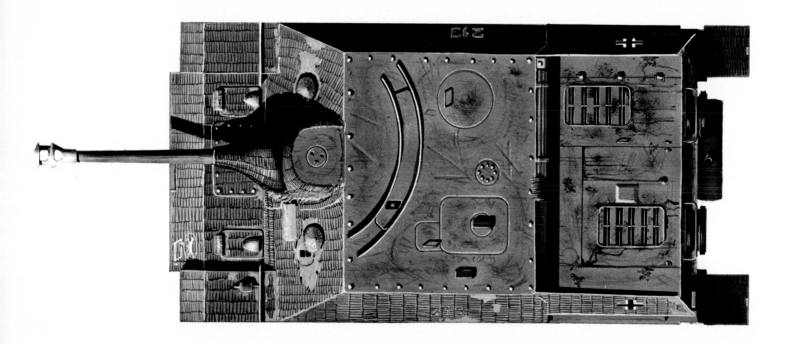

Danilo Renzulli

184

Jagdpanzer IV Ausf H (Sd Kfz 161)

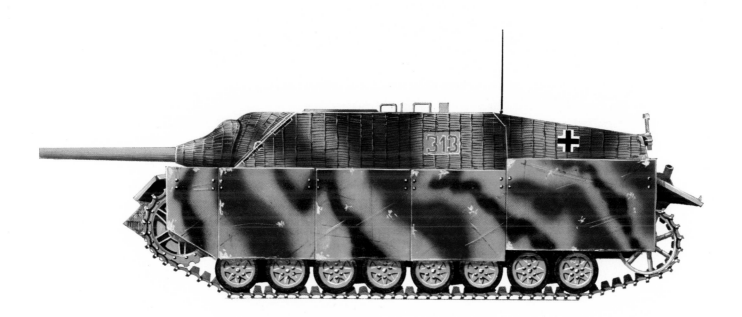

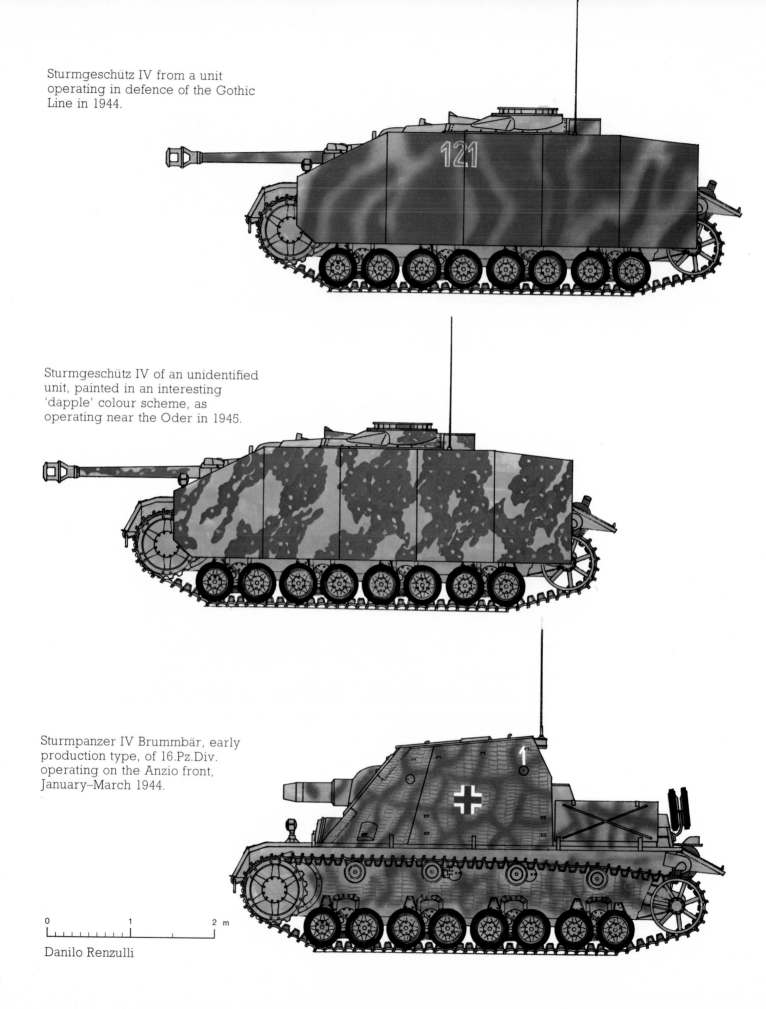

Sturmgeschütz IV from a unit operating in defence of the Gothic Line in 1944.

Sturmgeschütz IV of an unidentified unit, painted in an interesting 'dapple' colour scheme, as operating near the Oder in 1945.

Sturmpanzer IV Brummbär, early production type, of 16.Pz.Div. operating on the Anzio front, January–March 1944.

0   1   2 m

Danilo Renzulli

Sturmgeschütz IV, Jagdpanzer IV and Sturmpanzer IV

Sturmpanzer IV Brummbär of an unidentified unit as operating on the Eastern Front in 1944.

Jagdpanzer IV L/70 (Sd Kfz 162/1). This version has the longer 7·5cm gun of the same model as fitted to the Panther tank and is typical of late-production vehicles. Note the steel leading bogie wheels to counter-balance the extra nose weight of this gun. Standard wheels suffered excess wear in this position. This example was in action on the Ruhr in April 1945.

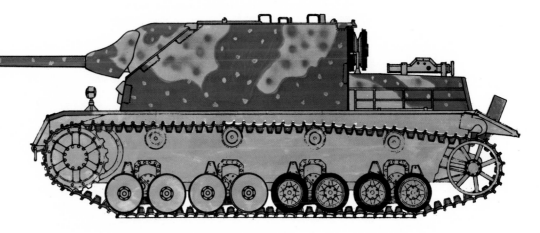

Panzer IV L/70. This was the very late-production stop-gap model built by Niebelungenwerke, utilizing chassis intended for tank production rather than purpose-built chassis. As these chassis had an unmodified nose it was necessary to mount the standard superstructure higher than on the Jagdpanzer IV, and build up the front and sides accordingly. The basic chassis was that of the PzKpfw IV Ausf J. At the time when these vehicles were built, the Germans were desperate, and any vehicle with a powerful gun was considered to be worthy of the designation 'tank', as reflected in the name given to this type.

Combat and air recognition flag of the Red Army.

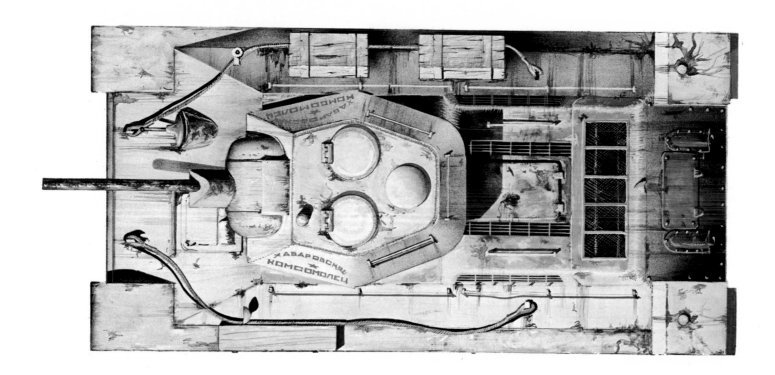

Danilo Renzulli

T-34/76B

This is the second production model, the T-34/76B, which came out in 1941 and had a longer, more powerful Model 1940 L/41·5 76·2mm gun than the T-34/76A. Later vehicles of this type had twin horn periscopes instead of the single periscope previously used. Finally, the cast gun cradle was replaced by a fabricated bolted assembly, which was easier to produce. The 1942 production programme included a B version with a cast, instead of a welded, turret. Some of these were equipped as flame-throwers under the designation ATO-41, having an armoured fuel tank on the hull rear. The vehicle illustrated here is a typical re-worked tank of the later war period, being a T-34/76B which has been refitted with a turret from the T-34/76D. This vehicle is from a Guards Tank Regiment and bears the inscription of a presentation vehicle from the Khabarovsk Komsomol.

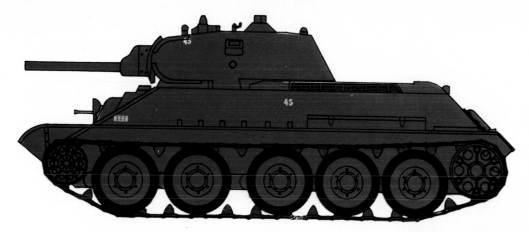

This T-34/76A was captured by the Germans in the early stages of Operation Barbarossa in summer 1941, and later handed over to the Italian Army for evaluation at their Central Establishment of Motorization. The small numbers indicate the armour thicknesses at various points, but the number on the yellow panel is the Italian Army number. The cast mantlet and short calibre were characteristics of the A model.

A T-34/76B captured by the Germans in Russia and later used by the occupation forces in Norway. Besides being prominently marked with German crosses, it carries the insignia of Waffen-SS division Totenkopf (death's head).

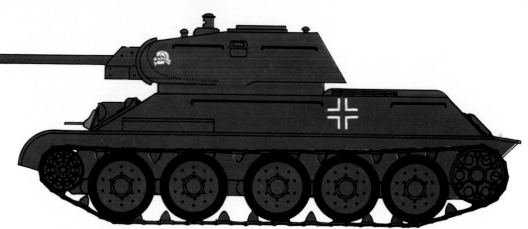

A T-34/76B presented by the people of the Bjelgorod Republic and used in action in the Battle of Kursk. It is seen here later in temporary winter whitewash camouflage.

A T-34/76B captured by Italian troops on the Eastern Front and then put into service as a command vehicle with 62 Gruppo of the 120th Artillery Regiment. It is marked with prominent white crosses on sides, front, rear and turret top.

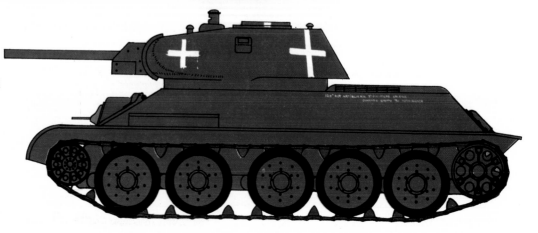

0   1   2 m

Danilo Renzulli

190

T-34/76

Late in 1942 a new type was produced, identified as T-34/76C. This had a larger cast turret, webbed and spudded tracks, and two small hatches replacing the original single big turret hatch carried on previous models. The vehicle illustrated served on the Baltic Front and carried the inscription 'For the Estonian Soviet'.

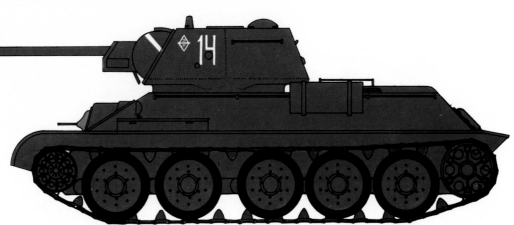

The T-34/76D had an entirely new welded hexagonal turret intended to eliminate the shot trap which existed under the overhang of the original turret. There was a new mantlet in a bulged housing, and some tanks of this type had all-steel wheels when new. This vehicle, of an unknown unit, saw action at Kursk.

A T-34/76D, of an unknown unit, which took part in the Orel offensive.

A T-34/76D, of an unknown unit, which was involved in the defence of Moscow. It has a temporary white winter finish.

191

The Soviet BT 'fast tanks', copied from the original American Christie design, led directly to the development of the T-34, one of the most famous and widely used tanks of all time. The process of evolution from the BT first involved a modernized version of the BT-7 tank, known as the BT-7M, which appeared in 1936. The original adapted aero-engine used in the BT-7 was replaced with a V12 four-stroke diesel unit which was developed specifically for tank use in the 1920s. Increased range, reduced maintenance needs, and better cold-weather performance resulted from this motor, which was known as the V-2, and in various forms, it has powered all principal Soviet tanks until recent times. Hull shape and hence shot-deflection in the BT-7M was improved by replacing the boat-shaped hull front by a slightly-angled, sloping nose plate.

A hull machine gun was fitted and a 76·2mm partly stabilized gun was carried in the turret.

Next came an experimental tank, BT-1S, which had sloping hull sides extending over the top of the tracks to the full width of the vehicle. A slope-sided turret was also used. After some running of the BT-7M and BT-1S, a new vehicle, the A 20, was built based on the BT-7M chassis. It had the new sloped hull shape but still retained the option of wheel or track-running, a distinctive ability of the BT series. However, there proved to be design limitations in the A-20 which would prevent the fitting of a larger gun. An enlarged prototype was therefore produced, the A-30, later called the T-32, which ran on tracks only, had armour up to 60mm thick, and a 76·2mm gun. In 1939 this prototype was tested and, after modifications to the transmission, was finalized in design as the T-34. The T-34 ran on tracks only and the conventional clutch and transmission brake system of steering replaced the steering wheel and pivoted front road wheels used in the earlier Christie-based vehicles.

The first T-34s were ready in March 1940 and were successfully tested in a tough but trouble-free trial run from Kharkov to Smolensk and back. The original T-34 mounted a 76·2mm gun, and was a well-shaped vehicle with sloping armour all round. Of simple design, and rough but serviceable finish, it lent itself to mass-production and easy maintenance (the engine and transmission were at the rear with good accessibility). Because of the war situation in 1940, though Russia had then been involved only in the brief Russo-Finnish War, the T-34 was put into production with great rapidity, so quickly that many of the early models suffered numerous mechanical defects. A large tank arsenal for making T-34s was specially built at Kirov.

The T-34's existence remained a close secret, however. When Germany invaded Russia in June 1941, the first Soviet tanks encountered were the lightly built and obsolescent vehicles of the 1930s. The Germans claimed to have destroyed or captured 20,000 of them. The T-34 did not appear on the battlefront until July 1941, when it instantly outclassed all German tanks then in service. It was superior in firepower, armour and performance, and its appearance led to rapid German efforts to produce a new tank to combat it.

The first production model (T-34/76 by German designation – the Soviets did not bother with individual designations) had a rolled plate turret and short L/30·3 Model 1938 tank gun. It was carried in a cast and contoured cradle which was welded very simply to an external mantlet. In the first 115 vehicles there was a ball-mounted machine gun in the turret rear (as in the KV), but this was discarded in all later vehicles. There was 45mm of front armour with 40mm side armour. Many parts were interchangeable with the KV, including, of course, the engine. On the early T-34s the large disc wheels had solid rubber tyres, but because of ever-increasing shortages, steel-tyred wheels were soon adopted.

Later in the war, however, when rubber became more plentiful the original tyres were once again used.

MODEL T-34/76.

COUNTRY OF ORIGIN USSR.

WEIGHT 26·7 tonnes (26·3 tons).

LENGTH 6·5m (21ft 4in).

WIDTH 2·97m (9ft 9½in).

HEIGHT 2·4m (7ft 10in).

GROUND CLEARANCE 0·32m (1ft ½in).

ARMOUR 14–45mm.

ENGINE V-2-34 500hp, diesel.

MAXIMUM SPEED 49km/h (30mph).

RANGE 302km (188 miles); 450km (280 miles) with additional fuel tanks.

CREW 4.

ARMAMENT 1 × 76·2mm gun, 2 or 3 7·62mm MG.

AMMUNITION 76·2mm: 80 rds, MG: 2,394 rds.

TRENCH CROSSING 2·99m (9ft 10in).

TRACK WIDTH 0·48m (1ft 7in).

MAXIMUM ELEVATION 30°.

FORDING DEPTH 1·09m (3ft 7in).

T-34/85 and SU-100

An up-armoured version of the T-34 was produced in early 1943. It had 110mm front armour and 75mm armour at the sides, as well as the late-pattern turret and a new five-speed gearbox. Because of the changes it was designated T-43, but it still retained the old 76·2mm gun. It was thought, however, that a heavier weapon was now essential since the new German 75mm and 88mm high-velocity tank and anti-tank guns were being deployed in increasing numbers.

The answer was to fit a new high velocity gun in the existing T-34, and the turret already designed for the new KV-85 was adapted to fit. This had a ring diameter of 1·58m (5·2ft) and room in the turret for an extra crew-member – so that the crew could now consist of driver, hull gunner, turret gunner, loader and commander. The gun was the Model 1943 85mm, a development of an older AA gun, the Model 1939. This gun had an effective range of over 1,000m (1,100yd) and could penetrate 100mm of armour, so was in theory able to take on the German Tiger and Panther tanks on equal terms. Subsequently a special armour-piercing 'Arrowhead' round was produced for this gun, which proved very effective, though it was not particularly accurate at long range.

Designated T-34/85, the new vehicle went into production during the 1943–4 winter and the first vehicles were issued to Guards units in the spring of 1944. When production was in full swing, the T-34/85 soon outnumbered the German Panther, output running at over twice the rate of the Panther in 1944–5. Because of the heavier turret the performance of the T-34/85 was rather poorer than that of the T-34/76 but the available power meant that fall-off speed was insignificant.

The T-34/85 rapidly became the standard Soviet medium tank and some older T-34/76s were also re-worked as T-34/85s, production continuing in the immediate post-war years. About 40,000 T-34s of all types were built (representing 68 per cent of Soviet tank production in World War 2), and of these 12,000 were T-34/85s. In 1947 an improved model was developed, which was designated T-34/85-II. It had improved transmission, armour, vision devices and fire control equipment. This type was used in action by North Korean and Chinese forces in the Korean War of 1950–3. The T-34/85-II and its predecessor were used by all armies of the Soviet bloc.

The SU-122, based on the T-34 chassis, was the first of several SP developments. The gun in this case was the Model 1938 field howitzer adapted to fit a limited traverse mount in the nose of the vehicle. A simple box-like superstructure was formed following the slope of the T-34 nose, and the gun was held in a cast mantlet with a fabricated armour cover for the prominent recoil system. This vehicle was designed in 1942 and Stalin ordered mass-production, the first vehicles coming into service in January 1943. Used in platoons of three vehicles, the SU-122 gave close fire support for tank divisions, but from late 1943 this vehicle was phased out and replaced by the SU-152 which was based on the KV chassis.

A tank destroyer was produced in August 1943 by fitting the 85mm gun into the limited traverse mount in the new SU superstructure as used in the SU-122. By the end of 1943, 100 SU-85s had been built, and in 1944 they were made in vast numbers, quickly replacing the SU-76 which was relegated to infantry support work. Once the T-34/85 was in service in large numbers, the SU-85 had no worthwhile advantage over the tank, so an up-gunned SU, the SU-100, was built from September 1944. This was essentially the same as the SU-85, with a 100mm Model 1944 high-velocity gun replacing the 85mm weapon, and fixed in a larger mantlet. The SU-100 became the major type of Soviet tank destroyer; it remained in first-line service until 1957 and has been used by some Warsaw Pact and Soviet satellite armies since then. The 100mm gun had an effective range for HE fire of 20,000m (12·4 miles).

MODELS T-34/85 and SU-100.

COUNTRY OF ORIGIN USSR.

WEIGHT **T-34/85:** 32 tonnes (31·5 tons); **SU-100:** 31·4 tonnes (31 tons).

LENGTH **T-34/85:** 7·5m (24ft 8in); **SU-100:** 9·75m (32ft).

WIDTH 2·99m (9ft 10in).

HEIGHT **T-34/85:** 2·38m (7ft 10in); **SU-100:** 2·25m (7ft 6in).

GROUND CLEARANCE 0·4m (1ft 4in).

ARMOUR 18–110mm.

ENGINE 12-cylinder, water-cooled, 500hp, diesel.

MAXIMUM SPEED 48km/h (31mph).

RANGE 299km (186 miles); 353km (220 miles) with additional fuel tank.

CREW **T-34/85:** 5; **SU-100:** 4.

ARMAMENT 2 × 7·62mm MG plus **T-34/85:** 1 × 85mm gun, **SU-100:** 1 × 100mm gun.

AMMUNITION MG: 2,394 rds, 85mm: 55 rds, 100mm: 40 rds.

TRENCH CROSSING 2·51m (8ft 3in).

TRACK WIDTH 0·48m (1ft 7in).

MAXIMUM ELEVATION **T-34/85:** 25°; **SU-100:** 20°.

FORDING DEPTH 1·32m (4ft 4in).

Combat and air recognition flag of the Red Army.

0   1   2 m

Danilo Renzulli

The main illustration shows a T-34/85 of the Soviet Army as operating in the winter of 1944–45. The side elevation below shows an SU-100 of the Egyptian Army captured by British forces during the Suez operation of 1956.

In addition to the standard gun tanks illustrated, several special purpose variants of the T-34 were produced. Old T-34s with turrets removed were used for recovery – simply as towing vehicles. Another variant had a boom to act as a crane. The recovery version was designated TT-34. There were at least three models of Bridgelayer based on the T-34, designated T-34/MTU. One was an 'ark' type bridge fixed to the vehicle, one a rigid arm-launched bridge, and the other a folding scissors bridge, the latter being a post-war model. For mine clearing there was a roller-equipped variant in both T-34/76 and T-34/85 form, which was designated T-34/PT-3. The rollers were propelled ahead of the vehicle on arms in the conventional way for this type of equipment. Also produced was a mine-clearer with chain flails similar to the British Scorpion equipment. Finally there was a dozer-equipped vehicle designated T-34/STU.

T-34/85-II of the Soviet Army used in action during the uprising in East Berlin in 1953.

T-34/85-II of the Army of the People's Republic of Korea in 1957.

T-34/85-II of the Egyptian Army in 1956.

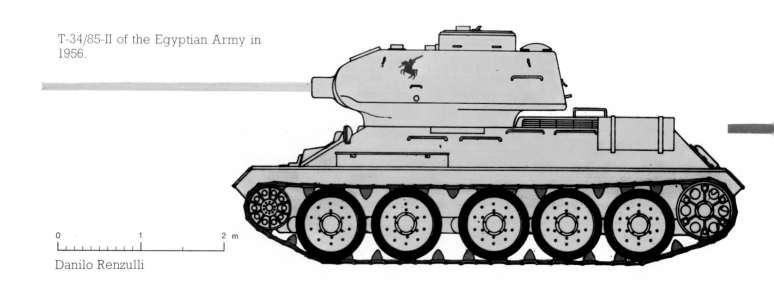

0   1   2 m

Danilo Renzulli

T-34/85 and SU-100

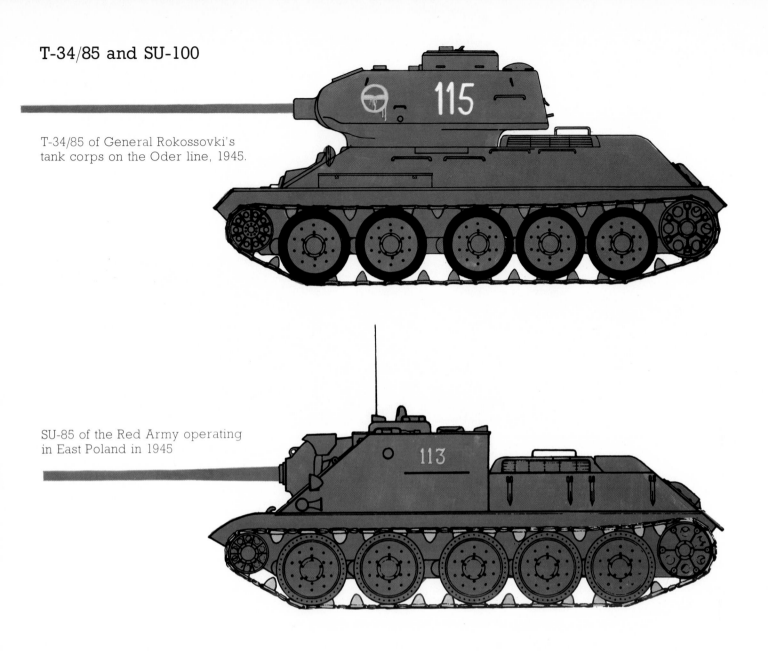

T-34/85 of General Rokossovki's tank corps on the Oder line, 1945.

SU-85 of the Red Army operating in East Poland in 1945

SU-100 of the Red Army in 1945. This was the first Russian vehicle to enter Vienna at the start of the tripartite occupation of Austria.

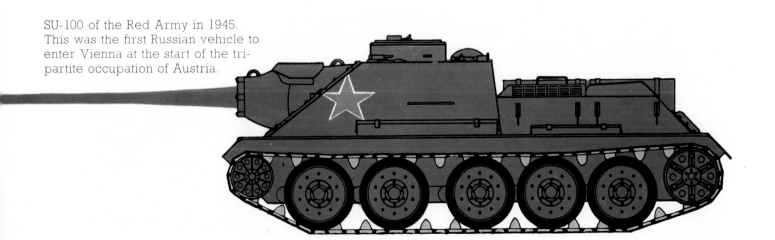

The Red Army had a series of light tanks which were used in the reconnaissance role, starting with the T-38 about 1931, then leading to the T-40, T-60 and finally the T-70 of 1942. A T-80 was produced as a prototype but did not see service. The final service light tank was the T-70A and this example shows one on the Finnish front in the winter of 1944.

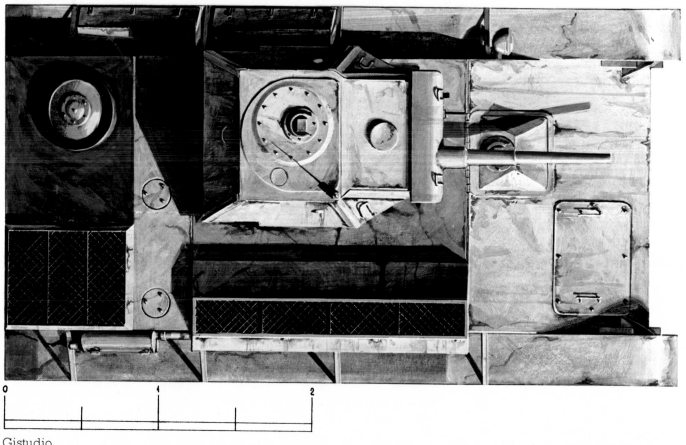

0　　　　　　1　　　　　　2

　　Gistudio

T-70A

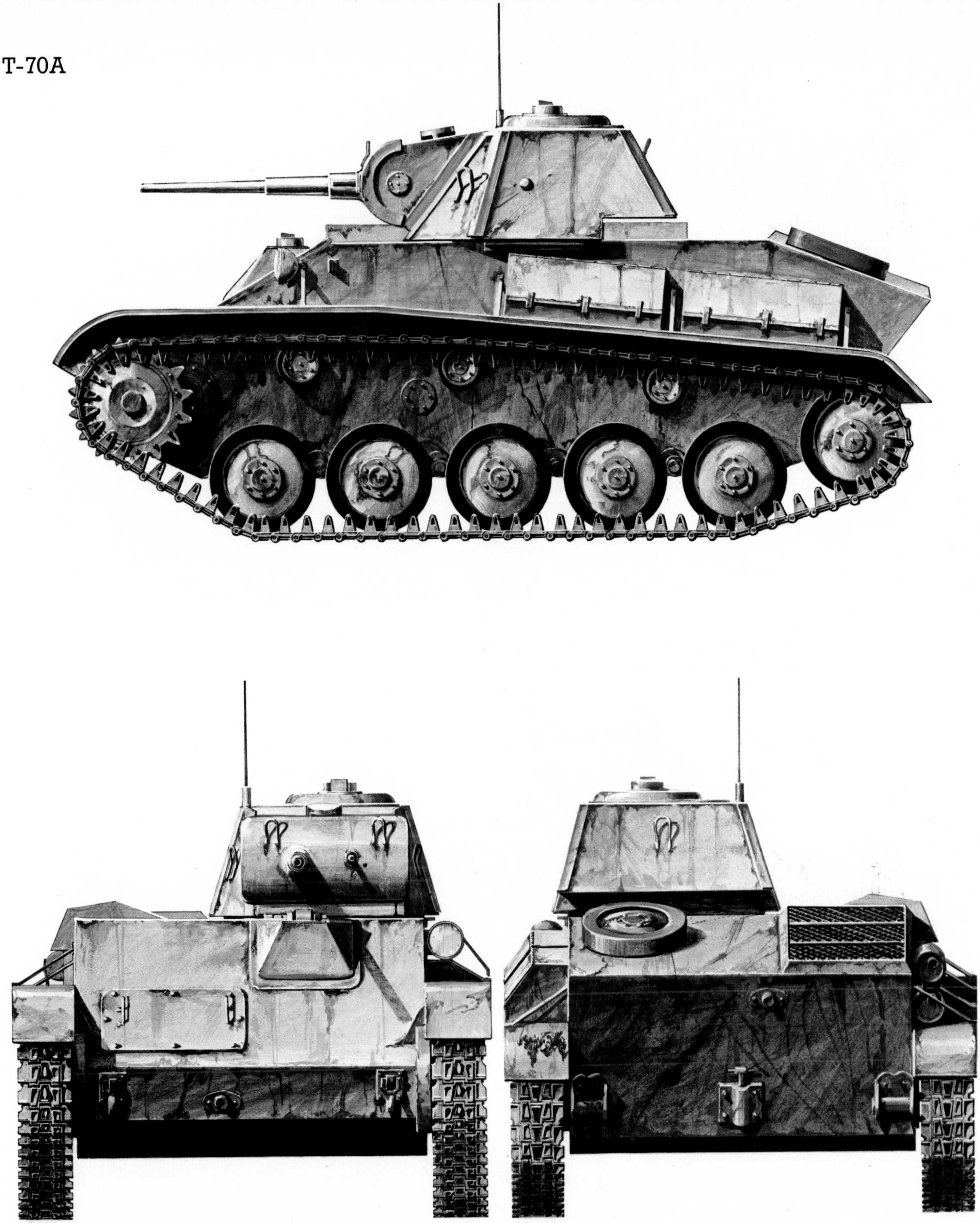

A T-40 light tank captured by the Germans; the numbers show armour thicknesses marked for test purposes.

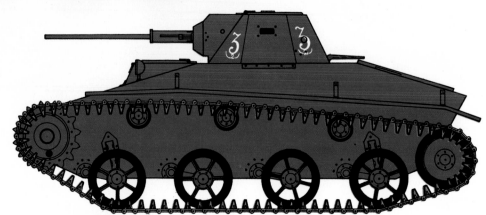

Light Tank T-60, early production type, of an unknown unit.

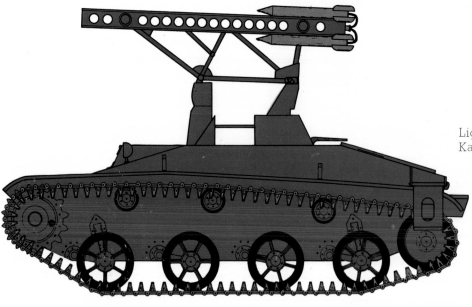

Light Tank T-60 modified to fire Katyusha rockets (Stalin Organ).

Light Tank T-60, later production type, at the Donetz Basin, 1942.

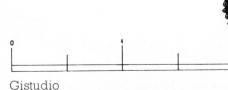

Gistudio

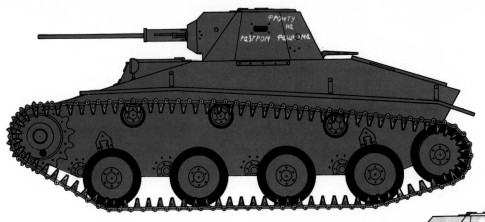

Light Tank T-60, Battle of Stalingrad, 1942.

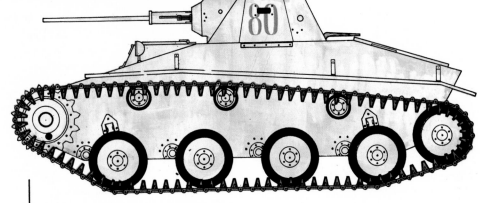

Light Tank T-60, Manchurian front, winter 1944.

Light Tank T-70 of the Moscow Defence Brigade, 1944.

SU-76, modified with higher side shields, Vistula front, 1945.

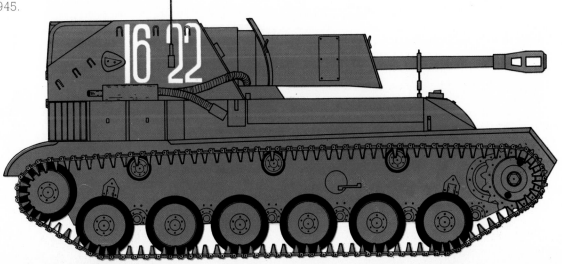

T-40, T-60, T-70 and SU-76

To fulfil the need for a light tank to replace the obsolete versions then in Russian service, a non-amphibious light tank was built, based on the chassis of the T-40 light amphibious vehicle. Designated T-60, it was internally identical to the T-40, but had increased frontal armour, the hull and the turret being welded throughout. A high-velocity 20mm ShVAK aircraft machine gun with co-axial 7·62mm DT MG was mounted. This vehicle entered production late in 1941 and was issued to reconnaissance units.

An improved model, the T-60A, appeared in early 1942. This was fitted with extra armour, and the road wheels and idlers were solid, in contrast to those on the T-60 which were of the spoked type. T-60s were later used as artillery tractors and self-propelled mounts for rocket launchers. Most light tanks were withdrawn from service as reconnaissance vehicles from 1943, their function being taken over by armoured cars and US Lend-Lease half-tracks.

The next major type was the T-70, projected as a light tank with increased armour and a more powerful gun to cope with the new German tanks that were being encountered. It was fitted with a 45mm gun and co-axial 7·62mm DT MG in a redesigned welded turret and modified hull armour. Powered by twin truck engines, the T-70 began to replace the T-60 in light tank units early in 1942, and was built at the Gorki arms plant, which was principally a manufacturer of trucks. A T-70A version was produced in mid-1943, having increased armour and more powerful engines. The turret had a squared off rear, in contrast with the rounded type of the T-70. Production was discontinued during late 1943, by which time more than 8,000 had been built, the chassis later being used as mounts for self-propelled guns. With a top speed of 45km/h (28mph) and maximum frontal armour of 44mm, the T-70 had only a short service life before light tanks were generally withdrawn from service with reconnaissance battalions. In late 1943 a prototype appeared, designated T-80, which was essentially a T-70 with thicker armour and a bigger turret. However, it was only put into production in limited numbers and few were used.

The most important member of this series of Soviet light tank designs proved to be a self-propelled gun variant, the SU-76. When the war in the east began in June 1941 Russia had no SP guns, but the Red Army was impressed by the Germans' extensive use of this class of vehicle. Accordingly, as soon as tank establishment had come up to strength, the Defence Ministry, in October 1942, turned its attention to the procurement of self-propelled guns in the German fashion. Since the light tank had been found to be the least effective of AFVs, the T-70 chassis was chosen as a basis for a conversion with a view to using existing vehicles for the production run. The conversion was quite extensive since engine, fuel tanks and driving position were all changed and moved right forward. This gave a clear space to the rear to take the M1942-43 76·2mm anti-tank gun which was to be carried. The length was increased, with one more suspension unit being added on each side. The basic mount and fire control equipment (sights, etc) were identical with the field equipment from which the gun was adapted.

There were a number of variations as production proceeded; some vehicles had rear access doors, others had open backs; and some had external radiators mounted on the track covers instead of in the engine compartment. Later vehicles had twin GAZ 203 in-line, air-cooled gasoline engines in place of the truck engines of the original T-70. A distinctive feature was the armoured cover over the prominent recoil mechanism of the 76·2mm gun. The SU-76 could fire about 20 rounds a minute. Though first envisaged as a tank destroyer, it was soon displaced from this role by later vehicles and was then used widely as a true assault gun. It was still in use by the Chinese in Korea in the early 1950s.

MODELS Light Tank T-40 and Light Tank T-60.

COUNTRY OF ORIGIN USSR.

WEIGHT **T-40:** 6·3 tonnes (6·2 tons); **T-60:** 5·8 tonnes (5·71 tons).

LENGTH **T-40:** 4·2m (13ft 8in); **T-60:** 4m (13ft 1in).

WIDTH **T-40:** 2·3m (7ft 8in); **T-60:** 2·28m (7ft 6in).

HEIGHT **T-40:** 1·98m (6ft 6in); **T-60:** 2m (6ft 8in).

GROUND CLEARANCE **T-40:** 0·35m (1ft 2in); **T-60:** 0·30m (1ft).

ARMOUR **T-40:** 10–14mm; **T-60:** 7–25mm.

ENGINES **T-40:** GAZ 202, 85hp, gasoline; **T-60:** GAZ 202, 85hp, gasoline.

MAXIMUM SPEED **T-40:** 40km/h (25mph); **T-60:** 43km/h (27mph).

RANGE **T-40:** 337km (210 miles); **T-60:** 113km (70 miles).

CREW **T-40:** 2; **T-60:** 2.

ARMAMENT **T-40:** 1 × 12·7mm gun or 20mm cannon, plus 1 × 7·62 MG; **T-60:** 1 × 20mm gun, 1 × 7·62mm MG.

AMMUNITION **T-40:** 12·7mm: 550 rds, 20mm: unknown, MG: 2,016; **T-60:** 20mm: 780 rds, MG: 945 rds.

TRENCH CROSSING **T-40:** 1·72m (5ft 8in); **T-60:** 1·72m (5ft 8in).

TRACK WIDTH **T-40:** 17·78cm (7in); **T-60:** 17·78cm (7in).

MAXIMUM ELEVATION **T-40:** 40°; **T-60:** 40°.

FORDING DEPTH **T-40:** floats; **T-60:** 0·86m (2ft 10in).

Valentine

Early in 1938, Vickers was asked to build the Infantry Tank Mk II (A12). As an alternative, the company was invited to build a design of their own based on the A10. The A10, which had been the first 'infantry tank' to be developed from the 1934 General Staff specification for this type, had later been reclassified as a 'heavy cruiser' since it was much less heavily armoured than the A11 and A12 designs. Vickers chose the latter alternative since they already had production facilities and experience for an A10-based design, which would have been wasted if they had switched to building A12s. The new vehicle utilized a chassis, suspension, engine and transmission identical to the A10, but had a lower, more heavily armoured superstructure and a new turret mounting a 2pdr gun. Plans for the tank were very quickly drawn up and submitted to the War Office just prior to St Valentine's Day in February 1938, so inspiring its name.

There was no production order for over a year, however, the main shortcoming in the design being the small turret which would only accommodate two men. In July 1939, with war fast approaching and an urgent need for tanks in quantity, an order for 275 vehicles was placed with Vickers. Quick production had been promised by Vickers since the chassis had already been proven with the A10, so that no lengthy development period was required. The first vehicle was delivered to the Army for trials in May 1940 and proved to be a stable gun platform and mechanically reliable. Production deliveries were made in late 1940, and for a time in 1940–41 Valentines were used in the cruiser tank role. The first Valentines appeared with tank brigades in the 8th Army in June 1941 and then played an important part in the remainder of the desert fighting.

Valentine production was stopped early in 1944 after 8,275 vehicles had been completed. By late 1942, however, the Valentine was largely obsolete because of its low speed and small turret, which restricted the fitting of larger calibre armament. Mks III and V had the turret modified to accommodate three men (a loader in addition to commander and gunner), but the third turret member was, of necessity, dropped when the 6pdr gun was fitted in later marks (VIII-X). In this case the disadvantage of a two-man turret crew was accepted in the interests of increased gun power in 1942. Other modifications included an improved engine installation (a GMC diesel unit) and a change over from all-riveted to all-welded construction. In March 1943 a Valentine was used for the test installation and firing of the British 75mm tank gun, intended for the A27 cruiser tanks and the Churchill. The success of these trials in the Valentine led to the development of the Mk XI, the final type, mounting this gun.

Valentines were also built in Canada by the Canadian Pacific in Montreal. Of the 1,420 vehicles produced, however, all but 30, which were retained for training, were delivered to the Soviet Army.

The Valentine was one of the most important British tanks and in 1943 totalled nearly one quarter of British tank output. Valentines formed the basis of many special-purpose AFVs including bridgelayers, mine clearers, and amphibious (DD) tanks. Two SP guns were also put into production on the Valentine chassis, and these are shown on page 207. These were the Bishop, with 25pdr howitzer in a large housing, and the Archer with 17pdr anti-tank gun fitted to fire to the rear.

In 1944 there was also the Valentine OP/Command vehicle, a converted gun tank with dummy gun and extra communications equipment for battery commanders and OP officers of Archer-equipped SP units. Valentines were also adapted to take the Scorpion minesweeping flail equipment developed for the Matilda and there was a Valentine bridgelayer (used in Burma), several experimental types, and the very important first 'swimming' tank, the Valentine DD.

MODELS Valentine Mk I-XI.

COUNTRY OF ORIGIN Great Britain.

WEIGHT 16·2–17·2 tonnes (16–17 tons).

LENGTH 5·4m (17ft 9in).

WIDTH 2·63m (8ft 7½in).

HEIGHT 2·27m (7ft 5½in).

GROUND CLEARANCE 0·40m (1ft 4in).

ARMOUR 8–65mm.

ENGINE AEC 135hp, gasoline or AEC 131hp, diesel; or GM 138hp, diesel; or GM 165hp, diesel (**Mk X, XI**).

MAXIMUM SPEED 24km/h (15mph).

RANGE 295km (183 miles).

CREW 3–4.

ARMAMENT 1 × Besa ·303 cal. or Browning ·30 cal. MG; plus: 1 × 2 pdr (**Mk I-VII**), 1 × 6pdr (**Mk VIII-X**), 1 × 75mm (**Mk XI**).

AMMUNITION Besa MG: 3,150 rds, 2 pdr (**Mk I-VII**): 60 rds; 6 pdr (**Mk VIII-X**): 53 rds; 75mm (**Mk XI**): 48 rds.

TRENCH CROSSING 2·36m (7ft 9in).

TRACK WIDTH 0·35m (1ft 2in).

MAXIMUM ELEVATION 20°.

FORDING DEPTH 0·91m (3ft).

The highly successful Infantry Tank Mk III, Valentine, was used extensively in the North African campaigns. It took its name from the fact that the design work was completed on St Valentine's Day in 1938. This vehicle, 'Ali Baba', is from 6th Armoured Division and is shown as it appeared in action in Tunisia, February 1943.

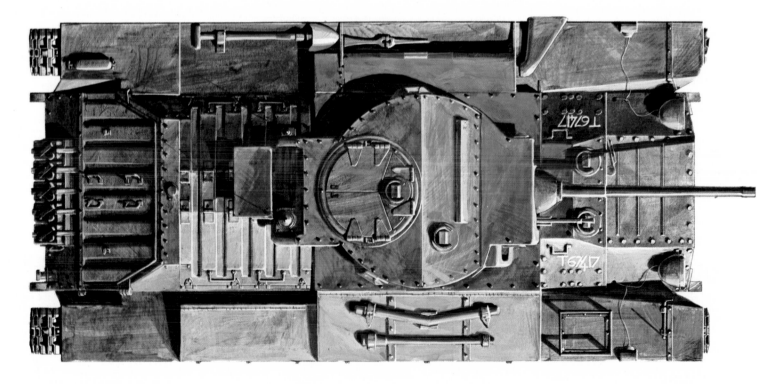

0   1   2 m

Gistudio – Tatangelo

Infantry Tank Mk III, Valentine V

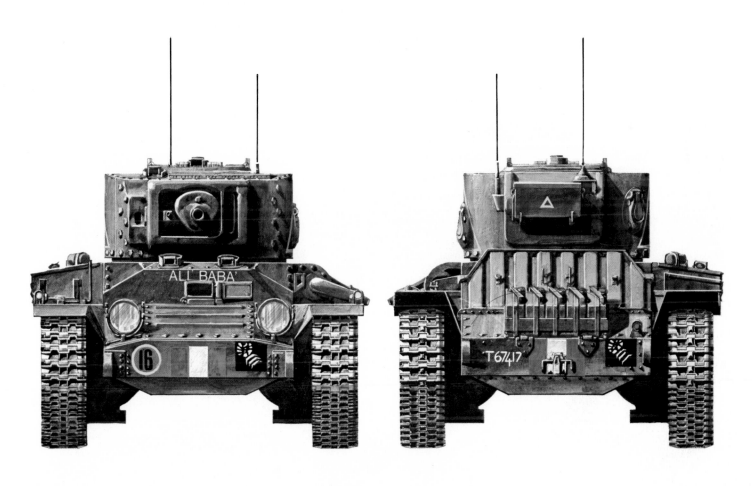

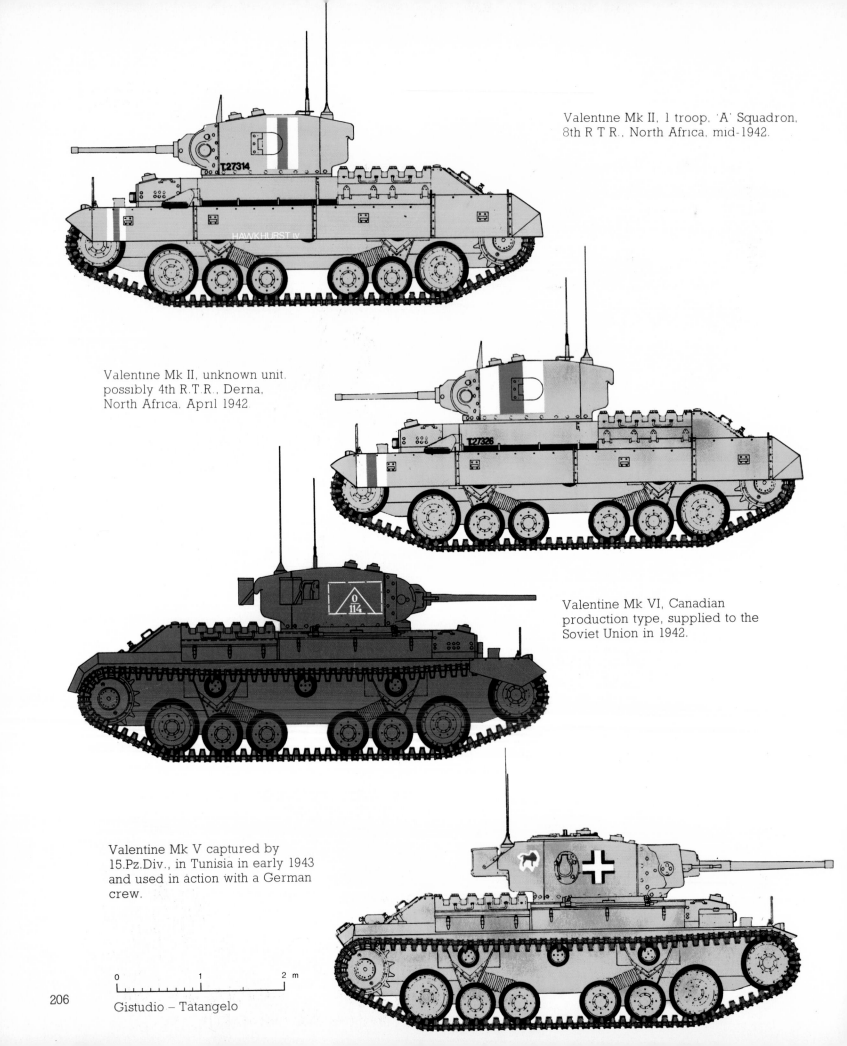

Valentine Mk II, 1 troop, 'A' Squadron, 8th R T R., North Africa, mid-1942.

Valentine Mk II, unknown unit, possibly 4th R.T.R., Derna, North Africa, April 1942.

Valentine Mk VI, Canadian production type, supplied to the Soviet Union in 1942.

Valentine Mk V captured by 15.Pz.Div., in Tunisia in early 1943 and used in action with a German crew.

0 1 2 m

Gistudio – Tatangelo

Valentine

Valentine Mk XI with a 75mm gun was the final production model.

Valentine Mk VIII DD tank, armed with 6pdr gun. The DD (Duplex Drive) idea was evolved by Nicholas Straussler, a Hungarian-born military engineer, and the system involved a propeller driven by power take-off from the vehicle's engine. To provide flotation, collapsible canvas side screens were fitted to the vehicle's hull which, when raised, gave a boat-like form to the vehicle. The actual tank hull was, in fact, suspended below the water surface. Valentines were used to develop this system.

17pdr SP Archer used by British troops in the Egyptian Canal Zone in the 1948–50 period.

25pdr SP Bishop of 5th Regiment, Royal Artillery; Sicily landings, July 1943.